£17.00

Enfield Libraries

GW00392034

S 1 0/06

2 9 MAR 2017

RZ

Please remember that this item will attract overdue charges
if not returned by the latest date stamped above. You may
renew it in person, by telephone or by post quoting the
barcode number and your library card number.

ENFIELD
Council

306.44

REL

RZ   LRUZ

30126 01632955 6

Polygons: Cultural Diversities and Intersections
General Editor: **Lieve Spaas**, *Professor of French Cultural Studies, Kingston University*

RELATIVE POINTS OF VIEW

Linguistic Representations of Culture

Edited by Magda Stroińska

Berghahn Books
New York • Oxford

First published in 2001 by
Berghahn Books
www.BerghahnBooks.com

Editorial offices:
604 West 115th Street, New York, NY 10025, USA
3 NewTec Place, Magdalen Road, Oxford OX4 1RE, UK

Library of Congress Cataloging-in-Publication Data

Relative points of view : linguistic representations of culture /
edited by Magda Stroinska.
    p. cm. -- (Polygons ; v. 5)
Includes bibliographical references and index.
ISBN 1-57181-202-4 (alk. paper) -- ISBN 1-57181-340-3
    (pb. : alk. paper)
    1. Language and culture. 2. Sapir-Whorf hypothesis. 3.
Intercultural communication. I. Stroinska, Magda. II Series.

P35.R44 2001
306.44--dc.21

            00-049348

British Library Cataloguing in Publication Data

A catalogue record for this book is available
from the British Library.

Printed in the United States on acid-free paper.

ISBN 1-57181-202-4 (hardback)
ISBN 1-57181-340-3 (paperback)

CONTENTS

ACKNOWLEDGEMENTS

In undertakings like this volume, it is difficult, or indeed impossible, to list all those who have contributed to its inception, evolution and final production. There are, however, always those without whom this book would have been impossible. Those are easy to name.

First of all, I would like to thank all those colleagues who contributed chapters to this volume. Without you, this book would not be possible. Thank you for your support and for your hard work to meet the deadlines. I am thankful for your understanding of my vision of this book and for your cooperation.

I would like to express my very special thanks to Lieve Spaas, who invited me to submit the proposal for this volume and who has been invaluable in offering advice and encouragement at all stages of its production. I would also like to thank colleagues, many of whom contributed to this volume, from Kingston University (England), where I spent a very productive and enjoyable year in 1996/97. My particular thanks go to François Nectoux for many interesting discussions, and to Teresa Lawlor, Head of School of Languages, for her support for this project.

I would like to thank the Department of Modern Languages at McMaster University for giving me a year off in 1996/97 so that I could take up the fellowship at Kingston University and for granting me extra time off in the last term of this century so that I could concentrate on the editorial work.

In the final two months of 1999, I could not have completed the work without the very able, highly professional and always cheerful assistance of Gordon Roberts. He was an invaluable help, full of initiative and enthusiasm. I would also like to thank Trista Selous for final editorial touches.

I think I should also thank the circumstances that did not prevent me from finishing the work. It is most likely the case with any project that involves several people and stretches over a long period of time that many unexpected and undesirable things happen. Probably, it is only to be expected. Here, we had illness, serious family problems, one hit-and-run accident, a move from one university to another (or from one country to another), the completion of a PhD thesis, a running of the New York marathon, and a strike of teaching assistants at McMaster in the final week before submission. Nevertheless, things could always have been worse, so I remain thankful.

My very special thanks go to my family: my husband Kris and my children Kubuś and Joanna, who always supported me and without whose encouragement I would not be able to persevere.

With all my indebtedness for ideas, discussions and support, the shortcomings are entirely mine.

Magda Stroińska
December 1999

PREFACE:
THE CONTENT OF THIS VOLUME

When I first began to think of this volume, I had a pretty well-defined picture of the field that I hoped the book would cover. I saw it as a collection of essays that would present some non-standard areas of interaction between culture and language. The aim was to show, using examples from several of those areas, that communication is an interplay of many factors that go beyond language and culture. On one hand, language itself is not transparent and neutral, and some of its properties and devices, such as the use of metaphor, may have an impact on our perception of issues and events. On the other hand, factors such as gender, profession, religion, social position, etc., along with our ethnicity and linguistic background, influence the way we speak and understand others.

When the first chapters started to arrive, I realised that the topic involved more instability, or, indeed, relativity, than I had initially envisaged, because I simply had not thought of all possible forces that may shape discourse. One such example is what happens to metaphorical expressions in reported speech (see Teresa Dobrzyńska's contribution). At the same time, a pattern began to emerge. Both the additional factors themselves – such as gender or religion – and the notions that we started with – those of language and culture – are concepts under construction and not stabile entities. They need to be constantly redefined to reflect the fact that they are not finished and ready-to-use products, but processes.

As the book developed, I realised that this kind of under-
taking is only meaningful when done as a collaborative interdisciplinary research. Every contribution brings someone's
perspective to the project, each represents a specific *point of
view*. Consequently, this volume is a collection of such points of
view, illustrating a variety of areas, which may reveal something interesting about our discourse practices.

My intention, as the editor of the volume, was that this collection of essays would look beyond the commonly explored
territory of the relationship between language and culture.
What the contributing authors are searching for is either linguistic patterns that we accept without realising their complex, often metaphorical origin, or the individual and
particular in this area, that is, what individual speakers and
(social, political or professional) groups of speakers bring into
discourse practice.

In order to show connections between individual chapters
the volume has been divided into several parts. They follow
the introduction, which outlines various areas of interest in
the study of language, culture and linguistic relativity. Part
one, *Thinking in words*, contains two papers that look at linguistic problems related to metaphor, but go beyond traditional ways of looking at this issue.

Jim Miller researches the area of linguistic representation of
spatial relations, which he sees as 'a cognitive bedrock' underlying a variety of cultural differences. Spatial relations could
be seen as a set of metaphors than can be applied to discussions of other areas of human perception. Languages from
many different families use the same grammatical constructions that describe location and movement in space to express
other concepts, such as causation, agency, instrumentality or
comparison. In many languages, this happens by applying
the same case marking on nouns or the same prepositions
with case suffixes. Spatial relations are also often found to
form the basis of expressions that describe time. The author
argues for a coherent localist framework for Russian cases
used for spatial and temporal expressions.

Teresa Dobrzyńska concentrates on what happens to
metaphoric expressions in reported speech. The author clearly
shows how the possibility of retaining a metaphor in reported
speech is related to the attitude of the person doing the reporting to the content of the message. The examples used by
Dobrzyńska, drawn both from Polish and from English, illustrate the thesis that reported speech is not a mechanical gram-

matical transformation, but must be based on an analysis of the message and its reconstruction from the point of view of the reporting speaker, taking into account the new addressee.

Part two, *Language and politics*, focuses on the use of language in political debates on issues related to social or national problems. Sakis Kyratzis looks at the use of metaphors of war and illness when public figures discuss drug policy. He compares public discourse on drugs in Greece and in the USA, noting that while in both countries the war metaphor is used, its interpretation would differ in the two contexts because of the different experiences of and attitudes towards war.

François Nectoux takes the case of language as a central component of national identity and social practices, and argues that a strictly relativist approach to nationalism would not only be flawed in social sciences terms, but also ultimately self-defeating. It would prevent the resolution of conflicts by picturing differences as impossible to overcome. He then focuses on how individuals within a given national group continuously negotiate, adapt and legitimise their national identity, and how this ongoing process of identity construction could be helpful in finding a key to understanding other nationalities.

Part three, *Divided by a common language*, contains papers that focus on discursive practices in some specific areas of social interaction. Chris Horrocks comments on the debate on the competence of writers who use scientific terminology in non-scientific texts, 'claiming the credentials of scientific rigour'. Horrocks argues that some forms of postmodern discourse cannot be easily analysed from the point of view of an empiricist and positivist tradition.

In her paper on gender identities, Lia Litosseliti takes the position that gender is socially constructed, and that discourse practices are instrumental in this process. As she examines only one particular group of people and their arguments about the institution of marriage, the results cannot be directly applied to groups that, due to age, religion or sexual preference, would have a different attitude to marriage. The mechanism of identity construction and gender as part of that identity, however, could be adapted to other groups and other topics.

The world of international business and global economy creates new problems in cross-linguistic and cross-cultural communication. In part four, *Different language, different thoughts*, Francesca Bargiela-Chiappini investigates the numerous factors that may determine the success or failure of multinational joint ventures. Some of them may remain hidden from managers not familiar with cross-cultural issues, but may in fact be more important to a company's success than market strategies. The author points out a possibly more promising way to understand organisational communication by suggesting basing our interpretation of communication across cultural boundaries on discourse used by the parties involved.

Libby Rothwell offers a valuable survey of techniques of teaching intercultural awareness and discussing cross-cultural communication with students who spent part of their study programme abroad. The author discusses several definitions of culture and how they can be useful in identifying problems related to language and culture as well as in teaching intercultural issues to language students.

The last part of this collection looks *Beyond the limits of language*. Stephen Smith examines the issue of emotional labour, questioning the universality of the ways feelings are conceptualised and lexicalised in different cultures and languages. He then asks the reader to re-examine the Western system of values in relation to the three types of labour – mental, emotional and manual – and to the authenticity of acting. This reveals some very interesting paradoxes in our system of evaluating different types of emotional labour.

Religion, sometimes disguised under different names, is a necessary part of human culture. In his paper on language about God, Ben Wiebe discusses the way people talk about the Supreme Being in Christianity and in Hinduism. The author argues that even when we talk about God, the goal of the communication is to understand the other man. This cannot be achieved without an attempt to understand the other person's 'framework'. A dialogue between individuals and between religions or cultures can only begin when all parties are prepared to put some effort into understanding that notions they use may have different meanings in different cultures.

This collection of themes, being of necessity very selective, may perhaps seem eclectic. Looking at discourse practices from a comparative point of view is somewhat like exploring a night landscape with a flashlight: we may see very little, but we at least come to realise that there is a lot there to discover. There are interesting discourse phenomena wherever we look, and any selection can offer only a sample of the overwhelming richness of problems and issues.

Introduction:
Beyond Language and Culture:
Relative Points of View

Magda Stroińska

The field of *diversity in mental individuality* is of measureless
extent and unfathomable depth.

(Wilhelm von Humboldt 1988: 163)

There seems hardly any need to argue at length against the two
most extreme views concerning the relationship between meaning and language: the view that meanings cannot be transferred at all from one language to another, and the view that
meanings can be fully transferred.

(Anna Wierzbicka 1992: 6)

Introduction

Language is more than just an innocent tool used for communication. It is a powerful instrument, which may be used to
enable exchange of thoughts and expression of feelings. However, it can also become a weapon for destruction, alienation,
exclusion or thought manipulation. Unfortunately, language
does not come with an instruction manual. We usually have
to learn about its powers by a trial and error method. In a
world of increasingly multicultural communication, we now

need to watch for dangers and pitfalls associated not only with our native languages, but also with those of the others.

It is easy to oversee the importance of language. We usually cannot even remember learning our first language. Although it is the most basic and indispensable medium of expression for thoughts and emotions, language seems so transparent and harmless that we hardly ever pay attention to the way its patterns influence our way of organising experience. It is not possible to separate cognitive processes and language. Language is also a marker of identity, by delineating group boundaries and revealing group membership of the speaker and being an important factor in the process of identity construction. Language may also be seen as a vehicle for action because certain acts, such as oaths or promises, complaints and apologies can only be performed through language and have to be given a linguistic representation.

Culture can be seen as a set of 'social experiences, thought structures, expectations, and practices of action', or simply some kind of 'mental apparatus' (Redder and Rehbein 1987: 20) and 'collective programming of the mind which distinguishes the members of one group or category of people from another' (Hofstede 1991: 4). If we take this, rather practical and pragmatic, perspective on culture, language naturally intersects with culture by providing means of expression for beliefs and value systems of groups and individuals. As Franz Boas points out in his introduction to Ruth Benedict's 1934 book *Patterns of Culture* 'we must understand the individual as living in his culture; and the culture as lived by individuals' (xx). All those forces shape the individual speakers' perspective and their relative points of view, which are the focus of this volume.

Linguistic relativity hypothesis

Over the centuries, the question about the nature of similarities and differences between languages and about the role of language in human thought processes has been addressed from a variety of perspectives and by people representing diverse fields. Can we communicate meaning across language boundaries, or is it so closely interwoven with words that, as the eighteenth century German philosopher Johann Gottfried Herder put it, every nation speaks the way it thinks and thinks the way it speaks? If thinking is a form of 'inward language', then language plays an active role in shaping thoughts, and we may be led to believe that translation from one language into another is close to impossible.

Wilhelm von Humboldt, another great German thinker of the early nineteenth century, inspired, among others, by the writings of French philosophers such as Condillac (cf. the introduction to the 1988 translation of Humboldt's work by Hans Aarsleff), developed the idea that every language necessarily contains a characteristic *worldview* (Germ. *Weltanschauung*) (1988: 60). This concept was not Humboldt's invention, but rather an extension of the common sense idea that concepts we use in our language are determined by our needs, and are therefore not arbitrary in relation to the people that use them:

> As the individual sound stands between man and the object, so the entire language steps in between him and the nature that operates, both inwardly and outwardly, upon him. [...] Man lives primarily with objects, indeed, since feeling and acting in him depend on his presentations, he actually does so exclusively, as language presents them to him. By the same act whereby he spins language out of himself, he spins himself into it, and every language draws about the people that possesses it a circle whence it is possible to exit only by stepping over at once into the circle of another one. To learn a *foreign language* should therefore be to acquire a new standpoint in the world-view hitherto possessed, and in fact to a certain extent is so, since every language contains the whole conceptual fabric and mode of presentation of a portion of mankind. But because we always carry over, more or less, our own world-view, and even our own language-view, this outcome is not purely and completely experienced. (Humboldt 1988: 60)

As an undergraduate student of German and linguistics in Poland, I was captivated by these theories of linguistic relativity. I immediately applied them to my own experience of living in a communist country, with all its propaganda and ideology. Was I a prisoner of language in addition to a hostage of a political system? Looking at the question of relativity from this narrowly defined social angle, the works of Edward Sapir and Benjamin Lee Whorf were perhaps even more revealing.

Sapir saw language as 'a guide to 'social reality'' (1949: 162), and anyone who lived in a totalitarian system or studied totalitarian propaganda would probably agree with this view. Language 'powerfully conditions all our thinking about social problems and processes' [ibid.]. Language is not only, often quite successfully, used to manipulate the thoughts of the people and their perception of the world, it is also used to create fictitious social realities that can take the place of the authentic one in the official media (for a more detailed discussion of this thesis, see Stroińska 1994). It is widely recognised that the first step towards political freedom and democracy is the liberation of language.[1] Where language is free, thoughts cannot be controlled either. This is why independent publications have always been banned in authoritarian regimes. The area of social activities and politics is where the linguistic relativity theory applies quite readily, but it is also an area that is usually studied from a sociological rather than a linguistic perspective.

Benjamin Lee Whorf is usually considered responsible for the much-criticised radical formulation of the idea that language influences thought. The extreme version of the Sapir-Whorf hypothesis attributes to the authors the view that speakers of different languages virtually cannot communicate with each other. Their worldviews are, in Sapir's own words, 'incommensurable' (Sapir 1931: 128) and differences in their worldviews insurmountable (see discussion on linguistic relativity in Devitt and Sterelny 1999: 217–228).

> Human beings do not live in the objective world alone nor alone in the world of social activity as ordinarily understood, but are very much at the mercy of the particular language which has become the medium of expression for their society. [...T]he 'real world' is to a large extent unconsciously built up on the language habits of the group. No two languages are ever sufficiently similar to be considered as representing the same social reality.[2] The worlds in which different societies live are distinct worlds, not merely the same world with different labels attached. (Sapir 1949: 162)

According to Whorf, however, the principle of linguistic relativity, modelled to some extent on Einstein's theories (as pointed out by Foley 1997: 192), stated simply that

> users of markedly different grammars are pointed by their grammars toward different types of observations and different evaluations of externally similar acts of observation, and hence are not equivalent as observers but must arrive at somewhat different views of the world. (Whorf 1956: 221)

Devitt and Sterelny (1999: 224) comment that 'Whorf's remarks are interesting and suggestive, but the argument for an important linguistic relativity evaporates under scrutiny. The only respect in which language clearly and obviously does influence thought turns out to be rather banal: language provides each of us with most of our concepts.' This to me is already an indication that by the very fact of providing key concepts, language does in fact influence our thinking about the world.

'Lexical discriminations [...] provide important clues to the speaker's conceptualisations,' writes Anna Wierzbicka (1992: 120), whose opinion can be trusted. She spent almost three decades researching the role of semantic primitives and explaining how cultures can be understood through their *key words* (Wierzbicka 1997). 'Words matter,' as the writer A.P. Herbert (1935) observed. Working on the assumption that there are no profound differences to be detected among languages, Devitt and Sterelny later agree that, as a product of historical development, different languages may have taken different shapes. They consent that 'of course once the linguistic difference exists it will influence the thought of those who come after' (Devitt and Sterelny 1999: 223).

It is easy to ridicule views of fundamentally different worldviews embedded in different languages, as our daily practice of communication across cultures clearly shows that it is possible to communicate across language boundaries. People learn foreign languages, documents are being translated, and travelling has never been easier. Living in the better-off part of the global village, it is easy to assume that we do, in fact, communicate across language and culture barriers. However, do we really communicate what we want to communicate, i.e., are we really getting our message across? Are we really interpreting correctly what the other person is trying to tell us?

Even though the developments in cognitive sciences in the 1960s discredited to a large extent the idea of linguistic relativity, emphasising instead what seemed to be the universal basis of human cognition, there has been 'a recent change of intellectual climate in psychology, linguistics, and other disciplines surrounding anthropology [...] towards an intermediate position, in which more attention is paid to linguistic and cultural difference, such diversity being viewed within the context of what we have learned about universals' (Gumperz and Levinson eds 1996: 3).

Whorf himself did not in fact deny, as aptly noted by Wierzbicka (1992: 27), the existence of a 'common stock of conceptions' (Whorf 1956: 36). The existence of these shared concepts was for Whorf 'a necessary concomitant of communicability of ideas by languages' and was 'in a sense a universal language to which the various specific languages give an entrance' [ibid.]. It is perhaps interesting to note that linguists interested in real language data, such as Wierzbicka, or anthropological linguists, such as William A. Foley, do not find Whorf's work on linguistic differences ridiculous. This is usually the opinion of philosophers and theoretical linguists, who have no interest in the messy stuff that others call language.

What, if anything, is universal?

If anything were universal, it would perhaps be something like the 'alphabet of human thought' proposed in the eighteenth century by Gottfried Wilhelm Leibniz (1903): a set of primes, semantic primitives, found in every language. Such primitive notions would not require definition; in fact, they could not be defined without recourse to more complex notions, thus making definitions circular and therefore absurd. In her 1992 book *Semantics, Culture and Cognition: Universal Human Concepts in Culture-Specific Configuration*, Wierzbicka develops the concept of semantic universals, and proposes a set of primes based on extensive research and on the examination of several languages from different language families. She warns strongly against attempting to analyse semantic universals using concepts originating within one specific culture and then declaring that one has arrived at what is universal in human thought. She is very critical of the use of analytical tools that are not 'culture-free', as they distort the result of analysis. At the same time, she is aware of the inherent difficulty of a culturally unbiased research in this area:

> As human beings, we cannot place ourselves outside all cultures. This does not mean, however, that if we want to study cultures other than our own all we can do is to describe them through the prism of our own culture, and therefore distort them. We *can* find a point of view which is universal and culture independent, but we must look for such a point of view not *outside* all human cultures (because we cannot place ourselves outside them) but *within* our own culture, or within any other culture with which we are intimately familiar. (Wierzbicka 1992: 26)

This, in a way, reiterates Whorf's observation that language gives an entrance to the study of what could possibly be universal. There may be several such entrances and several relative points of view on what is the common stock of human conceptions and the realisation of this multiplicity of perspectives is important.

The search for universals in the way humans conceptualise the outside world has to go deeper than the shallow waters of the lexicon. Lexicon is just a way of signalling differences. The fact that a word to describe a concept is missing in a language might point to the concept's relative lack of significance in the culture. This topic is developed in Stephen L. Smith's chapter on cross-cultural perspectives on emotional labour in this volume.

Lexical distinctions are rooted in a deeper system of structures. These structures determine the way we organise our experience but are themselves also, at least to some extent, products of the culture we live in. Some principles of the organisation of experience may be more or less easily recognised, as for instance the Western focus on individualism and the significance of the *I*. Individualism, with its high value attached to the speaker's *I*, is one of the qualities that are not universal but culture-specific.

Other underlying principles of the organisation of experience escape our attention and are simply assumed as having a universal validity. One such significant concept and *core system* of culture (cf. Hall 1983) is that of time. In his 1983 book *The Dance of Life*, Edward T. Hall observes that Western civilisation takes the objective existence and linear nature of time for granted and attaches to it a high value. *Time is money*. It can be *wasted* or *invested*, *spent* or *saved*. Time organises our lives and is a fundamental category in our way of perceiving the internal and external world. The Western time, however, differs from its counterparts in other cultures, that may conceptualise it differently and that may place it at a different level in their value systems.

The way many Indo-European languages represent time, however, is further related to another fundamental dimension in human cognition, that of space. In his chapter in this volume, Jim Miller argues that linguistic representations of spatial relations constitute 'a cognitive bedrock' underlying a multitude of cultural differences. Spatial relations, being a basic dimension in our representation of reality, provide us with a set of metaphors that can then be used and is used for representing other important relationships, such as for example causation or instrumentality. Indo-European languages apply the concepts of location and movement to time, transforming time into another kind of space.

Our Western way of conceptualising space, however, is not the only possibility either, and localism is not the only possible metaphor used in language for grammatical purposes. Perhaps as pervasive as spatial relations is reference to body parts. Hollenbach (1990, reported in Foley 1997: 188–190) investigated how in Copala Trique, a Mixtecan language spoken in Mexico, names of body parts have been reanalysed as grammatical morphemes, roughly corresponding to prepositions in English. While we too may talk about 'the nose of the airplane' or 'foot of the mountain', we do not habitually associate the roof of the house with an animal's back and we do not see the beginning or end of a period of time (month or year) as its feet and head. This perspective can be further extended to notions such as *within* or *inside* represented by the name of another body part, 'stomach', while *in front* is represented by 'face', and *after* by 'back'.

What then, if anything, is truly universal? A thorough comparative analysis of many languages representing various language families may lead to discovery of semantic primitives, that is, basic concepts present in all human languages. This search for universals must not begin by imposing one point of view, rooted in one language and culture, on other languages and cultures. Finding such an alphabet of thought is indispensable for proper understanding of other cultures. Otherwise, we could only understand them in terms of our own culture, distorting and misinterpreting what we see. Obviously, we may not be able "to understand a distant culture 'in its own terms' without understanding it at the same time in our own terms," writes Wierzbicka (1992: 27), who is the leader in the search for semantic primitives. However, if we are armed with the understanding of what is universal, we shall be able to see what is human in it, and not only what is exotic, i.e., different.

Identity in cross-cultural contexts

The complexities of the relationship between culture, language and different aspects of human behaviour have always attracted interest, but probably never as much attention as over the recent years. We seem to have a great desire to explain the apparent idiosyncrasies of the way our fellow human beings behave or to excuse our own mishaps. Cultural and linguistic differences seem to provide an easy – sometimes way too easy – excuse.

We behave and speak in a way that has been to a great degree influenced by our upbringing and experience, sometimes imitating the patterns of speech we grew up with, sometimes rebelling against them. We want to belong to some social groups and want to distance ourselves from others. One of the ways of expressing our actual or desired group membership is by adopting or rejecting the group's language. Obviously, we do not have the full power of control in this respect, with some language features being easier to copy than others, and some people having a greater facility of imitation than others. One obvious example (with the editor of this volume being a good sample to illustrate this phenomenon) is that of non-native speakers trying to fit in linguistically in their adopted homeland. Though some may achieve a great degree of success in learning the new language and, in some cases blend in perfectly, the majority never reach even a close approximation of native fluency. And although the ability to use foreign language may have little to do with the speaker's intelligence, the sophistication of his or her linguistic expression will likely be interpreted as a reflection of their cognitive abilities, often becoming the basis of language-based stereotyping (cf. Stroińska 1998). As one immigrant woman put it, 'people believe that if you speak with an accent, you think with an accent.'

Language and culture are also said to be instrumental in defining our individual and group identity. We become who we are through the process of interaction with others (or the lack of thereof). 'We see ourselves as others see us,' argues Hewitt (1984: 55). We grow up surrounded by other people's attitudes toward us and we construct our self-awareness by internalising those attitudes (cf. Stroińska forthcoming 2000). Our identities are always under construction because the world around us is changing, and so is the language we are exposed to and the language we use.

Two areas where the construction of identities seems to offer particularly interesting insights are gender studies and the question of national identity and nationalism. Gender, ethnicity and social class used to be taken 'as given parameters and boundaries within which we create our own social identities,' observe John Gumperz and Jenny Cook-Gumperz in their influential paper on language and the communication of social identity (Gumperz and Cook-Gumperz 1982: 1). If language is studied as a tool of interaction, it is possible to demonstrate that 'these parameters are not constants that can be taken for granted but are communicatively produced' (ibid.).

Deborah Tannen (1996: 3) warns that 'entering the arena of research on gender is like stepping into a maelstrom' because of the interdisciplinary nature of the field. When researchers from different disciplines try to communicate, they encounter similar problems to those found in cross-cultural communication. The study of gender and discourse, that is the linguistic perspective in gender studies, although only a small fragment of research in this area, is further divided between those who support the *dominance* model and those who work within the model of *cultural difference*. Both approaches look at the communicative or conversational styles of men and women.

Judith Butler (1990) sees gender as 'performative', a notion borrowed from Austin's (1962) speech act theory. This means that femininity or masculinity are the effects produced by our behaviour and that gender is not given but socially constructed. Language is acknowledged as an important element in the process of identity construction. Deborah Cameron (1997) suggests that we interpret the gender-related behaviour of others through the discourse they use and through our own discourse habits and expectations. Discourse thus becomes what constructs gender differentiation.

National identity may also be seen as a socially constructed entity, with language, culture, religion and ethnicity as some of the key factors that contribute to its definition. The need to assert national identity occurs mostly when there is some crisis situation, usually linked to threats against what is considered important for the nation's survival, stability or wellbeing. The twentieth century has witnessed several examples of nationalism and, despite renewed hopes created by the end of the cold war, conflicts surrounding national issues are far from being over. While sensitivity to differences seems desirable in almost all areas of social studies, a relativistic approach to the study of national identities and nationalistic movements, especially those involved in conflicts, would do nothing to resolve, or even clarify, the problem. As all elements listed as key factors could be seen as parts of dynamic social and political processes, the radical view that national differences are insurmountable and national aspirations irreconcilable would only make conflicts seem unavoidable. It certainly makes more political sense to look for similarities and to learn how to interpret differences.

Even though the language we speak influences our way of thinking, if through nothing else then by the repertoire of concepts it provides, it does not determine or limit our cognitive abilities. There are different political or religious groups within one national or linguistic community and, with technology making communications faster and easier, the diversity, hidden under the surface of apparent uniformity, will only be growing. While Humboldt, and later Sapir and Whorf, spoke of worldviews of different peoples, represented through and in their respective languages, it seems that perhaps we are now moving away from homogeneous national or group perspectives and towards distinctive but also constantly changing individual points of view.

The globalisation of culture?

As much as we may detest the word *globalisation*, the world around us is changing rapidly, and we are more and more parts of one global community. The events in one part of the world may easily have global implications. This is happening mostly due to economics and politics, technology and telecommunications, and only partly due to culture, as we used to understand it. Global culture still sounds like an oxymoron, because what has been growing at an international scale is rather a variety of subcultures (e.g. popular music, film, fashion industry, etc.).

Marshall McLuhan, the theorist of media, predicted the birth of the *global village* in the 1960s, well before anyone was talking about information highways (cf. McLuhan 1964). Technological changes in our immediate surroundings may give us the impression that the world is shrinking and may have blurred the perception of time and distance. The new 'infomedia revolution,' as Frank Koelsch puts it (1995), is already upon us, triggered by the convergence of information technology and media. It is rapidly changing the way we live, work, think, and communicate, and it is shaping the way our children will see the world. However, we should perhaps also be reminded that the technological revolution has not yet touched most people in many less fortunate parts of the world, and that for half of the people living on Earth, the next phone call they make would be their first. The world, which for many centuries seemed mysteriously big, was suddenly, over a few decades, transformed and 'became united [...] so that shocks or inflammations in one part are instantly passed on to the other portions – some of which may lack the appropriate immunity', writes Alexander Solzenitzyn (in Dunlop et al.

1973: 562). This 'lack of proper immunity' of the people who come in touch with new forces is often matched by the lack of sensitivity of those who introduce new technologies or new social concepts.

The media talk about a constantly growing degree of globalisation of many aspects of the world economy and politics, with cultural developments allegedly following the global patterns as well. Since it is relatively easy to bring new technologies or products into new markets (the success of such ventures is a different matter), one may be easily misled into believing that cultural convergence is an equally facile process, which may be a natural consequence of economic processes. Despite the failure of any effortless technological and economic convergence of different regions of the world, many people believe that the world is sufficiently uniform in terms of culture and civilisation to warrant a successful global communication. This belief is made to look more acceptable with a relatively small number of languages recognised as means of international communication.

With English emerging as a *global* language, it is easy to forget that even when people from different linguistic and cultural backgrounds communicate in English, they continue to communicate from within their distinctive frameworks. It is not surprising that the better English they speak, the more intolerant native-speakers may be if they spot inconsistency in the linguistic behaviour of the foreigner. Foreign accent is a self-defence device that alerts the native-speaker to the possibility of misunderstanding. However, even if there is nothing to alert us to the possibility of cross-cultural miscommunication, we should not assume that we share the same values and use the same parameters for, say, politeness. It is only our impression, promoted by the development of new communication technologies, that the world is getting smaller and cultural barriers no longer exist.

The translatability of worldviews

There are thousands of professional translators and interpreters and their very existence could be seen as evidence for the translatability of ideas from one language to another. Yet, at the same time, translators never tire of attempting new and, as they believe, improved translations of the same books or poems, as if there was something inadequate or missing in the existing versions. A popular Italian saying – *traduttore, traditore* – compares a translator to a traitor, pointing to the belief that expressing the same thoughts in a different language affects the meaning of what was said. James Merrill (1977) concludes his poem *Lost in Translation*, where he ponders life in a number of languages, with the statement, 'But nothing's lost. Or else: all is translation/And every bit of us is lost in it/[...] Or found...' Stanisław Barańczak (1994) changes the title of Merrill's poem and calls his own book on the practice of translating poetry *Saved in Translation*, showing that it is possible to recreate poems from one language and culture in another, without losing much of their appeal.

There are, however, numerous problems related to translating literary and non-literary texts. Often even the simplest and apparently unambiguous expressions, those that seem to have direct equivalents in the other language, may prove treacherous. I was once asked to interpret at the investigation for discovery involving a murder charge. The prosecution's case was partly based on the fact that, in the initial interrogation, the accused never asked how his wife died. This, for the police, and later also for the prosecutor, implied that he must have known how she died, and so he must have been the killer.

I had the opportunity to listen to the tapes with the full text of the interrogation, conducted with the assistance of a Polish speaking police officer (whose Polish was rather basic), and I must agree that the accused never posed the question 'How did my wife die?' This, however, does not mean that he never asked how she died. He repeatedly asked in Polish 'Co się stało?', which was translated into English, without any hesitation, as 'What happened?' There is no doubt that 'what happened?' is a correct, word-for-word translation of the Polish *co się stało?*, and that the Polish speaking officer had not done anything wrong translating it that way. However, he missed an important point in his interpretation. In Polish, *co się stało?* is not only a possible way to ask about a tragic event of this kind; it is practically the only way to ask. The equivalent of the English question 'How did she die?' (*jak ona umarła?*) sounds very technical and could be asked by a police doctor or a forensic examiner, but not by a concerned relative. How do we account for this type of translation trap?

There are many other traps there as well. For many years after the Second World War, Victor Klemperer's 1947 book on the language deterioration in the Third Reich, *Lingua Tertii Imperii* ('Language of the Third Reich'), could not appear in Polish (cf.

introduction to my 1992 translation). This may seem odd as Poland was a victim of the Nazi regime, and there seemed to be no reason for not allowing publication of a book by someone who was as critical about Hitler's regime as Klemperer. Yet there was a reason. The language of the Third Reich had so much in common with the Polish language of the communist propaganda, that anyone familiar with communist style would have noticed the shared repertoire of metaphors and other stylistic devices. However, as Sapir had warned, 'no two languages are ever sufficiently similar to be considered as representing the same social reality' (Sapir 1949: 162). It would be misleading to simply translate seemingly easy Nazi key words, such as *Blut* and *Boden* as *krew* and *ziemia*, because Polish equivalents lack all the culture- and political-formation-specific associations and connotations. When I undertook the task of translating Klemperer's book into Polish, I chose to use equivalent communist newspeak when it seemed harmless and an extensive system of footnotes when using a seemingly obvious Polish communist equivalent would have been misleading (Klemperer 1992).

We usually discuss translation as a transfer of content and form from one language to another. The word 'interpretation' is also used and applied to translation practices, sometimes restricted to oral presentation of what was said in another language. The term 'interpretation', however, could also be applied to the representation of one person's words by another person. This process often requires special linguistic strategies, such as the proper sequence of tenses in reported speech in English or the use of subjunctive in German. Like translation, reporting someone's words involves an interpretation process, where the attitudes have to be examined, compared and resolved. In her chapter, Teresa Dobrzyńska looks at the use of metaphorical expressions in reported speech, pointing to speaker's attitudes as yet another factor that shapes discourse practices. We are well aware of the importance of attitudes in direct discourse, however, the way they influence indirect speech remains largely covert.

Translation is not a mechanical replacement of words or strings of words in one language by words or strings of words in another language. It involves a transfer of culture and a high degree of sensitivity to language and context. It is hardly ever easy (if it seems easy, it is probably wrong), but it is possible. I strongly believe that we can always communicate with another human being, no matter whether we share or do not share their (constructed) point of view. If we do not share the same framework, communicating will simply require more effort, but, like translation, it is possible.

Notes

1. The importance of the liberation of language could be seen in presentations at a special session organised at Warsaw University, Poland as early as the fall of 1981, just one year after the strikes that led to the creation of the first free trade unions in the communist Eastern Europe. The main topic was language manipulation and defence against it.
2. This, for instance, nicely applies to the analysis of the language of totalitarian propaganda that was strikingly similar in, say, Nazi Germany and communist Russia. However, to say that the two systems were alike would be a very inappropriate simplification. For a discussion, see Stroińska 1994.

References

Austin, J.L. 1962. *How to Do Things with Words*. Cambridge, MA: Harvard University Press.

Barańczak, S. 1994. *Ocalone w tłumaczeniu* ('Saved in translation'). Poznań: Wydawnictwo a5.

Benedict, R. 1934/1989. *Patterns of Culture*. Boston: Houghton Mifflin Company.

Butler, J. 1990. *Gender Trouble: Feminism and the Subversion of Identity*. New York: Routledge.

Cameron, D. 1997. 'Performing gender identity: young men's talk and the construction of heterosexual identity', in *Language and Masculinity*, eds S. Johnson and U.H. Meinhoff. Oxford: Blackwell, 47–64.

Devitt, M. and Sterelny, K. 1999. *Language and Reality; An Introduction to the Philosophy of Language* (second edition). Cambridge, Massachusetts: The MIT Press.

Dunlop, J. B., Haugh, R. and Klimoff, A. 1973. *Aleksandr Solzhenitsyn: Critical Essays and Documentary Materials*. London: Collier Macmillan Publishers.

Foley, W. A. 1997. *Anthropological Linguistics: An Introduction*. Oxford: Blackwell.

Gumperz, J.J. and Cook-Gumperz, J. 1982. 'Introduction: language and the communication of social identity', in ed. Gumperz, J. J. *Language and Social Identity*. Cambridge, New York: Cambridge University Press. 1–21.

Gumperz, J. J. and Levinson, S.C. eds. 1996. *Rethinking Linguistic Relativity*. Cambridge: Cambridge University Press.

Hall, E.T. 1983. *The Dance of Life: The Other Dimension of Time*. Garden City, New York: Doubleday.

Herbert, A. P. 1935. *What a Word!* London: Methuen.

Hewitt, H. 1984. *Self and Society: A Symbolic Interactionist Social Psychology* (3rd edition). London: Allyn and Bacon.

Hofstede, G. 1991. *Cultures and Organizations*. London: McGraw-Hill.

Hollenbach, B. 1990. 'Semantic and syntactic extensions of Copala Trique body-part nouns', in eds Cuarón, B. and Levy, P. *Homenaje a Jorge A. Suárez: Lingüística indoamericana e hispánica*. Mexico City: El Colegio de México. 275–296.

Humboldt, W. 1988. *The Diversity of Human Language-Structure and its Influence on the Mental Development of Mankind*, translated by Peter Heath. Cambridge: Cambridge University Press.

Klemperer, V. 1992. *Lingua Tertii Imperii: Notatnik Filologa*, translated by M. Stroińska. Toronto: Polish Publishing Fund.

Koelsch, F. 1995. *The Infomedia Revolution: How it is Changing our World and your Life*. Toronto and Montreal: McGraw-Hill Ryerson.

Leibniz, G.W. 1903. *Opuscules et fragments inédits de Leibniz*, edited by L. Couturat. Paris.

McLuhan, M. 1964. *Understanding Media: The Extensions of Man*. New York: McGraw-Hill.

Merrill, J. 1977. *Divine Comedies*. Oxford: Oxford University Press.

Redder, A. and Rehbein, J. eds. 1987. *Arbeiten zur interkulturellen Kommunikation*, Osnabrück: Osnabrücker Beiträge zur Sprachtheorie 38.

Sapir, E.1921. *Language: An Introduction to the Study of Speech*. New York: Harcourt, Brace and World.

———. 1931. 'Conceptual Categories in Primitive Languages', *Science* 74: 578. Reprinted in *Language in Culture and Society: A Reader in Linguistics and Anthropology*, ed. D. Hymes. 1964. New York: Harper and Row: 128.

———. 1949 *Selected Writings*. Berkeley: University of California Press.

Stroińska, M. 1994. 'Linguistic relativism and universalism: the language of ideologies', in *Socialist Realism Revisited*, eds N. Kolesnikoff and W. Smyrniw. Hamilton: McMaster University Press. 59–72.

———. 1998 'Them and us: on cognitive and pedagogical aspects of the language-based stereotyping'. in *Stereotype im Fremdsprachenunterricht*, eds M. Löschmann and M. Stroińska. Frankfurt am Main: Peter Lang. 35–58.

———. forthcoming 2000. 'Self-reflection through language'. in *Echoes of Narcissus*, ed. L. Spaas. New York and Oxford: Berghahn Books.

Tannen, D. 1996. *Gender and Discourse*. New York and Oxford: Oxford University Press.

Whorf, B.L. 1956. *Language, Thought, and Reality; Selected Writings of Benjamin Lee Whorf*. Cambridge, Massachusetts: The MIT Press.

Wierzbicka, A. 1992. *Semantics, Culture and Cognition: Universal Human Concepts in Culture-Specific Configurations*. Oxford: Oxford University Press.

———. 1997. *Understanding Cultures through their Key Words*. Oxford: Oxford University Press.

PART I

THINKING IN WORDS

Space and Time in Natural Language: Some Parallels between Spatial and Temporal Expressions in English and Russian

Jim Miller

Introduction: grammar and cognition

This paper rests on three assumptions: language is central to all culture and cultures; the study of language-use and language-users must take account of cultural variation; underlying cultural differences is a cognitive bedrock of spatial relations. What evidence supports the last assumption? Brain surgery does not reveal mental representations of the non-linguistic world but the codes, the syntax and morphology, by which speakers talk about the world can be inspected and reveal that the syntax and morphology, and even vocabulary, that are used for talking about spatial relations are also used for talking about non-spatial relations of all sorts. Many central grammatical structures in many languages are based on constructions relating to location or movement; although this paper focuses on temporal relations, the constructions to be examined are part of a much larger and pervasive phenomenon. To bring out the parallel treatment of space and time the discussion must draw on linguistic data. Non-linguists are assured that the English and Russian data are central to the respective languages and that the minutiae are excluded.

Language system and language behaviour

Humans regularly perform miracles of communication, using the limited resources of human languages in situations that vary subtly and infinitely. All languages possess a small number of syntactic and morphological constructions relative to the number of different situations in which their speakers take part, and equally they possess a relatively small number of lexical items.

How then do humans perform their linguistic miracles? The answer lies in the distinction between language system and language behaviour (see Lyons 1977a). We will focus on language system, but first draw attention to one important facet of language behaviour: speakers produce utterances in context and in each context speakers and listeners collaborate to determine the reference of lexical items. Listeners work hard to interpret which speech acts are performed, and whether the speaker is being ironical or not (see Clark 1992). Speakers and listeners belong to social groups ranging from small groups such as football teams to larger groups such as Edinburgh lawyers, and the Mayan community in Oxkutzcab (Hanks 1990), not to mention other groupings based on gender, age and so on. They share a linguistic code guiding, e.g., their syntax, their pronunciation, their choice of vocabulary, the way they tell jokes, and what counts as a narrative or a rational discussion with a view to deciding a course of action, and so on.

Since the work of Austin (1962), Goffman (1959), Sacks et al. (1974), Grice (1989), admirably reviewed in Schiffrin (1994), much research has focused on language behaviour. We argue here that humans are able to deal with the ever-shifting details of context and situation partly because certain properties of linguistic systems constitute an anchorage point for their linguistic behaviour. The properties of interest here are (i) content and contrast within linguistic systems and (ii) the relationship between spatial expressions and concepts and a large range of other expressions and concepts.

Language system and contrast

We will begin with content and contrast. Items in a linguistic system contrast with each other, and the content of each item is not determined in detail but just enough to preserve the contrasts. 'Contrast' does not apply just to lexical items; indeed, at first it was not even applied to lexical items, but mainly in the analysis of phonological systems. What were regarded as crucial were the contrasts between phonological units, not a complete specification of the properties of phonetic segments. The concepts of co-occurrence and contrast have been applied to the analysis of vocabulary, the pioneering work being Lyons (1963).

The role of contrast can be demonstrated by the denotation of the lexical item CHAIR. Chairs come in all shapes, sizes and materials, but the normal adult members of any given group have a prototype concept that enables them to work out what is being referred to as a chair by a particular speaker in a particular context. The contrast between CHAIR and, e.g., SOFA, TABLE and BED, guides the listener to a particular conceptual area; once in that area, listeners can start to relate to the context the utterance they have just heard, and speakers can begin to choose an appropriate lexical item for the utterances they are planning.

This paper is concerned more with grammatical codes. These are interesting for two reasons: they provide evidence for a central property of human cognition, and speakers of any language are obliged to use them. Case suffixes and prepositions, the two types of element to be examined here, form closed systems, closed sets of contrasts. Individual cases and prepositions carry very general meanings; the contrasts guide language users to the relevant general meaning, which they refine using the (general) meanings of the lexical items in a given clause and by (re)constructing the relationship between clause and context.

Spatial relations are fundamental both cognitively and linguistically, that is, that the basic concepts on which all others are built are location in a place and movement to or from a place. This localist hypothesis is held to apply to all languages (or all speakers of all languages) and in all cultures, and it takes spatial relations and concepts to be a major cognitive anchoring point in the flux of situations. We will see that the concept of contrast is important in localism, since localists, like some other schools, interpret contrasts in syntax and/or morphology as signalling contrasts in meaning. A lack of syntactic or morphological contrast is taken as indicating a basic meaning underlying all the uses of a particular syntactic or morphological construction. The presence or lack of contrast is taken by some analysts as signalling the presence or absence of meaning in morphemes and words.

The assumption that the hypothesis applies universally might seem rash in the light of recent work on spatial orientation (see Levinson 1991, 1997; Pederson et al. 1998). Levinson (1997: 30–31) reminds his readers of Kant's argument that spatial concepts are fundamental intuitions presupposed by the rest of our ideas about the material world, and that they are inevitable and universal concepts. Levinson maintains that Kant's argument is destroyed by the existence of languages with no system of relative expressions such as *left* and *right*, *front* and *back*, and with no system of intrinsic coordinates that enable speakers to talk of items being located, e.g., *at the rear of the lorry* or *at the front of the pub*. Instead, these languages (e.g. the Pama-Nyungan family of Australian languages) have only a system of absolute coordinates, East–West, North–South.

Levinson's fears are not justified. None of the localist work, in whatever framework, depends on systems of coordinates; it does depend on concepts such as location and movement, and distinctions such as those between location inside an entity, location near an entity, movement away from an entity (out of/off), movement into/onto an entity, movement to a location near an entity. These concepts do appear to be universal in human societies and in human ways of talking about the world.

The localist hypothesis

An essential point is that the localist hypothesis did not emerge from idle speculation, but was developed because of the large amount of data throughout the languages of the world demonstrating the use of spatial constructions to express and manipulate non-spatial concepts. Over a wide range of languages from many different language-families throughout the world, constructions that express location or movement are used to express concepts such as cause, agency, instrumentality (in brief, all the relationships signalled by case suffixes or prepositions), verb aspect, comparison.

A major principle of localism is that patterns of one and the same case suffix or preposition expressing spatial and non-spatial meaning should be found over a wide range of languages. This principle ensures that general theories are not proposed on the basis of the idiosyncracies of one language. For example, the use of identical markers for the goal of a movement, as in going to a place, and for recipient, as in giving something to someone, is very widespread, being found, for instance, in Indo-European languages, in Turkish, in Austronesian languages (see Hooper 1996: 23), and in Australian languages (see Donaldson 1980: 95–96; Austin 1981: 114–137).

A second major principle of localism is that all differences in form, all contrasts, are significant. This can be illustrated by means of the much-cited 'loading hay' examples. *The farmer loaded the wagon with hay* and *The farmer loaded hay onto the wagon* differ as to which noun phrase is the direct object, *the wagon* or *the hay*, which noun phrase is the oblique object, (*with*) *hay* or (*onto*) *the wagon*, and which preposition occurs, *with* or *onto*. These grammatical differences were initially thought to be minor but it turns out that the sentences have rather different truth conditions. The first is true if the wagon is completely full of hay, and the second leaves it open whether the wagon was completely full or part-full. The apparently minor grammatical differences turn out to signal important differences in meaning.

The principle sketched in the previous paragraph is important. Linguists divide into those for it and those against it. The latter hold to the view that the elements in clauses divide into items with 'lexical' meaning, nouns, verbs and so on, and items with no lexical meaning and even no meaning at all. These are words such as *the* and *a*, prepositions such as *of*, *with*, auxiliary verbs such as *be* and *have*.

Matthews (1981: 50–70) regards *of* as not contrasting with any other preposition and as being simply a cue by which a construction is identified. He argues that *the speeches of Cicero* is not parallel to *the speeches from Cicero* and *the speeches by Cicero* because the latter have functions from which *of* is excluded; they occur in finite clauses as the modifiers of verbs, as in *The speeches have arrived from Cicero* and *The speeches were composed by Cicero*. The lack of contrast between *of* and any other preposition indicates that *of* carries little information.

Similarly there is a long tradition whereby no semantic meaning is assigned to certain case suffixes and prepositions. The division is clearly seen in the treatment of genitive and dative case in Indo-European languages such as Icelandic and Russian. Some analysts see the case suffixes as simply unusual markers of direct object; localists see them as contrasting with the accusative case and as expressing different relationships.

A particularly clear example of the difference in approach is found in Lewis (1967), who employs traditional grammatical concepts for the description, but otherwise has no theoretical axes to grind. Discussing the Turkish ablative case, Lewis says that where the English verbs *suspect, loathe, fear,* and *like* take a direct object, the corresponding Turkish verbs require a noun in the ablative case. That is, the English clause *Osman fears Mehmet* presents Mehmet as the entity towards which Osman directs his fear; the Turkish clause *Osman Mehmetten korkiyor*, as Lewis (1967: 38) puts it, presents Mehmet as the source of the fear. An appropriate gloss would be 'Osman is frightened and this situation comes from/is caused by Mehmet'.

Contra Matthews (1981: 59–68), it is important to distinguish meaning and quantity of information. In a given context, even a particular full word may be predictable and therefore contribute a small amount of meaning, but it does not lose its content; in *I asked him to move along but he wouldn't* ___ there is a high probability that the gap will be filled by *budge*. The predictability of the second phrase does not rob it of its meaning. Matthew's approach leads to an analysis of the Turkish *korkmak* (fear) as entirely determining the ablative case, which therefore contributes nothing to the semantic interpretation. This approach overlooks the fact that the Turkish ablative suffixes occur in a number of constructions; it is legitimate to ask whether its occurrence in these constructions is accidental, or whether they share some element of meaning. The localist answer is that the various meanings are all built on the concept of movement-from. Going back to the second principle described above, localists further ask whether it is accidental that over a wide range of languages structures with a movement-from meaning are used as the source of structures for expressing, e.g., reason, cause, agent and comparison.

To sum up the above, localism is a set of hypotheses concerning basic semantic structures, the relationship between grammatical code and semantic structures, the handling of grammatical code (paying attention to differences in form, and so on), and the relevance of historical change. It also includes a hypothesis that spatial relations are basic both cognitively and linguistically. This thesis is independent of the argument as to whether Piaget's or Chomsky's views afford the better understanding of how children acquire language, but it is compatible with, and supported by, the evidence on which Piaget bases his idea of a sensorimotor period of cognitive development. The sensorimotor period precedes language (at least if by 'language' we understand the production of recognisable words); in it, children come to recognise permanent objects and relationships of various sorts, and, importantly, achieve a basic understanding of location and movement in space and of causality (for an account and comparison of the ideas of Piaget and Chomsky see Piatelli-Palmarini 1980: 25; see also the classic work [not Piagetian] by Miller and Johnson-Laird 1976). Levinson (1991: 2) adds the argument that the centrality of spatial cognition is shown by the way in which non-spatial problems are transferred into spatial ones, in particular the use of alphabets and diagrams for the representation of knowledge on paper, and the use of maps, charts and plans. The intense use of diagrams in many mathematics classrooms is a striking example to be added to Levinson's list.

Localism and case: case in Latin and Russian

It appears to be the case generally (even universally) that the markers of relationships between nouns and verbs in clauses, whether case suffixes, prepositions or postpositions, have either only spatial meanings or spatial and non-spatial meanings. The sort of evidence supporting the part of the hypothesis relating to prepositions is exemplified by the English preposition OVER: the sentences *The dog leapt over the wall* and *The children ran over the lawn* exemplify the spatial meaning, while *Over twenty students crammed into the phone box* exemplifies the non-spatial meaning. The spatial meaning has to do with movement through space, while the third example is interpreted as though movement were involved. The movement metaphor is not confined to OVER; we can say *There were under twenty students at the lecture*, using the opposition OVER-UNDER, and we talk of numbers rising and falling – *The number of injured rose above sixty* vs. *The number of unemployed fell below one million*. ABOVE and BELOW are not now used with reference to numbers without verbs such as RISE, FALL and SINK, but Jane Austen would have written *above twenty students*. This particular metaphor is persistent.

With respect to case suffixes, the hypothesis requires a more subtle analysis. One difficulty is that many, perhaps all, languages with systems of case suffixes have one or two suffixes that carry no spatial meaning and that cannot be shown ever to have carried spatial meaning. Turkish, for example, has a set of accusative suffixes whose sole function is to mark the direct object noun (alternatively, to mark the noun denoting the Patient in a given situation). It has a set of genitive suffixes whose sole function is to mark possession (in the very broadest sense). Subject nouns (which often denote Agents) have no case suffix. The other sets of case suffixes – dative, locative and ablative – do carry spatial meaning.

Analysts of case systems have for a long time drawn a distinction between grammatical and local cases (see Lyons 1968: 295–302; Blake 1994: 32–33, 119–156). Grammatical cases marked grammatical functions, for instance whether a noun functioned as the subject or direct object of a clause or as a possessor. Local cases marked location and direction (which, as examples given below will show, are not simple concepts). The distinction between grammatical and local cases applies well to, e.g., Turkish but in many languages the distinction between grammatical and local cases does not apply as easily; since the distinction was developed by scholars of Indo-European languages, it is ironic that it does not apply neatly to these languages. Russian is a good example of the difficulties. Although subject nouns are in the nominative case, which carries no spatial meaning, all the other case suffixes have spatial interpretations. For instance, the accusative case suffixes that mark direct object also signal the goal of a movement.

The reason for the two uses of accusative case is incorporated in traditional terminology. Direct objects go with transitive verbs, and the term 'transitive' derives from the Latin verb *transire* 'go across'. The metaphor is that of an action passing from an Agent to a Patient; this is a localist view, that as people move to places so actions move from one person to another. What is central, it is worth reminding ourselves, is the linguistic data: the fact that in Russian, and in many other languages, the same case marking is used for direct objects/Patients and for goals of movement.

The local uses of case suffixes present metaphorical extensions similar to those found in prepositions and discussed in the paragraph on OVER. These extensions reinforce the hypothesis that notions of location in and movement through space are the basic building blocks of the mental representations by means of which humans interpret themselves and the world they live in.

Location, movement and metaphor

We turn now to the last topic in this discussion of prepositions and case suffixes: to what extent do properties of concrete location and movement carry over to the abstract, metaphorical uses? King (1988) discusses the German prepositions *von* (from), *mit* (with), and *durch* (through). Grammars of German usually state that *von* is used for personal agents, as in *von Franz* (by Frank), *mit* for instruments handled by a personal agents, as in *mit einer Säge* (with a saw), and *durch* for abstract or impersonal causes, as in *durch ein Erdbeben* (by an earthquake).

King observes that in both spoken and written German, *durch* regularly occurs with nouns denoting personal agents and nouns denoting instruments. Examples are given in (1) and (2).

(1)   Caesar wurde durch Brutus getötet
       Caesar became through Brutus killed
       Caesar was killed by/through Brutus
(2)   Caesar wurde durch einen Dolch getötet
       Caesar became through a dagger killed
       Caesar was killed by a dagger

King collected interpretations of the above and other examples from a set of native speakers of German. They understood from (1) that Brutus is presented as an intermediary carrying out an instruction. If *durch* is replaced by *von*, Brutus is interpreted as the primary agent. The informants understood from (2) that, e.g., Caesar stumbled and fell on his dagger; the killing was accidental. If *durch* is replaced by *mit*, the interpretation is that the dagger was wielded by an agent. King suggests that the different interpretations build on the differences in meaning relating to actual movement; *von* marks the starting point of a movement, whereas *durch* marks the path along which the movement takes place. *Durch* presents a participant as merely the path along which an action travels and not as the source from which the action originates. The differences in spatial meaning are put to metaphorical use in the presentation of causation.

As an example of how differences in location and movement are projected onto time, let us consider the accusative and dative cases of Russian. Both signal the end point of a movement, but accusative case is used when one entity moves into contact with another one. Accusative case frequently combines with *v* (into) and *na* (onto), which denote contact with the interior or surface of some object. Dative case is used when one entity moves into the space adjacent to another entity but without coming into contact with it. Compare (3a) and (3b).

(3a)   Elena voshla v kiosk
       Elena went-into (the) kiosk
(3b)   Ona podoshla k kiosku
       She went-up to (the) kiosk

(3a) describes a situation in which Elena goes into the interior of the kiosk, possibly in contact with a wall but certainly surrounded by the walls. (3b) presents Elena as not entering the kiosk or coming into contact with it but standing at the kiosk.

Other prepositions that take the accusative case are *cherez* (through, across) and *po* (up to), as in (4).

(4a)   Volk shel cherez les
        Wolf went through wood
        'The wolf went through the wood'
(4b)   Doma po okna zaneslo snegom
        houses up-to windows it-buried with-snow
        'The snow buried the houses up to the windows'

Contact with an entity is important not just in connection with movement onto surfaces or into interiors; it is crucial when we consider the use of accusative case to mark direct object/ Patient nouns. Prototypical Patients undergo a change of state, are affected by another participant, and may be stationary relative to the position of another participant, as in arrows hitting targets.

Prototypical Patient nouns in Russian are marked by the accusative case, and prototypical Patients are affected by Agents coming into contact with them and changing their state. Of course, many non-prototypical Patients are also marked by accusative case, but we focus on prototypes and on the contrast between object nouns with accusative case and object nouns that receive dative case from verbs such as *pomoch'* (help), *otvetit'* (reply), *sovetovat'* (advise), *sochuvstvovat'* (sympathise), *pozvoljat'* (allow), *napominat'* (remind), *verit'* (believe), *radovat'sja* (rejoice at), and *udivljat'sja* (be surprised at). These verbs do not cause a change of state and have in general a much smaller effect. None of them denotes actions involving physical contact with an entity. The underlying metaphor is that of someone putting something in someone else's personal space (as Janda (1993: 54) puts it, of someone receiving something, be it harm, help or hindrance).

Space and time

Spatial relations are central to the lives of human beings, but time, too, is central. The key fact here is that temporal expressions are typically identical with spatial expressions; the English expressions *on Friday*, *in October*, *by Christmas*, *over the next two months* demonstrate the use of prepositions that have spatial uses. Where prepositions do not have obviously spatial uses in Modern English, such as *after* in *after Christmas*, they can be shown to be connected historically with a spatial expression or to be cognate with expressions in related languages that have spatial uses. *After* is connected with *aft*, which is used, with a spatial meaning, only in nautical contexts (apart from fixed expressions such as *run after someone*). *After* is cognate with the Afrikaans *agter*, which corresponds to *behind*.

Examples from English

Consider the English temporal expressions in (5) and (6).

(5a)   next week, last month, today, tomorrow, yesterday
(5b)   on Monday, on Saturday
(5c)   in January, in March, in 1953, in the holidays
(5d)   at Christmas, at Lammas
(6a)   For two years the city was under siege
(6b)   We are going to Moscow for a week

The examples in (5a) show that some English temporal expressions have no preposition while others require one, the question being why days of the week take *on*, months and years take *in*, and the names of festivals take *at*. Similar problems affect the analysis of Russian temporal expressions. The examples in (6) demonstrate the use of *for* where the speaker emphasises that an event extends over a particular period of time. The central feature of the construction in (6b) is that this occurrence of *for* can be analysed as parallel to the spatial use of *for* in (7). (7a) describes a situation in which the event of travelling through a gloomy forest lasted over a distance of twenty miles; (7b) describes a situation in which the event of cycling will last over a distance of twenty miles and the event of skiing over a distance of ten miles.

(7a)   For the next twenty miles we travelled through a gloomy forest
(7b)   We are going to cycle for twenty miles and ski for ten miles

Spatial approximation is signalled by prepositions such as *about, around,* and *round about. About* used to have the same spatial meaning as *round;* while that usage is now archaic, it still has the spatial meaning exemplified in (8), although even this usage is confined to literary English. *Around* and *round* are neutral in register but *round about* belongs to informal spoken English.

(8a)   Round/around the house was a high hedge
(8b)   About the castle is a moat

(8c)   There are railings round about the school playground
(9)   Drive to the junction beyond Straiton. You'll find the
        new IKEA store round there.
(10)   The manager is around/about. I'll just see if I can find
        him

The usage in (8) can be taken as basic; the speaker chooses a landmark or point of orientation, here the house, the castle, and the school playground, and locates an entity somewhere in the space round the landmarks. The speaker who utters (9) takes Straiton as a landmark and asserts that the new IKEA store is located somewhere in the space surrounding Straiton. Similarly, the speaker uttering (10) places the manager in the space surrounding and 'belonging' to the location of the speaker and addressee.

Compare now the temporal expressions in (11).

(11a)   We left around ten past six
(11b)   I'll be there about/around seven

In uttering (11a) the speaker places the event of leaving in the temporal space surrounding the specific clock time 'ten past six'; not at that time exactly but close enough to permit ten past six as a landmark. (11b) can be treated in a similar fashion.

Examples from Russian

Like English prepositions, Russian prepositions have spatial and temporal uses, and Russian case suffixes have spatial and temporal uses. All the Russian case suffixes apart from the nominative occur in expressions of time and space. (3a) exemplifies the use of *v* and accusative case for movement. (12) exemplifies *v* and locative case for location. (Analogous examples could be given for *na* (on).)

(12)   Elena v kioske
        Elena in (the) kiosk
        'Elena is in the kiosk'

We consider first the expression of spatial and temporal limits, as in the English examples in (13).

(13a)   Winter lasts from the beginning of December to the end
        of February in Edinburgh (though March, April, and
        May regularly bring unpleasant surprises)
(13b)   We flew from Edinburgh to Toronto

(13c)   I will be in the library from 9 o'clock
(13d)   She worked until/till midnight on the report.

(13a,b) demonstrate the occurrence of *from* and *to* in sentences describing the beginning and end of a movement through space, (13b), and the beginning and end of an event's duration in time, (13a). The event's duration in time is presented as the event moving through time. (13c) mentions just the starting point of the temporal movement, while (13d) mentions just the finishing point. (*Until* and *till* derive historically from prepositions with a spatial meaning).

With respect to spatial and temporal limits, Russian is interestingly different from English. The beginning point of a movement is expressed by three prepositions, the choice being determined by the nature of the starting point, as in *iz jashchika* (out-of a-drawer), *s polki* (off a-shelf), *ot berega* (from shore). The choice between *iz*, *s*, and *ot* in spatial expressions is simplified in temporal expressions: only *s* is used to denote temporal starting points.

The end-point of a movement can be signalled by *do*, as in *do granicy* (as far as the frontier) or by *po*, as used in (16b). *Do* is appropriate where an entity moves up to a landmark, but not necessarily into it or into contact with it. *Po* in (4b) is of limited occurrence in the meaning of 'up to', but it is used regularly, and its interpretation is 'up to and including'; in the situation described by (4b) the snow came up to and over the windows. This contrast between the spatial meanings of *do* and *po* is paralleled in temporal expressions. The examples in (14) are taken from Wade (1992).

(14a)   On otdyxaet s 26 marta do pervogo aprelja
        he is-resting from 26 March to 1st April
        'He is on holiday from the 26th March to the 1st April'
        (reporting back on the 1st April)
(14b)   On otdyxaet s 26 marta po pervoe aprelja
        he is-resting from 26 March to 1st April
        'He is on holiday from the 26th March to the 1st April'
        (reporting back on the 2nd April)

American English has the contrast between *till the 1st April*, corresponding to (14a), and *through the 1st April*, corresponding to (14b). The latter presumably captures the idea that the event moves through the 1st April to the end of that day.

(3b) exemplifies the use of the preposition *k* and a noun in the dative case to express the meaning 'movement in the direction of a landmark but not necessarily into the space adjacent to the landmark'. Note in (3b) the verb prefix *pod-*. Now both *k* and the preposition *pod* turn up in temporal expressions with meanings related to the spatial ones they bear in (3). Examples are given in (15).

(15a) Ja dopishu stat'ju k koncu sentjabrja
I will-finish-writing article to end of-September
'I will finish the article by the end of September'
(15b) On vernulsja pod konec sentjabrja
he returned under end of-September
'He returned towards the end of September'

The speaker uttering (15a) moves the event of writing the article into the temporal space adjacent to the 30th September, but not into the 30th itself. (15b) presents the event of returning as moving towards the end of September, but not reaching that landmark in the calendar.

A final example of straightforward parallels between spatial and temporal expressions is the use of *cherez*. Its use in spatial expressions, equivalent to the English *over* and *through*, is illustrated in (4a). Its use in temporal expressions is exemplified in (16).

(16a) Koncert nachinaetsja cherez desjat' minut
concert begins through ten minutes
'The concert begins in ten minutes'

The metaphor available to speakers of Russian is that the relevant persons move through certain extents of time to reach particular events; the addressee has (only) to move through ten minutes to reach the beginning of the concert.

We turn now to the occurrence of *v* (in) and *na* (on) in temporal expressions. At first sight the patterns are baffling, with all combinations of *v* or *na* and accusative or locative case. The preposition *v* 'in' used with nouns denoting years, months, and days of the week.*Na* used with the noun *nedelja* 'week', and with nouns denoting religious feasts such as Christmas. The locative case used with nouns denoting years and months but accusative case with nouns denoting weekdays. The locative case used with *nedelja* 'week', but the accusative case with nouns denoting religious feasts.

To be sure, the general hypothesis that spatial concepts and expressions are the source of temporal concepts and expressions receives strong support. Events are located inside months and years. Accusative case can be explained in terms of an event being projected onto a unit of time.

Interestingly, spatial expressions exhibit a similar breakdown of pattern. It remains true that for most nouns, *v* signals a relationship with the interior of an entity, while *na* signals a relationship with the surface. With certain classes of nouns, however, both *v* and *na* occur, not substitutable one for the other with the same subsets, but partitioning the subsets. Wade (1992: 424–433) lists a number of sets – countries; republics and other territories in the USSR (now the CIS); natural features and climatic zones; mountain ranges; islands, archipelagoes and peninsulas; points of the compass; buildings, areas and workplaces.

A number of nouns denoting buildings, areas and workplaces require *na*. Wade (and others) relate the occurrence of *na* to the fact that the nouns denote areas that were historically associated with open spaces or complexes of buildings, e.g. *na vokzale/zavode/dache/ferme* (at the station/factory/dacha/farm). The explanation sounds plausible, but why do we have *na aèrodrome* (at the aerodrome) vs. *v aèroportu* (at the airport), *na ferme* (at the farm) vs. *v kolxoze* (at the kolkhoz), *na stadione* (at the stadium) vs. *v parke* (in the park)? Perhaps the conception of particular types of areas, mountain ranges and so on that motivated the use of *na* is no longer operative, or no longer powerful enough to preserve the original contrast.

With respect to temporal expressions, one justifiable view to take in the absence of detailed analysis (and possibly psycholinguistic experiments with native speakers of Russian) is that the original spatial distinction between interior and surface is not relevant to time nouns. This view becomes particularly attractive when we discover that, although *v sredu* (on Wednesday) has *v* combined with a noun denoting a weekday, the noun *den'* (day) itself combines with either *v* or *na* depending on what modifier occurs with it.

We conclude this discussion of prepositions and case in Russian temporal expressions by commenting on the fact that a number of time nouns occur in the instrumental case, not accusative or locative. Some examples are given in (17).

(17a) *zimoj* (in winter), *vesnoj* (in spring), *letom* (in summer), *osen'ju* (in autumn)

(17b) *utrom* (in the morning), *dnem* (in the daytime), *vecherom* (in the evening), *noch'ju* (at night)

(17c) *vecherami* (in the evenings), *celymi chasami* (lit. whole hours 'for hours on end')

Note first the contrast between accusative case (movement) and instrumental case (location), illustrated in (18).

(18a)   Petr uexal za granicu
       Peter away-travelled beyond frontier-accusative
       'Peter went abroad'
(18b)   Peter zhivet za granicej
       Peter lives beyond frontier-instrumental
       'Peter lives abroad'

The second point is that the instrumental case on its own can denote a spatial relation, as shown in (19).

(19)   Deti   shli   v shkolu lesom
      children were-going to school wood-instrumental
      'The children were going to school through the wood'

One problem is that the relationship can be one of straightforward location, as in (18b), or more subtle, as in (19), involving a path relationship; the children are located on a path located in the wood. The path interpretation seems more suited to (17c) and the non-path same-place interpretation to (17a,b). Whatever analysis turns out to be consistent, supported by coherent argument and applicable to all the patterns involving the instrumental, the key point for present purposes is the general connection between instrumental case and spatial relationships. This fits the wider pattern of temporal expressions (and concepts) being based on spatial expressions (and concepts).

Conclusion

The above discussion focuses on grammatical structures. These are central to natural languages and their use is obligatory. Patterns that turn up in the grammars of a large number of languages from different language families, and/or persist through historical changes, are important and provide a clue to the mental representations constructed by the speakers of this or that language. The range of languages examined above is very restricted but the use of the same grammatical blocks for both spatial and temporal expressions is widespread throughout the world's languages, though not necessarily present in absolutely every language.

The case system of the Australian language Diyari, for instance, is analogous to that of Russian (see Austin 1981).

Locative case is used for location in space and for temporal relationships – 'on the ground', 'near the tree', 'in the morning', 'at night', 'in summer' – are expressed by means of the locative case; 'from the camp', 'off the shin bone', 'after the drought', 'after being hot' and 'since long ago' require the use of the ablative case; 'to his camp', to the hole', 'until tomorrow' require the allative case.

Outside the central grammar of a given language, there may be patterns of expressions of the sort investigated by, e.g., Lakoff (1987). For instance, one metaphor widespread and possibly even universal throughout Europe is that of past events being behind us and of future events being ahead of us. Alternatively, events come towards us (to our faces) from the future and recede into the past behind us. We look forward and plan ahead; we talk of there being a long way to go until some event, or of the event being far off. This pattern of metaphors is not universal throughout the world; the Torres Strait Islanders apparently talk of facing into the past and going backwards into the future, a view that makes excellent sense if based on travel by canoe (Lesley Stirling, University of Melbourne, personal communication). Other general metaphors are possible. Dixon (1972: 115) remarks: "Clearly, 'past time' is correlated with 'up' and 'future time' with 'down' in the Dyirbal°an worldview."

We close the paper by expressing regret that it deals only with language system and not with language behaviour. It does not look at the regular use of a particular language by a particular group of speakers in the various contexts and types of situation they encounter in their daily lives. Such an account is available in Hanks (1990). He examines the system of deictics in Maya (spoken in Yucatan, Mexico), and the use of the deictics by a particular community of Maya speakers. Hanks argues that deixis is a social construction intelligible only in relation to a sociocultural system. He asserts that time and space interweave because the organisation of domestic, agricultural and religious spaces reflects spatial requirements and constraints at any given point in a particular cycle, but also reflects what he calls (1990: 391) the microdiachrony of an activity field, the different stages in a particular cycle. The use of deictics is determined by spatial factors (distance from speaker, etc.), social factors, and time factors (stages in a cycle and even stages in the evolution of a conversation). All the localist would wish to add to Hanks's detailed and absorbing account is the idea that the spatial relationships are basic and form the template for social and temporal relationships. People can be near or distant socially, and events can be near or distant in time.

References

Austin, J. 1962. *How to Do Things With Words*. Oxford: Clarendon Press.
Austin, P. 1981. *A Grammar of Diyari, South Australia*. Cambridge: Cambridge University Press.
Blake, B. 1994. *Case*. Cambridge: Cambridge University Press.
Clark, H. H. 1992. *Arenas of Language Use*. Chicago: The University of Chicago Press and the Center for the Study of Language and Information.
Dixon, R. M. W. 1972. *The Dyirbal Language of North Queensland*. Cambridge: Cambridge University Press.
Donaldson, T. 1980. *Ngiyambaa*. Cambridge: Cambridge University Press.
Goffman, E. 1959. *The Presentation of Self in Everyday Life*. New York: Doubleday
Grice, P. 1989. *Studies in the Way of Words*. Cambridge, Massachusetts: Harvard University Press.
Hanks, W. F. 1990. *Referential Practice. Language and Lived Space Among the Maya*. Chicago: The University of Chicago Press.
Hooper, R. 1996. *Tokelauan*. München-Newcastle: LINCOM EUROPA.
Janda, L. 1993. *A Geography of Case Semantics: The Czech Dative and the Russian Instrumental*. Berlin: Mouton de Gruyter.
King, R.T. 1988. 'Spatial metaphor in German causative constructions', in *Topics in Cognitive Linguistics*, ed. B. Rudzka-Ostyn. Amsterdam: John Benjamin, 555–585.
Lakoff, G. 1987. *Women, Fire and Dangerous Things*. Chicago: The University of Chicago Press.
Levinson, S. C. 1991. *Primer for the Field Investigation of Spatial Description and Conception*, Working Paper No. 5. Cognitive Anthropology Research Group, Max Planck Institute for Psycholinguistics. Nijmegen: Max Planck Institute.
———. 1997. 'From Outer to Inner Space'. *Language and Conceptualization*, eds J. Nuyts and E. Pederson. Cambridge: Cambridge University Press.
Lewis, G.L. 1967. *Turkish Grammar*. Oxford: Clarendon Press.
Lyons, J. 1963. *Structural Semantics: An Analysis of Part of the Vocabulary of Plato*. Oxford: Blackwell.
———. 1968. *Introduction to Theoretical Linguistics*. Cambridge: Cambridge University Press.
———. 1977a. *Semantics, Vol I*. Cambridge: Cambridge University Press.

———. 1977b. *Semantics. Vol II*. Cambridge: Cambridge University Press.

Matthews, P. H. 1981. *Syntax*. Cambridge: Cambridge University Press.

Miller, G. A. and Johnson-Laird, P. 1976. *Perception*. Cambridge: Cambridge University Press.

Pederson, E., Danziger, E., Wilkins, D., Levinson, S., Kita, S. and Senft, G. 1998. 'Semantic Typology and Spatial Conceptualization', *Language* 74, 557–589.

Piatelli-Palmarini, M. 1980. *Language and Learning: The Debate between Jean Piaget and Noam Chomsky*. Cambridge, Massachusetts: Harvard University Press.

Sacks, H., Schegloff, E., and Jefferson, G. 1974. 'A Simplest Systematics for the Organization of Turn-Taking in Conversation', *Language* 50, 696–735.

Schiffrin, D. 1994. *Approaches to Discourse*. Oxford: Blackwell.

Wade, T. 1992. *A Comprehensive Russian Grammar*. Oxford: Blackwell.

CHAPTER 2

RENDERING METAPHOR IN REPORTED SPEECH: PRAGMATIC CONTINGENCIES[1]

Teresa Dobrzyńska

Introduction

It is assumed that a discourse always identifies its object of reference from a definite cognitive point of view. This is especially evident in the case of rendering someone else's discourse, and also in transforming the direct speech (*oratio recta*) into reported speech (*oratio obliqua*). Reported speech is not just a particular grammatical form or transformation, as some grammar books might suggest. We have to realise that reported speech represents in fact a kind of translation, a transposition that necessarily takes into account two different cognitive perspectives: the point of view of the person whose utterance is being reported, and that of a speaker who is actually reporting that utterance.

Reporting someone's speech is one of several ways of introducing 'someone else's (alien) word' to a discourse, as Bakhtin taught. Such transposition carries some particularly interesting consequences in one specific area of communication, that of metaphorical discourse (for a more detailed presentation on metaphor see Dobrzyńska 1984, 1992, and 1994). When reported, metaphors reveal their pragmatic determinants, inasmuch as they exprime a particular manner of conceptualisation and evaluation. The ways metaphors are rendered in the indirect speech depend on the functional sentence perspective (their topic or comment function). The act of relating is not uniform and creates several possibilities. The different forms of discourse used then reveal semantic and pragmatic peculiarities of metaphors.

Oratio obliqua and *oratio recta* as a discourse about a discourse

All uses of both direct and indirect speech reveal a basic characteristic of a complex discourse,[2] namely the fact that its parts are not communicatively equiponderant, since a quoted or reported discourse becomes objectified in another discourse. In the case of *oratio recta* it is the very form of language expression, literally or almost literally repeated, that is objectified; in the case of *oratio obliqua* it is the content of the reproduced discourse.

In the type of discourse discussed here, a specific hierarchy of two discourses conveyed in a single sentence (and often incorporated into a broader context that develops one of them into a larger text) finds its extension in the hierarchy of the speaking subjects. One of them is a superior, dominant instance, the one that organises the main text, setting its communicative purpose, determining the point of view of the entire discourse, as well as the relevant scope of basic knowledge on which an interpretation of the whole text rests. The other is only local, degraded to the status of the theme of a given discourse (or, to be more precise, to the role of the speaker of the objectified discourse). In some types of reporting a discourse (in *oratio obliqua*), the cognitive perspective of that second speaking subject is radically inferior. Students of discourse distinguish several ways in which this subordination can manifest itself. I shall discuss them briefly, so that sense-changing mechanisms, which a metaphorical discourse can be subject to, may become clearer.

Scholars emphasise that subordination of a reported discourse finds its strongest manifestation in the sphere of occasional words, in the sphere of Jakobson's *shifters* (Jakobson 1957), which in their semantic structure contain a *deictic* element, relative to the actual speaker and communicative situation. In transforming direct into indirect speech, those shifters must be appropriately transposed, lest the personal, temporal and spatial parameters of the subordinated speaker threaten the perspective brought in by the dominant one. Thus, the latter transforms all deictic terms (pronouns, tenses and other expressions relative to the situation of the original discourse), subordinating them to his own 'I – here – now' framework and stressing the shifted point of view. This can be seen on any random example of transforming direct into indirect speech:

(1)   John said: 'I'll be there tomorrow'. → John said he'd be at the appointed place the next day (relative to the moment of John's speaking).

The illustration above reveals the spatial–temporal shift from the point of view of the speaker whose discourse is reported; his or her *hic et nunc* differ from those of the reporting speaker. Transposition of direct speech into indirect speech also involves the necessity of adjusting all terms relative to the speaker:

(2)   John said: 'My mother has come.' → John said his mother had come.

(3)   John said: 'Barbara is a nuisance.' → John said his sister (Mrs. Brown, my daughter-in-law, etc. – depending on who the 'Barbara' is for the dominant speaker and on how he/she calls her in language contacts with the interlocutor) was a nuisance.

In analysing semantic and pragmatic properties of direct and indirect speech, Fillmore (1981) introduces the concept of 'internal and external contextualisation'. By its sense a discourse produces situational sequences to which some expression in the text may refer; moreover, the discourse itself is part of a situationally determined speech act. In the case of *oratio obliqua* this external contextualisation manifests itself in the necessity of replacing indexical and referential expressions (in English, Romance languages and many other tongues some adjusting of tense forms is also necessary) by corresponding expressions that respect the perspective of the speaker. Such expressions, says Fillmore, are selected from the point of view of the reporter and not the reported speech act. Furthermore, Fillmore observes that the dominant speaker may introduce his/her own ways of identifying who or what is spoken about, which can be at variance with the point of view of the reported message. The dominant speaker may, for instance, use his/her own evaluative description 'that idiot' in the reported sentence 'Peter is a genius':

(4)   John said Peter was a genius. (exact report)

(5)   John said that idiot was a genius. (report that shows a
        difference in opinion between the two speakers.)

Finally, in this brief survey of primary structural-functional
characteristics of reported speech we must not overlook its
often-stressed analytical character. Transformation of direct
into indirect speech requires explication and verbalisation of
the modal and expressive contents.

The analytical tendency of reported speech, writes Bakhtin
in his book published under the name of Voloshinov (1930:
151),[3] shows primarily in that all *emotional-affective elements* of
speech, as far as they manifest themselves not in the content,
but in the *forms* of discourse, are not conveyed in the
unchanged form into the reported speech. They are transferred
from the form to the content of a discourse and only then
introduced into the indirect construction or even shifted to the
main clause as modifying the verb that introduces the
reported discourse (emphasis -V.). A little further we read,

> It is only natural that, by the same token, no constructional
> and constructional-accentual expression of the speaker's inten-
> tion can pass unchanged into the reported speech. This is why
> constructional and accentual features of interrogative, exclam-
> atory and imperative sentences are not preserved in the
> reported speech, being marked only in its content. (Voloshinov
> 1930: 152)

An exclamatory sentence 'Oh, I have a terrible toothache!' –
in *oratio obliqua* could be adequately rendered by the sentence
'Groaning, he complained he had a bad toothache'. Similarly,
the order 'Let him come here!' could be conveyed by the sentence 'He ordered that the man (a person known from the context) come there.'

Let us conclude this short review of essential structural features of direct and indirect speech with a general remark,
stressing the textual aspect of mechanisms that are at work
here. Subordinating the perspective of the reported discourse
and objectifying a quotation or its content ensure coherence of
the types of discourse under consideration: a loose dual text
becomes a single one – a product of a single speaker, the dominant speaking instance. Whatever the type of rendering
someone else's (alien) speech – as direct speech, indirect
speech or free indirect discourse – it always combines a discourse with a discourse about the discourse, and thus is based
on the metatext–text relation.[4]

Reporting a metaphor

I shall discuss now a number of characteristic phenomena that occur in reporting metaphorical discourse, that is, in including metaphor in a complex discourse and situating it in the subordinate clause. Most of the remarks in this section will be devoted to the specific character of indirect speech, since it is there where the juxtaposition of two communicative perspectives – that of the reporting discourse and that of the reported one – is most clearly seen. For clarity of the argument, the illustrative material will principally be chosen from simple suggestive metaphorical constructions in colloquial language. A closer analysis allows us to make the following observations:

When reported, a metaphorical expression can be treated in various ways, depending on whether it constitutes the *topic* or the *comment* of the discourse. Let us compare, for instance, possibilities of reporting sentences 'John is a sly fox' and 'That sly fox won't be outsmarted'. Metaphorical constructions with a nominal metaphor functioning as the predicate and constituting the comment of a sentence can be easily transposed into corresponding forms of reported speech:

(6)   John is a sly fox. → Peter said John was a sly fox.

Problems arise when the metaphorical predicate passes into the description constituting the subject of the sentence, i.e. to its topic:

(7)   That sly fox won't be outsmarted. → Peter said that sly fox wouldn't be outsmarted.

Grammatically, everything seems all right: a metaphor has been supplied with a deictic element that can function as identifying the subject of a discourse (someone who is metaphorically defined as a 'sly fox'). Yet a more thorough knowledge of the rules governing *oratio obliqua* will allow us to accept this form of reporting the above-cited discourse only when the metaphorical designation comes from the person who reports the discourse (the dominant speaker). It is namely his/her cognitive and linguistic perspective that determines the forms of referential elements. To put the matter more simply: it is for him/her that the person in question is a sly fox or not; it need not be the opinion of the speaker of the reported sentence. Thus the sentence 'That sly fox won't be outsmarted' can be reported (in a somewhat emasculating way, to be sure) by such sentences as

(8)   Peter said (e.g.) Smith wouldn't be outsmarted.
        Peter said his neighbour wouldn't be outsmarted (etc.).

An exhaustive report of the content, on the other hand, would take into account the possible difference in attitudes between the two speakers towards John (defined as a sly fox by the one, whereas the other does not subscribe to the definition). This, in turn, would require splitting the description 'that sly fox' into the element that identifies the person in question and the predicate. The person in question would be defined in the way chosen by the reporting speaker. The metaphorical predicate would be rendered as the expression used by the speaker of the reported discourse. Thus,

(9)   That sly fox won't be outsmarted. → Peter said that X
        was a sly fox and that he wouldn't be outsmarted.

The variable X opens up possibilities for all identifying expressions that are concordant with the linguistic, cognitive and evaluative perspective of the reporting speaker. These may even be descriptions contradictory to the content of the original sentence, for instance,

(10)   Peter said that fool was a sly fox and wouldn't be out-
        smarted. (To the dominant speaker X is a fool, while to
        Peter he is a sly fox.)

In the Examples 7–10 examined above, the metaphorical description complies with the same linguistic-referential rules to which all identifying expressions, i.e., all topics of reported sentences, must conform. A discourse not only identifies a person or a thing, it always identifies its object of reference from a definite cognitive point of view, transposing one way of classifying and evaluating into another. *Oratio obliqua* is not just a particular grammatical form or transformation. It is a communicative structure contingent on pragmatic factors – relative to the speaker, his/her cognitive abilities, language habits and attitudes.

Reporting exclamatory metaphorical expressions

Let us now take a look – keeping in mind our main concern – at exclamatory metaphorical expressions with the hypocoristic function (similar qualities are to be found in invectives based on metaphors). Mother says to her child: 'My little peanut!' This expression can be shifted to the *meta* level in the quotation form of *oratio recta*:

(11)   Mother said, 'My little peanut!'[5]

Obviously, other variants of the phrase are possible, describing the person who speaks in some other ways (which the actual speaker finds adequate on the occasion):

(11a)   Annie said: 'My little peanut!' or
         My wife said: 'My little peanut!'

In transforming this exclamation into *oratio obliqua*, it is necessary to transfer the expressive elements from the expression plane to the content plane and to define verbally the act of speech (Voloshinov 1930: 151). The element of expression resides in the metaphorical hypocorism 'little peanut'. Following Wierzbicka's argument (1980: 59), I identify it with the semantic element *feel*. Addressing her child with the pet name the mother conveys information about her feelings. If we want to report this endearing phrase in indirect speech, having fulfilled the above-mentioned condition (verbal description of the speech act and of the emotion expressed), we will get

(12)   Mother fondly addressed...

To make the sentence complete, we have to define the addressee – the 'little peanut'. A simple transferring of the pet name to our formula of *oratio obliqua* is not possible, for it would produce a comical effect, resulting from de-metaphorisation of the phrase

(12a)   *Mother fondly addressed the little peanut.

Anyway, this also would be unjustified in the light of the previous semantic analysis of the phrase. Once the expressive element is separated from it, what remains is just a semantic element identifying the addressee of the phrase. Consequently, in *oratio obliqua* every speaker is free to define that addressee in a way he/she finds fit. Thus many variants of reporting sentences are possible here, as formulated from various perspectives of various speakers:

(12b)   Mother (or Annie, my wife, the woman, etc.) fondly addressed her son (or Johnny, the little boy, my nephew, etc.).

Let us return for a while to a possible 'faithful' rendering of the analysed phrase in *oratio obliqua*. It could only take the form of preserving the literally quoted element

(12c)   Mother fondly addressed her 'little peanut'.

We shall leave for further analyses the interpretation of what kind of discourse results from introduction of a quotation into the reporting clause. Anyhow, it cannot be treated as a pure form of reported speech. For our present purposes let us note that the quotational use of the expression – in its vocal realisation shown by a specific intonation – reveals an ironic attitude of the speaker. The speaker suggests that the affectionate attitude to the child is the mother's, not his. Thus we have to do here with a discourse situation that could be verbalised by the sentence

(12d)   Mother fondly addressed her – as she used to call him – 'little peanut'.

Ironic use of hypocorisms – also of those based on metaphors – is frequently employed as a stylistic device serving to ridicule an affected way of addressing a given person. The device is based on transferring a pet name from a direct address in a private conversation to a discourse about that person in a different communicative situation. In the new context, the endearing form is out of place, either because of the change of the speaker (the new speaker is not on intimate terms with the addressee) or because of the official character of the discourse. For example,

(13)   'Don't be upset, pinkie!', says his girlfriend to the director.
(13a)   '"Pinkie" is upset today', informs the secretary who happened to overhear the conversation.

Reporting with or without quotations

Let us pass to yet another observation. It would seem that metaphorical constructions can be easily transformed into indirect or direct speech even when the person who performs the reporting speech act is not only unable to find the content motivation of the metaphor used, but does not understand a given expression at all, for it is taken from another language, is archaic, or belongs to an alien functional variety of language or to an alien stylistic register. For instance,

(14)　John is a hobbledehoy. → Peter said: 'John is a hobbledehoy'; Peter said that John was a hobbledehoy.

(15)　The empress's hands are lan flowers. → A Chinese poet said: 'The empress's hands are lan flowers'; A Chinese poet said that the empress's hands were lan flowers. [6]

These transformations seem to be perfectly correct – also in the case of *oratio obliqua*. After all, among acts of reporting there is an act of reporting words and sentences that make no sense to the reporting speaker. Reports of this kind are used, for instance, in court, in the interrogation of witnesses who do not fully understand the sense of the utterances they repeat or do not grasp it at all. The metaphorical character of the reported words would not, then, affect the way of their reproduction.

We should not, however, be misled by the easiness of grammatical transformations. While at a closer look the form of the quoted sentences in indirect speech is unobjectionable (the obscure metaphor enters into the discourse as a quotation), the 'translation' of these sentences into reported speech seems to violate the latter's basic structural principle. I have mentioned before that *oratio obliqua* reports the content of a discourse, not the form of expression. In the examples cited above we have, in fact, no access to the content. Therefore, the only way of including such an obscure metaphor within the reported discourse is – like in the case of metaphorical hypocoristic expressions – its literal quotation. It seems, then, that the adequate form of our examples 14 and 15 in indirect speech would be that with quotational use of the words 'lan' and 'hobbledehoy'. This use could be identified given the proper vocal realisation of the sentences in *oratio obliqua* and would allow the speaker to suggest that 'lan' and 'hobbledehoy' are someone else's words, alien to his/her own vocabulary:

(14a)   Peter said that John was 'hobbledehoy'.
(15a)   A Chinese poet said that the empress's hands were 'lan flowers'.

Such quotational interpolations in reported speech were discussed by Bakhtin-Voloshinov, who pointed out they could take two forms:

> [...] an analysis of indirect speech can go in two directions or – to be more precise – can apply to two essentially different objects. Someone else's (alien) words can be taken as a definite *attitude* of the speaker towards the *sense* – in such a case the indirect speech construction serves to convey analytically its *exact content* (what the speaker said) [...] But someone else's (alien) speech can be analytically taken and conveyed as *expression*, which characterises not only what is spoken about (or even has only slight relation to it), but the *speaker himself*: his manner of speaking, individual or typical (or both), his state of mind, expressed not through the content, but through the forms of speaking (e.g. fluency of his speech, ordering of words, expressive intonation, etc.), his capability to express himself (emphasis –V.). (Voloshinov 1930: 152-153)

The first of these tendencies of shaping reported speech, the author called the 'content-analytical (content-oriented) modification', the other, the 'word-analytical (word-oriented)' one. He characterised the latter as follows:

> It introduces into the indirect construction words and phrases of someone else's (alien) speech that bear the subjective and stylistic stamps of the someone else's (alien) speech as expression. Those words and phrases are introduced in such a way as to be distinctly felt as specific, subjective or typical, and most often are included simply in the quotation marks. (Ibid.: 154)

This is exactly the situation, which we have to do with in the case of an obscure metaphorical expression reproduced in its material form in the quotation marks. What comes to the fore in such a discourse is the metalinguistic function. Similar interpretations can be applied to less exotic and obscure metaphorical constructions in *oratio obliqua* – provided that a given expression belongs to language registers different from those commonly used by the person reporting the discourse or from those he/she would spontaneously use in a given situation. When reporting Dora's calling herself a 'child-wife' of David Copperfield, we put the expression in quotation marks;

these would probably not be used by David himself or someone closer to his linguistic perspective.

The possibility of expressions in quotation marks in *oratio obliqua* poses a theoretical problem of distinguishing the word-analytical (word-oriented) modification of reported speech from the so-called free indirect discourse. M. R. Mayenowa (1979: 300-301), in her *Poetyka teoretyczna* ('Theoretical Poetics'), illustrates the latter by several examples, all of them being, as she says, 'ambiguous from the point of view of the speaker or – to be more precise – ambiguous as regards the way of introducing someone else's (alien) words'. Discussing the types of discourse defined by the terms *style indirect libre*, 'free indirect discourse' and 'free direct discourse' (German *uneigentliche direkte Rede*), she writes (Ibid.),

> Such ambiguous structures [...] are hybrid, essentially incoherent, not preserving any uniform direction of the reported words or any constant distance between the two speaking subjects: the one who introduces someone else's (alien) words and the one whose words they originally are.

One of the examples cited by Mayenowa is,

> Then he started to talk about his old, unhappy love for Eve. There is no life for him without the girl! For all those years they have been apart, he hasn't stopped loving her for one single moment.

Here the narrator impersonates his character, assuming his way of thinking and feeling. Consequently, he tells about his character's experience adopting the latter's intonation and manner of speaking, blurring the distinction between his own and his character's stylistic perspectives. This situation is radically different from intonational signalling of the peculiar character of the reported discourse, where a quotation is often underlain by irony and suggestive of the speaker's attitude to the someone else's (alien) words. While repeating their material form, the speaker at the same time indicates they cannot be – or at least are not – his own.

As ironic quotations will appear in many further examples, I should like to treat them as premises of recognising in a given realisation of reported speech what Bakhtin-Voloshinov defined as its word-analytical (word-oriented) modification. He elaborated upon this variety of discourse as follows (Voloshinov 1930: 156):

Words and phrases introduced into the reported speech and perceived as distinct (particularly when put in the quotation
marks) are – to use the formalists' term – 'made strange', oriented so as to serve the author's purposes; they are objectified,
made more colourful, and at the same time tinged by the
author's attitude – irony, ridicule, etc.

Reporting metaphor by explication or paraphrase

I shall pass now to the peculiarities of metaphorical discourse
reported in *oratio obliqua*. I shall consider the case when the
dominant speaker perfectly understands the metaphor contained in the sentence he reports, i.e. when there are no essential
discrepancies between his/her linguistic and cultural competence and that of the author of the reported discourse. In such a
case it is possible to transfer (translate) the reported discourse at
the level of content, to employ what Bakhtin-Voloshinov called
the content-analytical (content-oriented) modification of the
reported speech. Now it turns out that (instead of a simple reproduction) we may have to do with a more or less comprehensive
explication or a paraphrase of a metaphor.[7]

I should like to stress at once that this does not mean granting an ad hoc formulated paraphrase the status of an equivalent of the metaphorical meaning; a paraphrase does not
exhaust the metaphor's content. I do not believe the sense of a
living metaphor can be encompassed in an explicative formula. What we are interested in now is an entirely different
phenomenon – that of reporting a discourse in another discourse. This report can be faithful or unfaithful, adequate or
inadequate, exhaustive or not. It is just a fact of language
communication: transferring one discourse into another. In
this sense the sentence 'John is a bear' can be reported in *oratio obliqua* as

(17)   Peter said that John was clumsy and sluggish.

(In the word-analytical (word-oriented) modification, the transformation would take the form of: 'Peter said that John was a
"bear"'; in the content-analytical (content-oriented) modification the metaphor – though conveyed in the unchanged form –
would remain not explicated, imposing an interpretative task
on the audience: 'Peter said that John was a bear'.)

Thus, the possibility of paraphrasing metaphors is con-
ducive to production of still another type of transposing *oratio*

recta into *oratio obliqua* – one that can be called the 'interpretative variety of the content-analytical (content-oriented) modification' as distinguished by Bakhtin-Voloshinov. The same type of reporting would be found in the case of the non-metaphorical sequences cited by W. Górny (1966: 291) and discussed by M. R. Mayenowa (1979: 296):

(18) A: You're so slender, so downy now.
      B: So you're saying I've slimmed?[8]

The addressee of the first utterance analyses it and infers from it various conclusions – implicatures, to use Grice's (1975) term. Doubts whether the conclusions are adequate to the actual intentions of the first speaker – or perhaps simply seeking an acknowledgment of a desirable or undesired fact (of having lost weight) – make the woman ask the question that is a variant form of the reported speech. The form the question takes is the result of a rather far-reaching interpretation of the original discourse. It takes into account knowledge of the person whose looks are estimated, knowledge of antonyms slender/slim/thin – fat/plump/corpulent, as well as knowledge of possible conversational behaviour (of the fact that the interlocutor may euphemise or pay compliments). In a word, we have to do with a typical conversational situation (in Grice's sense of the term 'conversation'). The reporting is here combined with inferences from the preceding utterance.[9] It is perfectly understandable. Literal repetition of the first part of the dialogue would make sense only in particular communicational circumstances, e.g., if the first speaker forgot what he had just said:

(19) A: You're so slender, so downy now. [...] What was I say-
          ing?
      B: You said I was slender and downy.

This example leads to a more general conclusion, compatible with both recent linguistic pragmatics and the earlier excellent analyses of language interactions to be found in the works of Bakhtin-Voloshinov. We must realise that forms of reporting someone else's (alien) speech are one of the important techniques of communication. Scholarly reflection has not to date fathomed its multiformity or its mechanisms.

Final questions about the scope of responsibility in reporting metaphors

Let us pass now to summing up our observations, answering the question: what should we be apprehensive of in reporting a metaphorical expression in indirect speech? (Quoting it in direct speech gives no grounds for fear that the content of the message is deformed, since *oratio recta* renders the message literally.) Up to this point, our examples of reporting constructions have mostly been chosen from the colloquial speech. Now I shall try to shift to the sphere of journalism, which commonly offers opportunities for repeating and explaining someone else's discourse. On the one hand, the analytical properties of *oratio obliqua* help to isolate and verbalise some elements of the content of the reported discourse, or even its implicatures, and consequently, its journalistic rendering can be made more clear and understandable. On the other hand, however, the interference of a new speaker – another speaking subject – involves specific dangers connected with the introduction of a different cognitive and evaluative perspective. This applies to both literal and metaphorical expressions, but in the case of the reporting of metaphors, the dangers manifest themselves in a peculiar way. This is the result of a distinct content of such an expression, and depends on the place of the metaphorical expression in the topic-comment structure of the reported sentence. Thus various types of manipulation are possible here, even when the original message is faithfully rendered.

Let us consider the following example:

(20)   Amin's political short-sightedness is a disease, which will bring about many serious consequences.

Now let us assume that the sentence was originally uttered by a BBC commentator and was then reported in three different communicative situations: 1) to the readers of a serious political magazine – in a press review; 2) at a rally organised by Amin's opponents; 3) to Amin himself – in a report on current events, presented by his flattering secretary. The subject of our concern would be two metaphors contained in the sentence: 'short-sightedness' in its topic and 'is a disease' in the comment.

Situation 1 (a press review in a serious political magazine):
(21a)   A BBC commentator said that Amin's political short-sightedness was a disease, which would bring about many serious consequences.

(21b)   A BBC commentator said that Amin's activity was marked by 'political short-sightedness' which would bring about many serious consequences.

(21c)   A BBC commentator said that Amin's activity was marked by his failure to see major political problems and this would bring about many serious consequences.

In variant 21a, the point of view of the report is identical with that from which Amin's policy is seen as political short-sightedness, i.e. as a dangerous disease. In variant 21b, the point of view of the report is somewhat removed from that of the BBC commentator, while his very words and intent are accurately rendered through introducing the quotation. In variant 21c, the subject of the BBC commentator's reflection is neutrally named and the content of the metaphors he used is paraphrased. This last version offers us no way of finding out what exactly the BBC commentator said; all we are given is a general sense of his discourse, deprived of the expressive tinge originally brought in by the metaphor with its negative connotations.

Situation 2 (a rally organised by Amin's opponents):

(22a)   A BBC commentator said the political short-sightedness of that scoundrel Amin was a disease that would bring about many serious consequences.

The speaker who reports the BBC commentator's sentence shares the latter's opinion and also defines Amin's policy as 'political short-sightedness'. At the same time he/she seizes the opportunity to strengthen the negative reference to Amin in the extended topic description in the reported sentence by introducing appropriate epithets. Characteristically, in this type of reporting, neutral naming of the BBC commentator's topic and rendering his words with a quotational intonation are avoided. As a result, an uninformed listener could hardly separate that portion of the information for which the BBC commentator himself is responsible from that added by the participant of the rally.

Situation 3 (report of Amin's secretary – an arrant flatterer – informing Amin what is said about him):

(23a)   A BBC commentator said that your wise and far-seeing policy, Mr. President, would bring about many serious consequences.

(23b)   A BBC commentator – such a journalistic nonentity! – dared to say that your activity, Mr. President, was marked

by 'political short-sightedness' and that it was 'a disease
which will bring about many serious consequences'.

Amin's secretary does not – at least officially – share the
opinion expressed by the metaphor 'political short-sightedness'. Taking advantage of the fact that the metaphor originally functioned as the topic of the sentence, in variant 23a,
he replaces it with another description of the topic – from a
radically different point of view. Instead of 'Amin's political
short-sightedness' we get the 'wise and far-seeing policy'. In
this version, the negative connotations of the metaphors used
in the original sentence are obliterated, but at the same time
it is impossible to learn from it what the BBC commentator
actually said about Amin. In this respect variant 23b is much
more informative: we are told what exactly was said, about
what, and how it was expressed. Since the opinion of the BBC
commentator is in a sharp contrast with that of Amin's secretary, the latter's report is marked by his ironic or even sarcas-
tic attitude towards it; moreover, he discredits the
commentator ('journalistic nonentity', 'dared to say'). Two dis-
crepant communicational perspectives clash here, the secretary's perspective being dominant over that of the
commentator, whose discourse is objectified and discredited.

I have presented several versions of a single sentence as
reported in three different communicative situations. They
clearly show that a report is subordinated to interests of the participants of the communication, to their evaluative systems; in
each case it reflects their individual, distinct worldview, while at
the same time reveals their respective efficiency in modifying
variable components of discourse. In passing to *oratio obliqua*, a
message undergoes various transformations and deformations.
The reports in Situation 1 turned out to be relatively the most
faithful and neutral ones. Because of their journalistic character, they are meant to convey the informational content of the
reported discourse. Therefore the reporter avoids any addition of
evaluative elements of his own; he may, however, tend to interpret and paraphrase the original discourse. Situations 2 and 3
offer an opportunity for more thorough reformulations, for they
make it possible to introduce elements of evaluation into the
topic part of the reported sentence, and thus the evaluation
employed by the original speaker can be strengthened or
entirely changed. In the case of the fundamental discrepancy
between opinions (Situation 3), the predicative elements contained in the topic and the comment of the original sentence

are put into the ironic quotation marks and thereby shifted to the metalinguistic level that changes the informational capacity of the discourse. It should also be noted that all the manipulations we have observed make use, in a subtle way, of simple linguistic mechanisms. All the reports remain in their own way faithful to the original and are not evidently deceitful. After all, what gets changed in them is only the description naming the object of reference, and such a change is a normal device of actualisation, regularly used in indirect speech. The discourse is shifted – merely! – from the level of objectified words to the metalinguistic one, which makes it closer, as it were, to the most faithful form of reporting someone else's discourse – to *oratio recta*. We only need to compare the two sentences

(20)   A BBC commentator said: 'Amin's political short-sightedness is a disease, which will bring about many serious consequences'.

(23c) A BBC commentator said that your activity, Mr. President, was marked by 'political short-sightedness' and that it was 'a disease which will bring about many serious consequences'.

to realise to what extent simple direct speech differs from the word-analytical (word-oriented) variety of indirect speech that is markedly removed from the original way of predicating and capable of calling it in question through the use of ironic intonation.

Let us return to the question asked at the beginning of this section: what should we be apprehensive of in reporting a metaphor in indirect speech? In the case under consideration Amin's fears would probably be quite different from those of the BBC commentator, the author of the analysed discourse. Amin should fear that information his confidential secretary provides him with is inadequate, stripped of the evaluative elements carried by the stinging metaphor; that the man makes light of serious political dangers by suggesting that someone's mentioning them is of little significance. He should also fear that on the occasion of reporting what is said about him (not to mention other occasions) his opponents would feel free to introduce various bitter (also metaphorical) invectives into descriptions identifying his person. The BBC commentator, on his part, should be apprehensive that his message can be deformed, deprived of its evaluative content and of the power of making statements about the reality. He should also, of course, be fearful of Amin's revenge – but that is another story.

Conclusions

Metaphoric expressions rendered in reported speech are subjected to different communicational procedures: their content can be accepted as one's own or questioned by a referring speaker; it can be explicated and paraphrased or quoted in its original form. The choice of one of these procedures depends on the position of the metaphor in an utterance (its topic or comment function). However, it is determined first and foremost pragmatically, because a rendered expression becomes a part of someone else's discourse and is subordinated to linguistic, cognitive, and ideological perspectives of this new (dominant) subject. Therefore, *oratio obliqua* is not just a simple grammatical transformation of an utterance.

With the developing of our knowledge of language communication, the description of a reporting discourse should depart from the patterns inherited from grammar, with their rigid juxtaposition of content and lexical counterparts of direct and indirect speech. Much has been done as regards more subtle differentiation of the forms of discourse that include quotations[10] and the credit here must go to writers themselves, although their achievements are also taken into account by stylistics. The model of including quotations has been made more flexible by introducing the contrast between their objectified and metalinguistic uses – i.e., with and without the quotation marks (owing mainly to Bakhtin, and especially to his works published under the name of Voloshinov). The third domain of problems connected with the reporting of speech – the sphere involving interpretation of a message and the way of inferring used in actual communication – still awaits more thorough studies. Vast potentialities for the stylistics of discourse lie in comprehensive employment of Grice's concepts and modern communication theory. A powerful inspiration might in this respect come from various forms of non-standard sequences of colloquial dialogues, which we observe flowing, with a stimulating effect, into literature, and which arouse an increasing interest of linguists.

Notes

1. This paper is a shortened and modified version of the paper 'Wypowiedź przenośna relacjonowana w mowie zależnej' ('Metaphoric utterance in reported speech') published in Dobrzyńska (1994: 29–55).

2. The term 'complex discourse' (in Polish *tekst złożony*) was introduced by Wojciech Górny (1966:289), to denote direct speech, indirect speech and free indirect discourse.

3. It is a widely accepted view that the book *Marxism and the Philosophy of Language*, published under the name of Bakhtin's colleague V.N. Voloshinov in 1929 and reprinted in 1930, has in fact been written by Mikhail Bakhtin. Bakhtin was at that time in exile in Kazakhstan and was likely unable to have the book published under his own name.

4. 'Someone else's (alien) speech is speech within speech, discourse within discourse, but – at the same time – speech about speech, a discourse about a discourse', says Bakhtin-Voloshinov (1930: 136). Jakobson repeats and elaborates this formulation, including a quoted discourse *oratio* in the category of phenomena where a message refers to another message (Jakobson, 1957). Possibilities of changing the level of discourse from that of objectifying into the meta-level are discussed by Mayenowa (1979: 289 ff.) from the point of view of the text coherence and the semiotics of language behaviour.

5. In Polish, mothers would say something like *My little chicken!*, since in that language endearing, pet names typically employ names of little animals (sometimes flowers) in their diminutive forms, alien to English (e.g. *piesek, kotek, rybka, żabka, kwiatuszek, różyczka* etc.) and based on stereotyping the emotional attitudes to such creatures or plants. The stereotypes of this kind are culturally determined and vary from language to language.

6. Lan flowers are orchids. The metaphorical phrase 'your hands are two lan flowers' was used by a Chinese poet of the seventeenth century, Shen Toutsan. See a paraphrase of his love songs in: L. Staff, (1982: 188).

7. J. R. Searle (1979) finds paraphrases of metaphors justified in some cases.

8. The example is taken from *Przedwiośnie*, a novel by Stefan Żeromski.

9. The inferences do not take into account all the elements of the preceding utterance, as they ignore its predicative element 'downy'.

10. A wide array of possibilities was presented by O. Šoltys (1983) on Czech material.

References

Dobrzyńska, Teresa. 1984. *Metafora* ('Metaphor'). Wrocław: Ossolineum.

———. 1992. 'Metafora w przekładzie', in *Podstawy metodologiczne współczesnej semantyki*, ed. I. Nowakowska-Kempna. Wrocław: Wiedza o Kulturze, 231-250.

———. 1994. *Mówiąc przenośnie: Studia o metaforze* ('Metaphorically speaking; Studies on metaphor'). Warsaw: Instytut Badań Literackich.

———. 1995. 'Translating metaphor: Problems of meaning', *Journal of Pragmatics*, 24: 595-604.

Fillmore, Charles J. 1981. 'Pragmatics and the Description of Discourse', in *Radical Pragmatics*, ed. P.Cole. New York: Academic Press.

Górny, Wojciech. 1966. *Składnia przytoczenia w języku polskim*. Warszawa: Państwowy Instytut Wydawniczy.

Grice, H. Paul. 1975. 'Logic and Conversation', in *Syntax and Semantics, 3: Speech Acts*, eds P. Cole and J. Morgan. New York: Academic Press. 41–58.

Jakobson, Roman. 1957. *Shifters, Verbal Categories and Russian Verb*. Cambridge, Massachusetts: Harvard University Press.

Mayenowa, Maria Renata. 1979. *Poetyka teoretyczna: Zagadnienia języka*, (2nd edition). Wrocław: Ossolineum.

Searle, John Roger. 1979. 'Metaphor', in *Metaphor and Thought*, ed. A. Ortony. Cambridge: Cambridge University Press. 92-123.

Šoltys, Otakar. 1983. *Verba dicendi a metajazyková informace* ('Verba dicendi and metalinguistic information'). Prague: Československá akademie věd, Ústav pro jazyk český.

Staff, Leopold. 1982. *Fletnia chińska*. Warszawa: Państwowy Instytut Wydawniczy.

Voloshinov, Valentin N. (a.k.a. Mikhail Bakhtin). 1930. *Marksizm i filosofija jazyka* ('Marxism and the philosophy of language'). Leningrad.

Wierzbicka, Anna. 1980. *Lingua mentalis: The Semantics of Natural Language*. Sydney: Academic Press.

Żeromski, Stefan. 1974. *Przedwiośnie*. (24th edition). Warszawa: Czytelnik.

PART II

LANGUAGE AND POLITICS

CHAPTER 3

POLITICIANS ON DRUGS: FUNCTIONS OF POLITICAL METAPHOR ACROSS CULTURES

Sakis Kyratzis

Introduction

Language is often the only means that is available to a politician for him or her to suggest, argue, persuade or impress. The language of politics has attracted the attention of many scholars from a range of disciplines. Rhetoric has long been associated with public discourse, and consequently, metaphor – being the favoured figure of speech – lies at the centre of a large number of such studies, most of them focusing on the rhetorical functions of metaphor.

More recent theories of metaphor highlight the cognitive aspect of metaphor. Perhaps the most influential work in this area was *Metaphors We Live By*, by Lakoff and Johnson (1980). Their main goal was to prove that metaphor plays an important role in understanding: this means that metaphor is not just a matter of language, as is usually suggested, but of thought as well. Their main argument is that metaphors are the 'filters' that help us structure abstract concepts so that we can understand them; in this sense, our conceptual system is to a large extent metaphorical, and consequently the way we live is largely based on metaphor.

I will approach the phenomenon of metaphor in politics from a cognitive angle, rather than just from a stylistic or

rhetorical aspect. I believe that only after Lakoff and his collaborators showed how metaphor can influence the way we
think (and not just ornament the way we speak) did the effects
of political metaphor become more fully appreciated. In what
follows, I will consider the connection between metaphor and
culture in general; I will then discuss the role of metaphor in
politics and explain why metaphor is so pervasive in political
discourse across cultures, I will show how political metaphor
can reveal, shape, and manipulate ideology, and, with examples from Greek and American politics, I will illustrate some of
the functions of metaphor in political discourse and how these
can vary between cultures.

Metaphor and culture

Lakoff and Johnson (1980), in arguing that metaphor underlies our thought, gave new shape to what was considered to be
culture. The fact that, according to them, the basis of most
reasoning, but also of perception, is mediated by metaphor
shows that the foundations of culture must also be metaphorical; however, this is something that is stated only implicitly in
Lakoff and Johnson (1980). The relationship between
metaphor and culture has only recently attracted the attention of researchers. The main preoccupation of such studies is
twofold: (a) to expose intercultural variation in metaphor use,
e.g., Kövecses (1999a) talks of 'cross-cultural' and 'intra-cul-
tural' variation of metaphor use. This variation can be mani-
fested in the range of metaphors used and the difference in the
level of elaboration for each metaphor in different cultures or
sub-cultures. Metaphorical use can be affected intra-culturally
by sociolinguistic, individual, diachronic and developmental
factors; (b) a larger part of studies in this area aim to explore
the relationship between cultural models and metaphor: do
the former define the latter or vice versa? Quinn (Quinn and
Holland 1987; Quinn 1991) has worked extensively in this
area and she grants culture a far more important place in the
theory of metaphor than Lakoff and Johnson ever did. According to her, culture is the 'missing level' in their theory. She
tries to stress the importance of culture in relation to metaphor
by making a strong claim:

> Metaphors, far from constituting understanding, are ordinarily selected to fit a pre-existing and culturally shared model. (Quinn 1991: 60)

This claim runs counter to some of the fundamental theses of Lakoff and Johnson's (1980) theory, namely that metaphors underlie understanding and that they give rise to new metaphorical entailments that enrich the cultural model they are structuring. In her article, Quinn (1991) is actually putting forward the exact opposite position: cultural models have priority over metaphors, the latter are governed by and are selected to fit the former. This has raised a number of objections in the area, mainly by Kövecses (1999b). I think that both positions are extreme: there is an interplay between the two levels that results in the shaping of our cognitive system. To grant priority to one over the other would be to give a speculative (even arbitrary) solution to the chicken and egg problem: who can say what was there first, the metaphors or the culture? As Gibbs states:

> Our understanding of what is conceptual about metaphor involves significant aspects of cultural experience, some of which is even intimately related to our embodied behaviour. Under this view, there need not be a rigid distinction between cultural and conceptual metaphor. (Gibbs 1999: 146)

From the above discussion, it becomes apparent that culture must be taken into consideration in the study of metaphor and that the relationship between metaphor and culture is not a straightforward one.[1] Culture plays an important role in the formation and interpretation of metaphorical utterances. This will become more apparent when discussing examples from political discourse: I will show how, although politicians from different cultures use metaphors in their speeches to attain their goals – and sometimes they even use similar metaphors – the way these metaphors affect and are perceived by their audience is highly dependent on the specific culture these metaphors belong to. First, however, I will discuss the importance of metaphor in political discourse across cultures, i.e., what may be considered universally true concerning the role of metaphor in politics.

The role of metaphor in political discourse

Why is it that metaphor is so pervasive in the political arena? According to Paine (1981: 187), metaphor fits the *basic strategy of political rhetoric,* which is 'to induce the appropriate context from which will flow the behaviour that the politician seeks from his audience.' Metaphor is capable of restructuring concepts and opinions, thus preparing the ground for new ideas; it is this opening of mind that Paine means, I think, by 'appropriate context'. However, it is not only this aspect of the political world that explains metaphor's pervasiveness. It is the political world itself that is permeated by metaphor; it is the foundations of politics that contain metaphor. Thompson (1996) argues for the indispensability of metaphors in politics in his appropriately titled article 'Politics without metaphors is like a fish without water.' He claims that involvement in politics is directly related to group membership, and since group membership is not experientially grounded, metaphors are fundamental. According to Thompson (1996: 186), only when the individual is treated *as if* they were part of a larger group does the first step towards political involvement take place; 'until and unless that metaphorical leap of understanding is made, there is no participation in politics nor in political discourse.' Thompson (1996: 188) suggests that metaphor helps make the central concepts of politics, such as ideology, influence, power, etc., more tangible and concrete for the people involved in politics, but also for those directly influenced by it.

Moreover, it can be argued that the political processes themselves are defined by metaphor. Miller provides a definition of politics that, I think, holds a lot of truth:

> We could describe national politics, in general, as the conflict between two forms of euphemism: the government of the day employing enhancing euphemisms for all situations no matter how unpropitious; the opposition employing demeaning euphemisms for all situations no matter how propitious [...]. The battle is to persuade the public to believe one set of euphemisms rather than the other. (Miller 1992: 24)

Miller refers only to euphemism, but I want to suggest that the battle is to persuade the public to believe one set of *metaphors* rather than another. This presents a somewhat different picture of the political arena of power: a ring for competing metaphors.

Paine (1981) shows how these two concepts, power and metaphor, can be related within the context of politics. Politicians who want to get into power have to introduce new options and to reject – rhetorically – the options established by the government. To do so, they might choose to use metaphor that has the power to break old boundaries and to establish alternative points of view, or, in Paine's (1981: 189) words, 'to open what is closed by the power of others.' Metaphor then is the means of political change. The political data that are discussed in this paper show ways in which metaphors in political discourse attain hegemony and shape ideology by altering their metaphoricity: conventional metaphors within a certain context may become deautomatised and create a vivid image in the hearer's mind; conversely, new metaphors can become within discourse crystallised and conventionalised in the hearer's conceptual system. As Miller (1992) has argued, it is the frozen metaphors, the ones of which we are not aware, that 'govern' our conscience and are taken to represent reality. In this light, I think the political arena can be reinterpreted as a metaphorical contest, whereby politicians who are in power strive – by using various techniques (that will be explored soon) – to make their new metaphors frozen, and those who want to come to power strive to break the established metaphors, to expose them as such, and to replace them with new ones. It is difficult to determine how conscious a process this is. It is true that by examining political data such patterns did emerge, but I do not want to make the strong – and rather unrealistic – claim that politicians decide consciously which metaphors to freeze or expose. However, what can be said is that in trying to establish their ideology and in argumentation politicians sometimes seem to be aware of the possibilities that metaphor can offer them. By studying the way metaphor is used in discourse, certain patterns can be detected. One can say that there is a certain alignment, motivation – some kind of design.

Political metaphor and ideology

Metaphor in politics can be a useful tool in exploring ideology. Miller and Fredericks (1990) discuss the way the metaphors used in an American educational report (*A Nation at Risk*) reveal the ideology that is hidden behind the text; they show that the use of metaphorical expressions in major policy statements reflects a largely unconscious process whereby implicit beliefs, attitudes, and ideological presuppositions concerning the desirability or utility of a course of action are made explicit. (Miller and Fredericks 1990: 68)

These ideologies are revealed by finding categories of metaphors that run through the text and that represent a certain way of thinking. Miller and Fredericks (1990) argue that this is largely an unconscious process. This certainly holds true for the more conventional or frozen metaphors politicians use in their texts (and it is mostly this type of metaphors that Miller and Fredericks have looked at).

In the following section, I will show that, apart from the use of frozen metaphors, there are two other processes that relate metaphor to ideology, *(de)automatisation* and the *creation of new metaphors*. In Table 3.1 below, I summarise the relations I believe exist between these three processes and ideology:

Table 3.1: *Metaphor and Ideology*

Process	Effect	Intentionality
1. frozen metaphors	reflection of underlying beliefs	unconscious
2. (de)automatisation	awareness of ideology: reinforcing/normalising beliefs	potentially intentional
3. new metaphors	shaping of ideology	intentional

As can be seen from the table, these three processes differ in possible effects and degree of intentionality. The use of frozen or conventional metaphors in ideology was discussed by Miller and Fredericks (1990). I will present the other two here briefly.

(a) (De)automatisation

The notion of (de)automatisation I am introducing here refers to the phenomenon whereby a frozen metaphor in a particular context can become deautomatised, i.e., its metaphoricity becomes apparent, and conversely, a new metaphor becomes automatised, i.e., its metaphoricity becomes illicit; I want to argue here that this process in political discourse reveals *awareness of ideology* on the part of the speaker and intentionality potentially comes into the picture. The examples presented in the following section show how the metaphors used by politicians to talk about drugs not only reveal their beliefs on the topic, but also affect the hearers' belief system. I will also show that the way the hearers' belief system is affected is dependent on the culture in which they belong.

(b) The creation of new metaphors

This process is a conscious effort on the part of the speaker to *shape* ideology rather than just to suggest it; by using a new metaphor, the speaker is suggesting a new perspective, which can either redefine existing ones, or even replace them completely.

The war on drugs

In the previous sections, I have presented in mainly theoretical terms the various functions metaphor can perform in politics. I will now proceed to illustrate these points by presenting specific examples of political metaphor. These examples come from two different political arenas: North American and Greek. The reason for presenting examples from two different cultures is to show what may be some universal tendencies in the use of political metaphor and what is culture-specific.

The topic of the speeches from where the examples come is the same in both cases: anti-drug policy. The Greek data come from a parliamentary discussion that took place on 30 August 1994. The American data are drawn from Elwood (1995), who studied the metaphors used by Reagan and Bush in their speeches on anti-drug policy. The analysis will focus mainly on the Greek data, in order to show some of the functions of metaphors; I will illustrate that metaphors in discourse do not work in isolation, but they are rather part of metaphorical chains that are introduced and developed within the boundaries of the conversation. I will then present similar examples from the American data, in order to expose differences and similarities.

In both the American and the Greek data, the predominant metaphorical chain consists of WAR metaphors, which are usually combined with ILLNESS metaphors. These metaphors are exploited, to attain the objectives of the politicians (namely to mobilise the government to take action against drugs), to persuade the public that this issue is of top priority and severity, and to prove that the whole of the political body is prepared to solve the problem. I will also show how these metaphors are related to ideology and persuasion and how, although they are present in both the American and the Greek data, their meaning and effects are strongly influenced by the culture in which they appear.

The WAR and ILLNESS metaphors

The fact that the most productive metaphor in the data is that of WAR is not surprising: the domain of war is a highly structured one and as such it is apt to serve as a fertile source domain[2] (cf. the ARGUMENT IS WAR metaphor in the English language presented in Lakoff and Johnson 1980). The WAR metaphor is a typical way of talking about anti-drug policies in both English and Greek. Although some of the expressions used in relation to anti-drugs policy are conventional metaphors deriving from the war domain, politicians also combine expressions from the same or different domains and extend existing metaphors, thus creating a more vivid war atmosphere. In other words, by combining and extending metaphors, speakers deautomatise conventional metaphors or create new ones, thus succeeding in creating live mappings in the hearers' minds, mappings that construct an altogether negative picture of drugs, drug-users and drug-dealers. This results in creating a sense of urgency and unity towards a common objective, and leads to mobilisation, which is what the politicians wish to accomplish with their speeches.

Looking at the Greek data first, the WAR metaphor is introduced early in the discussion in the Prime Minister's introductory speech:[3]

Extract 1: Papandreou
Our road must have a vision and principles. Our actions and our objectives must inspire. Every step forward is truly such, when it has as its target the improvement of the citizen's way of living and their personality. The political forces of the country, the employees, the world of science, the intellectuals and the artists, every living cell of our society with its weapons must be united in arms to face this wound of the scourge of drugs.

The then Prime Minister is calling everyone to help solve the problem of drugs, but he is making his call stronger by using the WAR metaphor: according to this metaphor, every member of Greek society assumes a new role, in addition to the one they already possess; they all become soldiers united against a common enemy. What makes this call stronger than a more literal one (say, 'Let us all come together and suggest solutions to the drug problem') is the knowledge that is associated with WAR that comes into the picture and reshapes the concept of anti-drug policy. WAR is typically associated with strong feelings, such as fear and hatred, the enemy is usually someone threatening and dangerous, the soldiers fighting in a war are united in a grave common cause. This knowledge is mapped on the anti-drug policy and, in that way, aims become targets, means become weapons, and civilians become soldiers fighting against the dangerous enemy – drugs. Although not all the mappings are made explicit in this example, this metaphor is elaborated further on in the discussion as will be shown in Extracts 2 and 3 below. The point to be made here is that the speaker chooses to use a metaphor of WAR, in order to establish a sense of urgency and unity in the minds of the hearers (i.e., the general public and the other politicians).

Metaphors working in combination can be more effective (see Stibbe 1996). In this case, the WAR metaphor is combined with two other metaphors, the LIVING ORGANISM and the ILLNESS metaphors, each contributing in a different way to the overall effect. The LIVING ORGANISM metaphor (*every living cell of our society*) maximises the sense of unity. In the Greek language, it is a conventional way of stressing the importance of the family by talking about it as the cell of society. Cells are the smallest parts of a living organism and it is due to their existence and cooperation that the whole organism is enabled to live. In this example, this metaphor is further extended to include every single member of the society, focusing mainly on the importance of cooperation. In the LIVING ORGANISM metaphor, society is seen as an organism and, therefore, its well being and life is dependent on its cells, its members. By calling the politicians, the employees, the intellectuals and the artists cells of society, the Prime Minister is creating a strong bond between them, as strong as the biological bonds that exist between the cells of an organism. This sense of unity is maximised by the WAR metaphor. These two metaphors work together in a complex way, one on top of the other, as it were:

> the politicians, etc., are the cells of the society
> > ⇒ UNITY
> the cells of the society are the soldiers against drugs
> > ⇒ UNITY + URGENCY + IMPORTANCE

The second metaphor that works in combination with the WAR metaphor is ILLNESS (*this wound of the scourge of drugs*).

The ILLNESS metaphor is quite pervasive in both the American and the Greek data. Sontag (1978) shows how three ILLNESS metaphors are common in American rhetoric: the EPIDEMIC metaphor for social disorders, the SCOURGE metaphor that carries judgmental overtones, and the CANCER metaphor. These three metaphors are present in Greek political discourse too. Both Greek and American politicians refer to drugs as a *contagious disease*, an *epidemic,* or *cancer* and drug takers are considered to be *patients.* In this way, they try to establish the unpleasantness of drugs drawing from the common distressing experience of illness. By restructuring the drug domain in terms of the illness domain, knowledge that is typically related to disease is now attached to drugs: this probably results in the creation of a sensation of aversion, fear and stigmatisation of drugs and the drug-user in the minds of the hearers. They also contribute to the sense of urgency established by the WAR metaphors: drug-use is not just a disease, it is a contagious disease and it is spreading fast like an epidemic. Within this context, the image of coming in physical contact with a contaminated person and contracting their disease is conjured up. One could argue that the ILLNESS metaphor, when related to the drug situation, is responsible for the social marginalisation and contempt towards drug-users and probably the reluctance to take immediate action to solve their problems. The ILLNESS metaphor compels us to hate and avoid people using drugs for fear of contracting their disease. Unfortunately, over the last decade, these fears have been reinforced by the fact that illness is no longer a metaphor in some instances.

Returning to Extract 1, notice how the WAR, LIVING ORGANISM and ILLNESS metaphors are linked to each other: if society is a living organism, then it can even be a soldier fighting in a battle and getting wounded. The LIVING ORGANISM metaphor provides the 'unity' element, which is in line with the WAR metaphor (people are typically united when fighting a common cause), which in its turn is related to the ILLNESS metaphor (people are typically wounded in battles). Although in isolation these metaphors might be considered as frozen, when they are clustered with the aid of contextual and cognitive links, they are potentially revitalised, resulting in more active mappings and images that are more effective.

It can be said that the Prime Minister sets the theme for the rest of the speakers. The mappings of the WAR metaphor are presented gradually as the discussion evolves and are elaborated by the other participants of the discussion. Sensing that the conventional expressions in relation to anti-drug policy are not sufficient for their purpose, politicians start looking for new expressions elaborating and deautomatising in this way the initial conventional metaphors,[4] such as:

Extract 2:
1. It's time we officially declared war on drug-dealers, the great enemy of the Greek youth. (Samaras)
2. Importance must be given to all fronts of the fight against drugs. (Koutsikou)
3. Let's all unite in arms in an effort to mobilise the Greek population to armour the Greek youth against this great danger. (Lentakis)

As the discussion unfolds, the WAR metaphor gradually becomes deautomatised, thus generating a genuine atmosphere of war, unity and urgency. This can be attested in the following example, which comes from the final part of the discussion. The speaker is the Minister of Health.

Extract 3: Kremastinos
Mr President, ladies and gentlemen Members of Parliament, I am certain that tonight's discussion unites the Greek people against a new common enemy, namely the dangerous invasion of drugs in the Greek society, an enemy that threatens today every advanced society and one that no society has managed to defeat no matter how many weapons it has used.

Again the unity theme is present, only this time it is generalised to include every society and not just Greek society. Drugs are seen as enemies, which is a strong personification. As Thompson (1996: 188) remarked, metaphors 'clothe the intangible, giving life to abstractions.' In this case, drugs are seen in a precise and concrete way – not just as a person, but as an enemy as well. By using a personification, a clearer image is created in the hearers' minds that helps them deal with the problem of drugs much more easily, but it also serves the purpose of the speaker more effectively. If drugs are the enemy, then they can be feared, despised and even exterminated. These emotions and notions would have been more difficult to associate with drugs as an abstract concept, or indeed with drugs as a simple entity. There are other powerful personifications of this kind in the American data that will be presented later on.

Returning to the WAR metaphor, it is possible to see how it has been activated by clustering expressions such as *invasion*, *common enemy*, *threaten*, *defeat*, and *weapons*. I think this extract provides good evidence for the process of deautomatisation. I want to suggest that it is possible for a frozen metaphor to become more active within a certain context, and, in this way, it acts as an indicator of ideology. The clustering of the WAR metaphors that have been presented so far can be considered as such a context. At the beginning of the discussion (see Extract 1), the WAR metaphor was still frozen. But through a process of elaboration and combination with other metaphors (Extract 2) the WAR metaphor's metaphoricity changed and what was an automatised metaphor became a vivid image. By the end of the discussion (Extract 3), it becomes quite difficult to see a difference between this discussion about drugs and a discussion about waging war against a country. This development of the WAR chain shows the politicians' attitude towards drugs, their beliefs about drug-traffickers, and the way they wish to deal with the situation: the metaphor positions the people involved in such a way that drugs are vilified, the government is powerful and the actions taken are urgent, efficient and maybe violent, as in a state of war.

Similar observations on the exploitation of the WAR metaphor when discussing anti-drug policy were made by Elwood (1995). In the speeches of Ronald and Nancy Reagan and George Bush, the WAR metaphor is used in a similar way in order to create a sense of unity and mobilisation against a common cause:

Extract 4:
1. Well, now we're in another war for our freedom, and it's time for all of us to pull together again. [...] When we all come together united striving for this cause, then those who are killing America and terrorising it with slow but sure chemical destruction will see that they are up against the mightiest force for good that we know. [...] We will vanquish the drug enemies that threaten us. We can achieve this victory because we always have believed in the values that are threatened; our enduring belief will lead to our victory.
                                    (Ronald Reagan in Elwood 1995: 101–102)

2. All of us agree that the gravest domestic threat facing our nation today is drugs.
                                    (George Bush in Elwood 1995: 103)

3. The inanimate enemy is a bandit, a murderer, a violator of the values our children embody, a threat to our children,

and a thief in the night who steals the American dream from
our hopes for the future.

(Nancy Reagan in Elwood 1995: 100)

Again, the same themes appear here as in the Greek data: the
sense of *threat* (example 2), seeing drugs as an *enemy* that *kills*
and *terrorises,* and the only solution is a *war* and a *victory*
against this *common* enemy (example 1). Notice also the use of
personification by Nancy Reagan in example 3: although in
the Greek data drugs were only seen as an enemy and any
hatred towards drugs was created by the connotations of the
word 'enemy', here things are more explicit. Reagan qualifies
this enemy as *a murderer, a violator, a threat* and *a thief,* thus
creating an even more powerful and odious image of drugs in
her audience.

Although both groups of politicians use similar means, in
this case the WAR metaphor, to achieve their goals, I believe
that the meaning of the metaphors used is intended and perceived differently in the U.S.A. and in Greece. This has to do
with the differing experience of war these two peoples have,
which led to a different perception of the concept of war. This
difference is attested in the fact that the most commonly used
word that comes from the WAR domain in the speeches of the
Reagans is *crusade,* whereas in the Greek data is *battle.* According to Elwood (1995: 100), 'the invocation of the word used to
define the medieval wars sanctioned by the Pope to reclaim
the Holy Land resonates with the American proclivity to
endow our secular wars with religious significance'. In other
words, the use of the CRUSADE metaphor justifies any action
against drugs by claiming that it has a holy cause. In the
Greek data, religious overtones are not evident.

Apart from the religious connotations of the CRUSADE
metaphor, there is another difference between the American
crusade and the Greek *battle* that I believe is more significant
in terms of cultural differences. A crusade is a war that is
fought *away* from the home country; it is more an *expansive*
war and an *invasion* rather than a defensive war. It is a form of
intervention to rectify a wrong, rather than an act of protection
of one's own country. Looking at the recent histories of the
U.S.A. and Greece, it can be noted that the Americans' experience of war mainly relates to such *interventions,* whereas the
Greeks had mainly to deal with *defensive* wars. This difference
in the perception of war is evident in the language of the
metaphors used by the American and the Greek politicians. In

the Greek data (see Extracts 1–3), politicians talk of an external *threat* or an *invasion* and the main objective of this war is to *armour our youth* against this enemy. In the American data, politicians elaborate the CRUSADE metaphor and turn it into the INTERVENTION metaphor:

Extract 5:
1. We Americans have never been morally neutral against any form of tyranny. Tonight we're asking no more than that we honor what we have been and what we are by standing together.

    (Ronald Reagan in Elwood 1995: 101)

2. If the impoverished people who live in the projects cannot master their surroundings and eliminate drugs with promised help from the Federal Government, then they are drug war enemies who deserve a miserable existence or the punishment the law provides.

    (George Bush in Elwood 1995: 104)

Reagan in example 1 above reminds his audience of similar past interventions; justification of such interventions comes in the form of *moral rights* rather than religious ones, as in the CRUSADE metaphor. One could say that these interventions are the modern equivalent of crusades: the latter were done in the name of religion, the former in the name of morality and freedom. Both metaphors make the war against drugs seem inevitable and justified. The notion of military intervention is more prominent in Bush's speech (example 2): his words position the people who are related to drugs as an internal enemy and this situation can only be rectified by intervention from the Government, who is seen as the sole possessor of power and the administrator of retribution. In Bush's case, crusades and interventions did not remain metaphorical actions: Operation Just Cause, America's invasion of Panama, was a literal military action against drugs, and Operation Desert Storm, the Gulf War, was a modern day crusade (without a holy cause, however).

From the above discussion, it becomes apparent that due to different cultural experiences of war, the intended and perceived meaning of the same metaphor varies between the Greek and the American political world. For the former, war is more a means of defending yourself from something you fear might destroy you; for the latter, war is a crusade or a military intervention against something you consider to be wrong and that religion or morality gives you the right to rectify.

This contrast could be the basis for the differing attitudes and policies concerning drugs in both countries. Political discourse that is dominated by defensive war metaphors in combination with contagious disease metaphors has created a sense of hatred, fear and reluctance to deal with the drug problem in Greece. Drug users are marginalised, stigmatised and looked upon with contempt, and the public tries to shut its eyes fearing to deal with the problem. Drug rehabilitation clinics are banned from the centre of cities and can only be found in surrounding areas. In the U.S.A., the use of invasive war metaphors has contributed to the hatred of minority groups that are associated with drugs and the declaration of war metaphorically against internal drug gangs and literally against external drug barons (Elwood 1995).

Conclusions

Politicians often have language as their only means to attain their objectives – namely, to shape ideology and to achieve persuasion. Metaphor, with its potential to rearrange conceptual domains, seems to be the perfect tool to attain their goal. By choosing various metaphors, politicians try to create new realities, in the sense that they endeavour to make their hearers see situations and ideas in a new way. It should be kept in mind that metaphor is not a mere comparison: knowledge is also transferred from one domain to the other, thus creating a rich and effective new image. In the discussion presented above, the speakers employed various metaphors to establish a negative picture of drugs. Drugs, drug-users and drug-dealers were 'transformed' into anything from wounds, enemies, bombs to disease and death. Another means of shaping ideology and of persuading the public – apart from creating a new reality with the use of metaphor – was found to be the careful selection of familiar source domains, such as illness, to explain clearly the situation. By using well known domains, a better understanding of the situation can be attained, but also the hearers potentially become and feel more involved.

Metaphor can also be used to aid in other objectives. In the examples discussed, it was shown how politicians created a sense of urgency and unity concerning the drugs issue. Personifications were used to concretise the topic (i.e., drugs), which facilitated the attribution of negative characteristics to drugs. Personifications also had the effect of rendering the

issue of the discussion more real, more close and more threatening. This was more evident in the American data, where
drugs were not only seen as enemies, but also as bandits, mur-
derers, thieves and violators.

Concerning more general issues of metaphor and ideology,
it was shown that, due to the fact that metaphors restructure
partially the target domain, politicians were able to use different metaphors in combination to shed light on various aspects
of a concept. In this way, it is possible for metaphors to create
chains within the boundaries of the conversation. What is
meant by 'chains' is a string of metaphors that share a common source domain. In the drugs discussion, two such chains
were discussed briefly, the WAR and ILLNESS chains. Such
metaphorical chains can be developed collaboratively within
discourse: in the Greek data, speakers from all political parties
contributed to the creation of the three predominant chains.
According to Thompson (1996: 191), 'shared and reinforced
metaphors help create a sense of community and solidarity
among elites, and common metaphors become the vehicle for
institutionalizing policy and patterns across generations.'
Since anti-drug policies are one of the few topics all political
parties seem to agree on, it can be argued that the collaborative development of the three metaphorical chains and the
use of compatible, rather than conflicting, metaphors by all
speakers could count as evidence that endorses this agreement, but also as a sign to the audience that the whole of the
Parliament is united in this cause. Such chains provide cohe-
sion to the whole of the discussion, not only by keeping constant two conceptual domains (WAR, ILLNESS), but also by
putting forward one predominant and consistent ideology
concerning drugs that unites all political parties. From the
data analysed, it becomes apparent that the predominant ideology, when it comes to drugs, is that which relates to war,
both in Greece and in the U.S.A.

It was said earlier that the process of deautomatisation can
reveal ideology. In the examples discussed from the WAR
chain, evidence was found to support this claim. As was found
in other studies (see, for instance, Stibbe 1996), the clustering
of metaphorical expressions in discourse may render the
metaphor more active, i.e. ,it can become deautomatised. This
could be seen in Extract 3, where a collection of various WAR
metaphors resulted in the creation of a vivid 'polemical'
atmosphere, which contributed to the mobilisation of the
political world against drugs. Apart from clustering, however,

it was also found that deautomatisation of a metaphor can be achieved in the wider boundaries of the whole conversation by the *cumulative effect* created by consistent use of metaphors sharing a common source domain (in this case, that of war). In the anti-drugs discussion in the Greek parliament, politicians were continuously using metaphors from the WAR domain, and although the WAR metaphor at the beginning of the discussion was frozen, by the end it had become 'defrosted'. The same could be said for the American data: most metaphors used from the WAR chains were conventional and through constant use and accumulation they became deautomatised, thus revealing awareness of ideology on the part of the politicians. In other words, the politicians' metaphorical behaviour is reinforcing the existing ideology and shows their attitude and beliefs concerning drugs, i.e., that they are as bad and dangerous as an enemy and that they should be eliminated.

However, deautomatisation was not the only process that relates to ideology. The data also revealed that metaphors, apart from becoming deautomatised in order to create emotional and vivid images, can become frozen or conventionalised within the limits of a conversation. This can be achieved mainly through constant repetition. Speakers in the anti-drugs discussion kept repeating that 'drugs is the enemy' or 'drugs is a contagious disease', which led to the conventionalisation of these metaphors. This is quite powerful: if metaphors have the power to conjure up vivid images, they can also crystallise the way we think about various concepts. In this case, the mapping between drugs and enemy or death with all concurrent knowledge becomes frozen and is called up automatically when talking about drugs. This effect is more permanent and deep than its opposite (i.e., deautomatisation). Most metaphors that belong to the ILLNESS chain were new in both the American and the Greek data: the politicians tried explicitly to shape their audience's ideology using this powerful metaphor. By constantly repeating them, they potentially automatised these metaphors, thus making them conventionalised in their hearer's minds and, in this way, they achieved normalisation of the new ideology they were trying to project. Our attitude towards drug-addicts may be explained by the freezing of the ILLNESS metaphor.

These similarities in the two corpora of data show that there may be some universal features of metaphorical behaviour in political discourse across cultures. This is in line with relevant research in the area that shows the indispensability of metaphors in political discourse. Politicians from Greece and the U.S.A. use metaphors in a similar way to achieve their goals, and even the metaphors they use are drawn from the same sources. I think this can be explained by the fact that war and illness are two concepts that affect people globally and are, therefore, quite central to our experience. Concepts and objects that are important in a culture will also be visible in the language of that culture. Hence, the strong presence of these two concepts in the political speeches examined. Also, the nature of these two concepts makes them appropriate for a speech against drugs in any culture. Talking about two distressing experiences known to most people will make the audiences relate more easily to these speeches and be persuaded by them. Although the same metaphors were used by both groups of politicians, it was also argued that the meaning of these metaphors and the consequent action are dependent on the culture in which they belong. It was shown that in the U.S.A., the WAR metaphor was used in its more active and invasive form, whereas in Greece, more defensive metaphors were used. This difference could be the basis of varying attitudes towards drugs in these two countries.

I hope to have shown that the study of metaphor can be a useful tool in relation to language and ideology across cultures. Metaphor has the power to bring together two different discourses from two different conceptual domains, thus achieving, at times covertly, intertextuality. Politicians, through the use of metaphor, bring into their speeches a variety of voices, be it war cries or hospital sighs. It is these other discourses on which politicians draw that reveal their ideology and it is their new metaphors that they are trying to establish that shows us the way they want to manipulate and shape ideology in order to persuade.

Notes

1. For more on the relationship between metaphor and cultural models see also Cienki (1999) and Emanatian (1999).
2. The terms source domain and target domain were introduced by Lakoff and Johnson (1980) to refer to the two concepts that are brought together in a metaphor. Source domain is the conceptual domain that is rich in information and/or is well structured. The target domain is usually abstract and in need of structure. Through the metaphor, information and structure is transferred from the source domain onto the target domain. The corre-

spondences that are created by the metaphor between the two domains are called the mapping. For instance, in the ARGUMENT IS WAR metaphor, the source domain is WAR and the target domain is ARGUMENT.
3. All Greek examples will be presented in an English translation. In translating the texts, I tried to remain as close to the original as possible. Therefore, the English text might seem awkward at times. When a point will either seem different in the translation or not evident at all, it will be signalled and explained.
4. It should be noted that the WAR metaphor is so closely linked to drugs that 'the *fight* against drugs' is the only expression available in Greek for anti-drug policy.

References

Cienki, A. 1999. 'Metaphors and cultural models as profiles and bases', in *Metaphor in Cognitive Linguistics*, eds R. W. Gibbs and G. Steen. Amsterdam: John Benjamin, 189–203.

Elwood, W. N. 1995. 'Declaring war on the home front: metaphor, presidents and the war on drugs', *Metaphor and Symbolic Activity* 10, no. 2: 93–114.

Emanatian, M. 1999. 'Congruence by degree. On the relation between metaphor and cultural models', in *Metaphor in Cognitive Linguistics*, eds R. W. Gibbs and G. Steen. Amsterdam: John Benjamin, 205–218.

Gibbs, R. W. 1999. 'Taking metaphor out of our heads and putting it into the cultural world', in *Metaphor in Cognitive Linguistics*, eds R.W. Gibbs and G. Steen. Amsterdam: John Benjamin, 145–166.

Kövecses, Z. 1999a. 'Cultural variation in conceptual metaphor', paper given at the *6th International Cognitive Linguistics Conference*, 10–16 July 1999. Stockholm, Sweden.

———. 1999b. 'Metaphor: does it constitute or reflect cultural models?', in *Metaphor in Cognitive Linguistics*, eds R. W. Gibbs, and G. Steen. Amsterdam: John Benjamin, 167–188.

Lakoff, G. and Johnson, M. 1980. *Metaphors We Live By*. Chicago: The University of Chicago Press.

Miller, D. F. 1992. *The Reason of Metaphor: a Study in Politics*. New Delhi: Sage.

Miller, S. I. and Fredericks, M. 1990. 'Perceptions of the crisis in American public education: the relationship of metaphors to ideology'. *Metaphor and Symbolic Activity* 5, no. 2: 67–81.

Paine, R. 1981. 'The political issues of metaphor and metonym: an exploratory statement', in *Politically Speaking: Cross-Cultural Studies of Rhetoric*, ed. R. Paine. Philadelphia: Institute for the Study of Human Issues, 187–200.

Quinn, N. 1991. 'The cultural basis of metaphor', in *Beyond Metaphor: The Theory of Tropes in Anthropology*, ed. J. W. Fernandez. Stanford: Stanford University Press, 56–93.

Quinn, N. and Holland, D. 1987. 'Culture and cognition', in *Cultural Models in Language and Thought*, eds D. Holland and N. Quinn. Cambridge: Cambridge University Press, 3–42.

Sontag, S. 1978. *Illness as Metaphor*. New York: Farrar, Straus and Giroux.

Stibbe, 1996. A. *Metaphor and Alternative Conceptions of Illness*. Unpublished Ph.D. thesis, Lancaster University.

Thompson, S. 1996. 'Politics without metaphors is like a fish without water', in *Metaphor. Implications and Applications*, eds J. S. Mio and A. N. Katz. Mahwah: Lawrence Erlbaum Associates, 185–201.

Chapter 4

Nationalism and Culture: Some Reflections on the Construction of National Languages

François Nectoux

Introduction

The great historian Eric Hobsbawm, writing in 1990, concluded his study on nationalism by arguing that

> ...in spite of its evident prominence, nationalism is historically less important. It is no longer, as it were, a global political programme, as it may be said to have been in the nineteenth and earlier twentieth centuries. It is at most a complicating factor, or a catalyst for other developments.

He continued by forecasting a twenty-first century world that

> ...can no longer be contained within the limits of 'nations' and 'nation-states' as they used to be defined, either politically, or economically, or culturally, or even linguistically. [...] It will see 'nation-states' and 'nations' or ethnic/linguistic groups primarily as retreating before, resisting, adapting to, being absorbed or dislocated by the new supranational restructuring of the globe. (Hobsbawm 1990: 191)

It is evidently too soon to test the validity of this prognosis. But the experience of the 1990s in Europe and across the world appears to indicate that, if nations and nation-states are retreating before globalisation and new supranational power forces, they are doing so kicking and screaming very loudly. Indeed, it seems that the twentieth century is coming to an end with as many nationalist conflicts as it started with, although the world environment has changed completely – global restructuring being a new factor that may exacerbate these nationalist conflicts.

In Europe, the 1990s were marked by the agony of countries of the ex-Yugoslavia, and by the inability of the largest countries of the European Union (EU) to go beyond their own national interest in order to prevent the crisis degenerating into the three wars in Croatia, Bosnia-Herzegovina and Kosovo. Other nationalist conflicts flared up across the Southern borders of Russia, such as those in Chechnya, Armenia or Georgia, and tensions around issues of national minorities simmer in many countries in Central and Western Europe.

The 1990s also saw a resurgence of debates around national identity, nationalist attitudes and politics, including in 'old' nations such as France. There, the first half of the 1990s was marked by developments such as the on-going reassessment of the legacy of the French Revolution, which founded the modern idea of the French nation, in the aftermath of the bi-centenary celebrations of the 1789 events (Furet 1978, 1990). Similarly, there was an intensification of debates on the extent, causes and consequences of French collaboration with the Nazi occupiers during the Second World War, largely exploding the myths of the resisting Nation in arms. At the same time, intense political divisions around the negotiations for the Maastricht Treaty, advancing the integration process of the European Union, largely focused on the theme of national independence and sovereignty, and the 1992 referendum on the adoption of the Treaty approved it by only a very small majority. Another issue that questioned national identity in France during the 1990s was that of international trade negotiations, first through the General Agreement on Tariffs and Trade (GATT, the so-called Uruguay Round) and then through the World Trade Organisation (WTO). French diplomacy, supported by most of domestic public opinion, took a much-criticised approach, seeking to keep communication and cultural industries out of the trade liberalisation process, coining the expression 'cultural exception', which was later replaced by 'protection of cultural diversity'. This should obviously be put into parallel with the policies for the 'defence of the French language' that led governments to implement protective measures against the penetration of English. In the background to all these debates and policies concerned with national identity, the Front National political party was gaining considerable popularity on a platform of extreme nationalism, racism and xenophobia.

Similar examples could have been highlighted in other European countries – and across the whole world. It has become apparent that nationalism, one of the scourges of the twentieth century, is rebounding on a kind of post-Cold War wave. This has obviously been the case in Eastern and Central Europe, with countries freeing themselves from the mantle of Stalinist totalitarian control, and recovering old national identities 'reconstructed' for new circumstances. It was also the case in many parts of the Third World, in which the tremors of the post-colonial era had not calmed down while the end of the Cold War allowed for the renewal of nationalist claims. However, there is a feeling of incomprehension towards aspects of this resurgence of nationalist politics and debates around national identity that the end of the Cold War could not fully explain. Nationalism is a multifarious, polymorphous phenomenon that cannot be simply reduced, in terms of cultural and social values, to a mechanistic or functional set of interacting social causalities. Beyond the old debate on the structural vs. cultural roots of national identity and nationalism, the most important question is to find the tools for an understanding of national identity and nationalism in its practice, discourse and evolution.

Much has been written on this topic in the fields of cultural and political studies, and particular attention has been given to the construction and resistance of national stereotypes and archetypes in European industrialised nations (Balibar and Wallerstein 1991; Brubaker 1992; Jenkins and Sofos 1996). However, the inability to cope with 'foreignness', or 'otherness', displayed to different degrees by a large part of all European populations, would seem to indicate that national identity, as a factor of both inclusion and exclusion, touches more complex aspects in the socialisation process.

It could be tempting to adopt a 'relativist' approach to study these in a social science framework. This would explain the near impossibility of resolving many national differences and conflicts by the impossibility of 'translating' values and behaviour from one identity to another. However, there are good grounds for upholding the hypothesis that there is no experiential impossibility of sharing values between national cultures and ultimately gaining understanding between foreign national identities. The difficulty and the numerous failures of communicating properly between national cultures in times of crisis are largely due to the management of these crises by competing social groups and elites. These usually seek to gain or preserve some form of social control, and use deep-seated and complex cultural traits in order to further the perception of threats to national identity and, when necessary, stir up nationalist fervour. This complexity does not signify the 'impenetrability' of national identity – complexity is not the same as immanence. The cultural factors referred to above are history-based, religious, issues of social interaction or linguistics and they need to be deconstructed in order to understand how resentment towards 'foreignness' and the perception of threat from 'otherness' can develop through manipulation of those cultural factors. Amongst these cultural forms, language and linguistic constructs have a pre-eminent place, as language is at the core of cultural identities and practices, often itself bound up with a national identity and its expression.

The case of language can therefore be used to argue that a relativist approach to issues of nationalism is not only methodologically flawed in social science terms, but also ultimately self-defeating, as it would prevent rather than help the resolution of conflicts. Language issues also form the basis for many 'relativist' approaches to comparative sociology, anthropology, etc. If it can be shown that language is not consubstantial to a given culture, but an evolving construct participating in social change, this will validate the hypothesis that national identity can itself be understood and negotiated.

Nationalism as a complex social construct

If history since the beginning of the modern age had not already convinced us of the baffling complexity and diversity displayed by national identity and nationalism as socio-political phenomena, the last two decades of the twentieth century have certainly provided us with a multitude of convincing demonstrations. They have glaringly shown that nationalism can only be understood as a dynamic social construct:

> National identity [...] is neither natural nor stable. While undoubtedly the repository of distinctive collective experience, it is finally an invention, involving the establishment of oppo-

sites and 'others' which are used as yardsticks for self-definition. National identity is a fluid entity, where categorisation of 'self' and 'other', inclusion and exclusion, is an arena of contest between competing groups and institutions within society. (Evans 1996: 34)

This complexity in part explains why there are so few convincing theories of nationalism. It is remarkable that many classic textbooks still define national identity by simply accumulating a number of traits. For instance, Smith starts by defining a nation as 'a named human population sharing an historic territory, common myths and historical memories, a mass, public culture, a common economy and common legal rights and duties for all members.' He goes on then to assert that

National identity and the nation are complex constructs composed of a number of interrelated components – ethnic, cultural, territorial, economic and legal-political [...] The nation, in fact, draws on elements of other kinds of collective identity, which accounts not only for the way in which national identity can be combined with these other types of identity – class, religious or ethnic – but also for the chameleon-like permutations of nationalism, the ideology, with other ideologies like liberalism, fascism and communism. (Smith 1991: 14, 15)

The problem is that the articulation and functional analysis of these elements is often limited to an unsatisfactory description of the characteristics that can be associated with specific national communities or historical circumstances, or to a focus on one or two of these elements. (Smith focuses on the 'ethnic' core of national identity.) Functionalist approaches do not explain why the whole is more than the parts, why nationalism manages to have such a hold on individuals and communities.

Many other analysts see nationalism as cultural politics. Gellner, for instance, defines nationalism as follows:

Nationalism is a political principle which maintains that similarity of culture is the basic social bond. Whatever principle of authority may exist between people depend for their legitimacy on the fact that the members of the group concerned are of the same culture (or, in nationalist idiom, of the same 'nation'). (Gellner 1997: 3, 4)

This definition is quite limited in scope – it simply describes nationalist ideology as it presents itself within its own discourse.

However, it implicitly insists on the importance of analysing the nationalist idea, and national identity, as cultural expressions of social forces in a wide range of modern social formations. Indeed, the nation, as we now know it, has become a quasi-universal form of identity and socio-political framework and has yet managed to take widely different forms.

There is, however, a crucial element somewhat lacking in the sometimes violent denunciation of nationalism as a faked construct by Gellner, who once wrote, 'Nationalism is not the awakening of nations to self-consciousness: it invents nations where they do not exist' (Gellner 1964: 168). This missing element in this approach is the development of an understanding of why a nationalist ideology can convince so many people, across such a wide range of cultures and socio-economic formations, that their national identity is their overarching, definitive identity, and that its defence is worth more than everything else in their lives. This usually happens in times of crisis – a perceived threat from whatever quarter, and for various economic, territorial, or internal reasons (economic crisis, break-up of consensual politics between various communities within a nation). At such times the varied elements of national culture (religion, languages, social behaviour and interaction) get hooked up to the 'defence' of the nation. A perceived threat or resentment can privilege one more relevant aspect in the cultural construct – for instance, religion may become the main pole of expression of nationalist discourse or action, or it may be language, or a territorial claim, or several elements at once.

Another important aspect of nationalist ideology is that it provides the underlying justifications for the 'closure' of the nation. This important concept of closure helps give currency to the specific characteristics of the nation as defined by the nationalist culture of the society. It specifies who and what is included and excluded from the fold of the nation. It delineates the borders, assigns nationality, and expels what is deemed to be foreign to, and dangerous for, the integrity of the nation and national identity (Brubaker 1992; Jenkins and Sofos 1996). A typical example would be the old, somewhat mythical difference between the French and German principles for access to citizenship, *Jus soli* (literally 'law of the land': citizenship is awarded to people born, or long term resident in the land) and *Jus sanguinis* (literally 'law of the blood': citizenship is only awarded to people whose parents are already citizens). Although political and legal reality has made matters far more complex and ambiguous, the national identity philosophies in the two countries, focusing more on political principles in France and more on ethno-cultural principles in Germany, still reveal the different constructions of attitudes (and policies) as far as interactions with 'others' are concerned (such as racism, xenophobia, acculturation, immigration and integration policies).

One of the most productive concepts in the cultural analysis of nationalism is that of 'imagined communities', as Benedict Anderson has called nations in his celebrated book with the eponymous title (Anderson 1983). 'Imagination' here does not signify a 'figment of the imagination' – the nation becomes a real, socio-political entity (on the role of social imagination as a political principle of social organisation, see Castoriadis 1975). What is 'imagined', built in the mind, is the sense of belonging, shared by members of a nation:

> It is imagined because the members of even the smallest nation will never know most of their fellow-members, meet them or even hear of them, yet in the minds of each lives the image of their communion. (Anderson 1983: 6)

Anderson, commenting on the millions of deaths provoked by nationalist wars in the last two centuries, asks a stark question:

> These deaths bring us abruptly face to face with the central problem posed by nationalism: what makes the shrunken imaginings of recent history (scarcely more than two centuries) generate such colossal sacrifices? I believe that the beginnings of an answer lie in the cultural roots of nationalism. (Anderson 1983: 7)

Because it is a polymorphous ideological and cultural construct, modern nationalism can be adapted to a wide range of social formations, and it has itself changed with societies since it first appeared as a powerful principle of political organisation in the eighteenth century. Most analysts agree that the modern nation (and nationalism) first developed in early capitalist societies, or, as Gellner (1964) puts it, through 'industrialism', although others have criticised this view, putting more emphasis on trade conditions or aspects of pre-capitalist, pre-national formations. Whatever the starting point, however, the social and economic changes of the eighteenth century in Europe seem to have transformed the social identity of individuals. From a fixed status, this evolved into a more uncertain integration, based largely on an individualised and market-based economic identity. In this context, the framework of the nation was able to develop as a successful political and ideological system.

National identities are thus culturally defined, even though the socio-historical circumstances of their emergence and development are to be found primarily in the economic and political processes affecting a territory, ethnic community or social class. Their evolution followed that of societies in the last two centuries and can be seen in terms of four phases. The first was that of 'civic' nationalism and national identity based on equal citizenship, which developed in its archetypal form during the French Revolution and was later famously celebrated by Renan (Renan 1882). The nineteenth century in Germany and Central Europe saw the development of another archetypal version, that of the 'ethno-cultural' national identity, largely rooted in Romantic philosophy. In practice these two versions interacted in all countries, with hybrid ideologies and their accompanying contradictions spreading all over Europe (including France and Italy) during most of the following century.

A third form of nationalism appeared in the twentieth century. This was the nationalism of the 'national liberation' movements that fought to overcome colonial rule and conquer independence. Nationalist elites, often influenced by socialist thought (although earlier national liberation struggles in Latin America used a rhetoric close to French 'civic' nationalism), and usually influenced by the nationalist philosophy of the colonial power, adapted this model to their own community, where the social exploitation of colonialism had all but destroyed traditional identities (Harris 1990). It can be quite interesting to examine the language used by these national liberation movements. A typical example is the well-known *Declaration of the 1st November 1954* published by the embryonic Front de Libération Nationale (FLN) in Algeria, which signalled the start of eight years of armed struggle by Algerian nationalists against France before the country won its independence. The text declares that the aims of the FLN are

> ..national independence through: 1) the establishment of the sovereign, democratic and social Algerian state within the framework of Islamic principles; 2) the respect of all fundamental freedoms without distinction of race nor religion. (...) (Courrière 1968: 568–9)

It addresses a number of demands to the French authorities, especially

1) the recognition of Algerian nationality by the way of an official declaration abrogating the edicts, decrees and acts that
have made Algeria a French territory in contempt of the history,
geography, language, religion and customs of the Algerian people; 2) the start of negotiations with the authorised representatives of the Algerian people, on the basis of the recognition of
Algerian sovereignty, one and indivisible. (Reproduced in Courrière 1968: 569–70.)

Beyond the general tone, which is typical of national liberation movements, it is interesting to note the use of expressions
that are directly inspired by French national rhetoric, such as
'fundamental freedoms', the 'Algerian people' and, even more
strikingly, 'Algerian sovereignty, one and indivisible'. This last
expression is directly inspired by a text present in all the French
constitutions: 'The French Republic is one and indivisible',
which establishes a constitutive principle of the nation in
France. These similarities and parallels do not imply that the
Algerian nationalists fighting for the independence of their
country were mimicking French nationalism, their foe. Instead
they were appropriating elements of nationalist ideology for
their own purposes – recognising the validity of a nationalist
model as a tool for liberation from colonial oppression. In the
long term the appropriation of this particular model by the
nationalist elite has brought the same problems to the independent Algeria as it had to other countries (Harris 1990).

We seem now to be entering a fourth period, in which the
model of the nation faces new challenges, including globalisation (Hobsbawm 1990, Castells 1997). As noted above, the various phases and models have been interacting within nations.
Michel Winock, for instance, analysing the changes in nationalist ideology in France, distinguishes 'open nationalism' from
'closed nationalism' – the first corresponds to an 'acquisitive'
form (such as that of the early periods of the French Revolution) and the second to a 'defensive' form (such as the right-
wing nationalism that developed in France after the 1870
defeat against Prussia and during the Dreyfus affair) (Winock
1982). The first model is obviously the 'civic' archetype of the
Revolution, whereas the second is closer to the 'ethno-cultural'
type developed in Germany. These two models have been in
competition, interpenetrating each other since their emergence, and it is particularly difficult to determine the influence
of each in the development of the nation. Both, for instance,
can be found in the mythical French history constructed in the
nineteenth century by the central figure of Michelet – with its

ethno-cultural archetypes of the 'Gaul' and Joan of Arc meeting the 1793 patriot-citizens of the French Revolution known as 'the soldiers of Year II'. This myth-building, hybrid historical reconstruction of France's past can be seen as one of the main sources of French nationalist ideologies.

One last point on the evolution of nationalism: one of the principle ways that it emerged and developed in the eighteenth and nineteenth centuries across Europe and throughout the world was through new forms of communication, notably the printed word. The diffusion of printed material encouraged the adoption of what often became the 'national' language in a given country (Anderson 1983; Thiesse 1999). The development of education and the diffusion of printed material, at least within the middle classes, contributed not only to the development of market capitalism, but also to the spread of nationalist ideas. The close interaction between language and national identity is an important element in the study of national identity and nationalism as cultural phenomena.

Languages and national culture

There are strong and complex interactions between language(s) and nations and national identity. This is inevitable; after all, language contributes to the formation of identities, often expresses them and helps to distinguish between them, and itself is a form of identity for both individuals and communities. It is also an easy tool for exclusion and closure – those who do not speak the language of a community are 'barbarians' (literally so in ancient Greece, where the term referred to non-Greeks who spoke in *borborygms*; in modern French the word *baragouin* – uncomprehensible, degraded language – reflects the same principle). In the fear and loathing of 'others', people bearing foreign identities that cannot be understood, linguistic markers are always present – through accents, pronunciation, spelling variations of personal names, etc.

However, these interactions are particularly ambiguous, largely because of the ways the concept of 'national' language is played up in the nationalist ideology and nationalist politics. An important and obvious point should be made: there is no direct organic, constitutive link between national identity and nation, on one side, and language on the other. Although languages are always part and parcel of a national culture in one way or another, there is no need for a 'national' language to accompany the constitution of a nation, nor is there a need for the various communities and social groups that come to constitute a nation to speak a 'national' language. Indeed in most nations several languages co-exist in a situation of 'diglossia', to use the concept as Fergusson and Fishman do (Fishman 1967). In some cases, this co-existence becomes one element of an open conflict between communities. In most other cases, 'diglossia' (with or without bilingualism) is a source of tensions and in any case is always part of complex power relationships between communities or ethnic or social groups.

Calvet (1987) adds to the concept of diglossia by showing that in many cases, there is a complex 'embedded' diglossia. This means that several languages within a society have layered relationships corresponding to a dynamics of power between several types of speakers and types or modes of communication. The clearest instance of such linguistic structure occurs in countries that have experienced colonisation. For instance, Tanzania has English, Swahili and vernacular languages, while French, Wolof, and other African languages are spoken in Senegal. In both cases, the ex-colonial language is that of the elite engaged in 'premium' activities. Swahili and Wolof are the languages of communication between communities and in most public arenas (for instance for trade); then the vernaculars are used in low-level communication. Sometimes, a dominant vernacular is promoted to the rank of 'official' or 'national' language, making the power dynamics within communication in society even more complex. Complexity can be made even more striking by arrangements concerning taught languages in education. This important phenomenon of embedded diglossia, which can be found in varied forms in many parts of the world, contributes to the development of complex and interlocked identities.

Fishman summarises the relationship between language and nationalism by identifying several categories of interaction (Fishman 1973). For most nationalist ideologies, the language is first the link with the glorious past – the only way the old history/myths can be told, and the language of the ancestors. Second, language is the link with 'authenticity': first through the language itself (the 'purity' of which is a continuous source of concern) and second through oral and written artifacts that are the repositories of the national collective greatness. However, language does not have the same place in the various nationalist ideologies. This is particularly well illustrated by comparing the approaches of two important eighteenth and nineteenth century figures, Herder and Renan. Herder especially, as noted by Hermet, took a 'relativist' position in relation to national identity (Hermet 1996). For him, the German language was consubstantial to the German national identity, part of its 'spirit' and nature. On the contrary, Renan, in line with his theory of national identity as a meeting of the wills of free citizens, insisted that 'There is in man something superior to language: his will. The will of the Swiss to be united, in spite of their various idioms, is a fact of far greater importance than linguistic similarity, often attained through persecution' (Renan 1882; in Woolf 1996: 54–55). Was he writing about France in this last sentence? It appears not. On the contrary, he continued by claiming that 'One worthy fact about France is that it has never sought to obtain linguistic unity by coercive means. Can we not have the same feelings, the same thoughts, and love the same things in different languages?' (Renan 1882; in Woolf 1996: 55). Renan was clearly taking his wishes for reality – as will be discussed later, the regional languages in France were subjected to severe restrictions in the last decades of the nineteenth century. Furthermore, there are innumerable proofs that in France the 'ethno-cultural' view of the consubstantiality of the national language within national identity has been and is still widely held, and that it is an important element of nationalist thinking.

In Europe, many linguistic conflicts with nationalist causes are still unresolved – the case of Belgium is only one example. Other slow burning conflicts exist in the case of many minorities, such as the continued skirmishes between the Slovakian authorities and the Hungarian minority in South Slovakia; other conflicts have been more open – linguistic issues had a central role in the development of the Kosovo conflict. The refusal by France in 1999 to put the European Union's directive on regional languages on the statute book, with the French Constitutional Council refusing to accept it because of its 'anti-constitutionality' even when the government relented, is another example of a nation-state implicitly assuming a total identity between nation and language.

It is relevant to note that modern nation-states, far from defending languages against the 'external', have contributed (even if they are not always fully responsible for it) to the disappearance or slow death of many languages across the world. Interestingly in this modern age, we are less and less a truly polyglot world – not only are whole families of languages disappearing, but also vernacular variations – idioms, dialects, etc. This does not mean that linguistic productivity is decreasing, but that the pressures of economic development, communication imperatives and social control in modern societies, and in many cases the centralist policies of national bureaucracies, are such that they are allowing a great many languages and dialects to disappear through forced or insidious cultural assimilation. Clearly colonisation destroyed many languages (the population of the Americas may have been as high as one hundred million people before European colonisation – two hundred years later, there were fewer than one million native Americans. It can be assumed that many languages disappeared too.) However, the trend towards linguistic homogenisation is continuing. David Crystal recently commented that, of the estimated six thousand languages that are currently spoken in the world, half are not expected to survive the next century. Currently, five thousand languages are spoken by fewer than one hundred thousand people, and some three thousand (half of the total) are spoken by fewer than ten thousand (Crystal 1999). There are less than three hundred recognised nations.

The production of languages

In the industrialised Western world, the phenomenon of nationhood is often perceived as a monadic archetype – one nation, one ethnic group, one mythological historical framework and one national language – as if the collective mind that created the 'imagined community' had been working with homogeneous material. Diglossia and pluri-linguistic practices are presented as deviations from the archetype, rather than the norm that they are. This is not surprising, especially at the linguistic level, as older European nations (and especially the three classical examples of France, England and Germany) have evolved within such a model.

In reality, however, we should follow Anne-Marie Thiesse when she writes about 'the manufacturing of national languages', as this is what has happened in most existing nations and is still happening across the world (Thiesse 1999: 68). Similarly, Fishman demonstrates how nationalist proto-elites seeking to establish the basis for the construction of a nation utilise a version of existing vernaculars in order to construct (manufacture) a national language, which is then reified as containing the national spirit (Fishman 1973).

There are many examples of such developments, such as that of Norway. When struggling to get full independence from

Sweden, as opposed to the autonomy granted in 1815, a major issue was the establishment of a Norwegian national language. The problem was that the elites were speaking Danish, that the capital, Oslo, was speaking Dano-Norwegian (Riksmaal, which has since evolved into Boksmaal), and that the popular vernacular of the rural areas (Landsmaal, now Nynorsk), preferred by nationalists as more 'authentic', was completely different (Baggioni 1997). During the whole nineteenth century, the intense political fight between supporters of the two languages permeated every political issue. Both versions became national languages in 1885, but the fight continued well into the twentieth century, even after independence in 1905, and recently during the debate about entry into the European Community (Thiesse 1999).

Another case could be dubbed the finest hour of philologists. In Central Europe in particular, the early nineteenth century was the golden age of 'vernacularizing lexicographers, grammarians, philologists and litterateurs' (Anderson 1983: 71). Elites of communities with strong historical (often mythical) roots, often politically and economically controlled by centralised empires, were seeking to create national identities through their reinterpreted cultural roots, and universities were hotbeds of linguistic nationalist radicalism (Hobsbawm 1962). This required them to research their national history and, more importantly in practical terms, to construct a 'national' language from vernacular version(s) in order to be able to communicate with the target populations. Languages such as Finnish, Ukrainian, Serbo-Croat and Rumanian were for all practical purposes invented from vernaculars previously mocked as the uncouth language of the local peasantry (Anderson 1983). The revision of Turkish and the complete transformation of its written version during the modernist (and nationalist) Ataturk regime in the early twentieth century is another case of language planning, part of a political strategy aiming at modernising the country. The case of Modern Hebrew is more striking still. This is the only example of a language that has been revived, re-developed and adopted as a national language. Re-developed in Palestine by Ben Yehouda in the 1880s from old religious Hebrew and increasingly used by Jewish people later returning to Palestine, it became the national language of independent Israel in 1947, after the intense political debate between the proponents of Yiddish (spoken by most European Jews) and those of Modern Hebrew had been won by the latter. This case of very successful language planning contrasts with Ireland's failure to redevelop the use of Gaelic, despite the importance of this language in the national identity and culture.

However, it is interesting to note that the generalisation of French language followed, rather than preceded, the emergence of the modern French national identity. As shown in the classic study by Eugen Weber on the transformation of rural society in France during the last few decades of the nineteenth century, the French language was in fact spoken by only a proportion of French citizens up to a century after the French Revolution. At the time of the revolution, the famous report of Abbé Grégoire conceded that French was the majority language in only sixteen of eighty-nine departments, that a quarter of the population (six million people) did not understand it at all, and that only three million people spoke it correctly (Hermet 1996).

In 1863, a survey by the Education Ministry revealed that 'French was still a foreign language for a large number of French people, including nearly half of the children...' (Weber 1976: 114). The mass of the French population, living in rural areas, understood only a little French and was still largely communicating through its array of local dialects, idioms and languages, in which it was often impossible to fully understand people from a neighbouring valley. The whole South of France, Brittany, the centre regions (Auvergne, Limousin), Alsace, as well as the northern and Ardennes fringes, were speaking 'foreign' languages, disparagingly reduced to *parlers*, *patois*, and *baragouins* by French speakers.

It was only the transformation of the rural economy as analysed by Weber, pressure from the French-speaking administration and the simultaneous impact of compulsory schooling with its militant 'Republican' teaching profession, that led younger generations to adopt French as their main language more or less willingly in the later years of the nineteenth century and early years of the twentieth century. Later, the trenches of the First World War brought together a whole generation of young men from all regions and forced upon them the need to communicate through French as a single medium (Balibar 1985).

Conclusion: towards a political economy of language in nations

The reflections above could be refined and details added; however, some points have been outlined which could be of use in the study of the politics of nationalism – a murky area, if ever there was one. Nations are transient, historically located socio-political entities and nationalisms tend to appropriate and reconstruct the cultures of communities for their own reification. In particular many examples show that language(s) in each national identity is (or are) complex construct(s), often socially manipulated and evolving, subject to power games and conflicts. Therefore, there is neither an 'innate', organic, substantive, natural relationship between a national identity and a language, nor an impossibility of 'translating' cultural values and concerns from one identity to another, since language itself evolves socially. Furthermore, individuals and groups within a given national identity continuously negotiate, adapt, legitimise and fight between themselves for linguistic identity and power.

This conclusion does not negate the experience that individuals or social groups may have of a quasi-organic relationship between language, identity and, in many cases, nationality – indeed, the embedding of this relationship is very deep, substantial and difficult even to be aware of in oneself. However, this difficulty does not preclude understanding – it simply makes it more difficult. It is always possible to understand and explain nationalist practices and behaviours using the frameworks of analysis offered by social science disciplines. The issue here is to differentiate 'experiential' relativism from analytical relativism. The first should not be a justification for the second. In the social sciences in particular, cultural relativism operates within the realm of values (Gellner 1985), and brings many dangers to the analysis.

National identity, as a cultural artifact, is continuously being reconstructed by the evolution of the national community, and particularly by nationalist groups/elites seeking to control national identity. Although it is only one element in the complex array of interlocking identities that are developed by individuals through socialisation (Smith 1991), it comes to the fore in times of crisis that affect individuals and groups within a nation. Nationalism is essentially reactive, a reaction against 'otherness', seen as a threat to identity. In this sense, it can be seen as absolutely relativist – perceiving the other as a strange being that cannot be fully understood, and will not understand the national culture. Nationalist discourse affirms that it is impossible to fully understand the other without being this other, without absorbing its natural substance. Therefore it is better to stay far away from other nations – as Gellner (1997) says, nationalism seeks to 'purify' its own identity: ethno-cultural differentiation is seen as absolute, with minor differences being exploited to create an image of total strangeness.

Nationalism is an ideology functioning on a social construct – there is nothing natural, given or substantive in it. In other words, like all ideologies acting in the realm of power, it exploits and uses various societal constructs such as religion, language, political frameworks and social behaviour as resources and tools to further its own ends. Therefore, a kind of political economy of nationalism needs to be developed, especially in relation to the dynamics of language, to come to a better understanding of how the distribution of power in society relates to the distribution and confiscation of linguistic resources within the nation.

References

Anderson, Benedict. 1983. *Imagined Communities*. London: Verso.

Baggioni, Daniel. 1997. *Langues et nations en Europe*. Paris: Payot.

Balibar, Etienne and Wallerstein, Immanuel. 1991. *Race, Nation, Class: Ambiguous Identities*. London: Verso.

Balibar, Françoise. 1985. *L'Institution du français*. Paris: Payot.

Brubaker, Rogers. 1992. *Citizenship and Nationhood in France and Germany*. Cambridge, Massachusetts: Harvard University Press.

Calvet, Louis-Jean. 1987. *La Guerre des langues et les politiques linguistiques*. Paris: Payot.

Castells, Manuel. 1997. *The Power of Identity (The Information Age: Economy, Society and Culture, Volume II)*. London: Blackwell.

Castoriadis, Cornelius. 1975. *L'Institution imaginaire de la sociètè*. Paris: Editions du Seuil.

Courrière, Yves. 1968. *La Guerre d'Algérie, Volume 1: Les Fils de la Toussaint*. Paris: Fayard.

Crystal, David. 1999. 'The Death of Language'. *Prospects* 46 (November), 56–59.

Evans, Martin. 1996. 'Language of Racism within Contemporary Europe', in *Nation and Identity in Contemporary Europe*, eds Brian Jenkins and Spyros Sofos. London: Routledge, 133–153.

Fishman, Joshua A. 1967. 'Bilingualism with and without diglossia, diglossia with and without bilingualism'. *Journal of Social Issues* 23/2, 29–38.

———. 1973. *Language and Nationalism*. Rowley, Massachusetts: Newbury House.

Furet, François. 1978. *Penser la révolution française*. Paris: Gallimard.

———. 1990. *La Révolution française*. Paris: Hachette.

Gellner, Ernst. 1964. *Thought and Change*. London: Weidenfeld and Nicolson.

————. 1985. *Relativism and the Social Sciences*. Cambridge: Cambridge University Press.

————. 1997. *Nationalism*. London: Weidenfield and Nicolson.

Harris, Nigel. 1990. *National Liberation*. London: Penguin.

Hermet, Guy. 1996. *Histoire des nations et du nationalisme en Europe*, (2nd edition). Paris: Editions du Seuil.

Hobsbawm, Eric. 1962. *The Age of Revolution 1789–1848*. London: Weidenfeld and Nicolson.

————. 1990. *Nations and Nationalism since 1870*. Cambridge: Cambridge University Press.

Jenkins, Brian and Sofos, Spyros, eds. 1996. *Nation and Identity in Contemporary Europe*. London: Routledge.

Renan, Ernest. 1882. *Qu'est-ce qu'une nation?*, (modern edition 1992). Paris: Presses-Pocket.

Smith, Anthony D. 1991. *National Identity*. London: Penguin.

Thiesse, Anne-Marie. 1999. *La Création des identités nationales – Europe XVIIe–XXe siècle*. Paris: Editions du Seuil.

Weber, Eugen. 1976. *Peasants into Frenchmen – The Modernization of Rural France 1870–1914*. Standford, California: Standford University Press.

Winock, Michel. 1982. *Nationalisme, antisémitisme et fascisme en France*. Paris: Editions du Seuil.

Woolf, Stuart. 1996. *Nationalism in Europe, 1815 to the Present – A Reader*. London: Routledge.

PART III

DIVIDED BY A COMMON LANGUAGE

BETWEEN RELATIVISM AND TRUTH: JEAN BAUDRILLARD, THE SOKAL AFFAIR AND THE USE OF SCIENTIFIC TERMINOLOGY ACROSS CULTURAL BOUNDARIES

Chris Horrocks

Brief outline

Recently, key exponents of postmodern theory have been crit-icised for misusing and abusing scientific terminology in their texts. This has not only given rise to debates on the compe-tence of these writers when they claim the credentials of scien-tific rigour, but has reinvigorated 'The Two Cultures' debate, which first identified the intellectual subordination of the sci-entific community to the literary one.

This essay examines the critiques of Jean Baudrillard by Sokal and Bricmont in order to suggest that the former's 'epis-temic relativism' is misunderstood by those who operate in an empiricist and positivist tradition, on account of their repres-sion of the historical and literary context from which Bau-drillard draws when using analogies and metaphors of science for specific and tactical ends.

I conclude that the division between constative and intran-sitive, and performative and transitive modes of discourse, has been overdetermined in their critique. The binary oppositions that they construct are both inadequate and irrelevant when applied to certain forms of postmodern discourse. Further-more, I suggest that the distinctions that are made lead to moralistic and non-scientific judgements in contradiction to the objectivist intentions that critics claim are foundational to their approach.

The return of two cultures

> Now and then one used to find poets conscientiously using sci-entific expressions, and getting them wrong – there was a time when 'refraction' kept cropping up in verse in a mystifying fashion, and when 'polarised light' was used as though writers were under the illusion that it was a specially admirable kind of light. Of course, that isn't the way that science could be any good to art. It has got to be assimilated along with, and as part and parcel of, the whole of our mental experience, and used as naturally as the rest. (Snow 1964: 16)

The two cultures debate, which C.P Snow instigated with his Rede Lecture of 1959 in order to claim that science and litera-ture were polarised fields, the latter being a 'traditional' culture that refused to countenance the intellectual viability of the for-mer, has recently re-emerged in an isolated but notable exam-ple, known as the 'Sokal Affair'. Alan Sokal, a Professor of Physics at New York University, successfully submitted what he later claimed was a parody of a postmodern text to an unwit-ting social theory journal (Sokal: 1996), in order to demon-strate the absurd misuse of scientific and mathematical terms in postmodern discourse, and the uncritical manner of their reception. Sokal and Bricmont's subsequent publication, *Intel-lectual Impostures*, capitalised on the revealed hoax in order to show how key intellectuals, including Lacan, Kristeva, Deleuze and Baudrillard, 'have repeatedly abused scientific concepts and terminology: either using scientific ideas totally out of con-text, without giving the slightest justification [...] or throwing around scientific jargon in front of their non-scientist readers without any regard for its relevance or even its meaning' (Sokal and Bricmont 1998: ix–x). The book therefore revitalises Snow's initial thesis, while operating within a quite different cultural climate that Sokal and Bricmont describe and dismiss as dom-inated by 'epistemic relativism,' which in their view maintains that 'science is nothing more than a "myth", a "narration" or a "social construction" among many others' (1998: x). Thus, postmodern theorists have succeeded Snow's wayward poets as irresponsible ransackers of scientific language in order to maintain a thoroughly relativistic version of knowledge and meaning. Baudrillard, for example, stands accused of getting science wrong, by employing the discourses of cybernetics or string theory to preposterous ends, and drawing absurdly from the pure and applied sciences, including human biology, physics, cosmology, astrophysics, genetics and immunology. His use of terms such as 'stellar nebula', 'metastasis', 'strange attractor', 'hypertelia' are familiar to readers of popular science and scientists from various disciplines (Baudrillard 1983). For Sokal, Baudrillard's untenable position is characterised by incompetence and irresponsibility: the charge of incompetence is levelled by the natural scientists, for whom Baudrillard is intruding on a system of thought and practice without adequate respect for the rules of that system; and one of irresponsibility is made by social science as a response to Baudrillard's improper deployment of metaphors that misrepresent the objects of social theory or serve to promote a reactionary ideology. For example, the trope of the social masses as a 'black hole', absorbing all meaning with complete indifference, is taken as evidence of Baudrillard's political indifference to issues of class, power and inequality (Callinicos 1989).

Sokal's allegation of Baudrillard's 'imposture' is one of many examples of criticism initiated by social scientists and philosophers, who berated him for confusing his categories and conflating rational enquiry with aesthetics – of merging Kant with Baudelaire (Norris 1990).

The backlash to the linguistic turn

I wish to examine the process that Snow and Sokal considered illegitimate: the translocation of scientific terminology to areas designated as external to scientific discourse. Here, in their view, its precise function to describe events, objects or states is undermined. I concentrate on the specific critique of the scientific content of the work of Jean Baudrillard, in order to account for the context that this writer provides when mobilising such concepts. My intention is to indicate how the supposed abuse of such language is not simply attributable to a failure of Baudrillard to subscribe to the rigours of scientific definitions, but must be seen as relative to the particular strategies, arguably literary in character, which Baudrillard has designated for that language. These strategies, I wish to claim, have historically

specific antecedents, which if foregrounded tend to problema-
tise Sokal's position. I will explore these below. However, it is
necessary briefly to place Sokal and Bricmont's critique in its
cultural context, in order to demonstrate that the terrain has
altered somewhat since Snow's famous lecture.

It can be suggested that Sokal's complaint of epistemic relativism is indicative of the hegemony of the 'linguistic turn',
which superseded the 'The Two Cultures' debate, and repressed
the voices of empiricism. Indeed, it is now commonplace to
suggest that this is the case, as recently philosophies of science
have generally favoured the conception of science as a set of
conventions, constructions and consensual or conflictual
communities, whose exertions turn the definition of science
from a positivist and empirical one into a nexus of social
dynamics, institutional politics, and linguistic and discursive
codes or regimes. At the heart of this shift lies a key question:
can science be promoted to provide an explanation of the
world that can remain constant beyond shifting cultural
processes? This issue has been present since Quine's critique of
empiricism, which stated that the philosophy of science is
incapable of deriving a method of linking theory to observation and its sentences in a clear way, beyond their functional
role in belief systems, or sets of truth-claims (Quine 1960). It
extends through Kuhn's lively debate with Popper (1959), in
which scientific validity is seen by the former to be built on
assent and dissent in alternating periods of revolutionary and
stable activity (Kuhn 1970). It persists today in Feyerabend's
argument that science is a mythology that asserts itself
through a privileged community, and that its authority must
be challenged by other social and cultural domains (Feyerabend 1987), and exists in Richard Rorty's neo-pragmatist
contention that scientific change is similar to transitions and
effects when poets and other writers develop new metaphors to
alter cultural perception and social meaning (Rorty 1991).

Given the structuralist and poststructuralist currencies that
have impacted on the debate, the focus is now on the role of
language, discourse and text in the examination of these bodies of knowledge. As the analyses of culture formations, institutions and disciplines that constitute regimes of truth and
knowledge indicate, recent thought has tended to consider science and culture as reducible to common denominators,
described in areas of philosophical thought as language
games or grand narratives. This perspective has held the centre ground, yet recent texts have begun to turn critical atten-

tion to its scope, or more accurately its limitations, in the context of the criteria of scientific study. Thus, there has been a reaction to the claims made by central figures of postmodern thought, such as those of Jean-Francois Lyotard, for whom science is a cultural construction or a language game amongst others, which has no innate or prior claim to truth, and which has historically lost its means of validation (Lyotard 1984). It is this reaction, characterised as a claim over the validity and viability of scientific knowledge, that I wish to illustrate here, with reference to the Sokal affair. This reaction is not an isolated one; for example, the recent Critical Realist movement (Collier 1994) has attempted to draw a line between scientific truth and cultural relativism by distinguishing between 'intransitive' processes beyond human agency (such as physical laws and states), and 'transitive', socio-cultural and ethical ones (such as belief systems). Roy Bhaskar argues that cultural relativists, when discussing science, confuse these processes, thereby collapsing ontological considerations (the existence of objects and forces) into epistemological ones (the possibility of acquiring knowledge of such objects, etc.) (Bhaskar 1989).

The rhetorical construction of conceptual borders

The Critical Realists attempt to separate transitive and intransitive processes. Sokal also tries to distinguish between scientific truth and cultural relativism. This effort is also echoed in the Kantian critique of Baudrillard by Christopher Norris, who similarly argues for a conceptual compartmentalisation that he insists Baudrillard has infracted, albeit in an ethical dimension:

> On a close reading – something rarely attempted by Baudrillard's admirers – one can see how the rhetorical trick is pulled off by a habit of constantly shifting across between [sic] different modalities of discourse or orders of truth-claim. Thus postmodernity is a *fact* of our present situation (constative mode), but also an attitude we *ought* to take up (performatively speaking) if we are not to lose touch with these exciting New Times. (Norris 1996: 184)

Leaving aside Norris's assumption that Baudrillard aligns himself with postmodernity (Baudrillard in fact distances himself from the term) or that Baudrillard's position is predicated on an acceptance of this condition or is necessarily founded on an association between a loss of sense and abnegation of responsibility (rhetoric may be a strategy that maintains its own form of political engagement), it is significant that the unnoticed error, 'across between' survives. It seems to indicate an uncertainty involved in Norris's task of selecting a preposition that adequately conveys the transition between domains of discourse or philosophical categories. Indeed, the nuanced difference between 'across' and 'between' reveals the extent to which the process of movement over the border between transitive and instransitive states of enquiry (between/across the domains of facts and opinions) in Baudrillard's work, or between scientific enquiry and cultural relativism, is itself a question of the rhetorical function of language even within the strictures of Kantian philosophical critique. It highlights the problems that arise when constructing a coherent description not just of the border between modes of discourse, but of the instability inherent to maintaining such strict divisions – of constructing that border – between those modes in the first place. Such rigid distinctions necessarily affect the subsequent attempts to describe the dynamics of Baudrillard's alternation between the two fields, and create more problems than they solve, not least in the uncertain selection of prepositions that attempt to suture the divisions created.

While Norris differs from Sokal in his Kantian urgency to separate ethical and epistemological categories rather than scientific and non-scientific ones, he shares with the latter an overarching concern for which such rigidity cannot properly account: the appropriate classification of Baudrillard's text. Their positions illustrate an unwillingness to conjecture that his work may operate in a realm wherein the task of distinguishing between the constative, performative, transitive and intransitive modes outlined above is less relevant than such critics suppose. Indeed, I suggest that Baudrillard's writing should be addressed not in terms of their transition between or across such categories, but according to a more ambivalent and ambiguous contamination of categories and erasure of boundaries. These features, while appearing inadmissable to the critics mentioned here, only gain their sense when viewed in a framework they do not discuss.

Postmodernism and science: the question of literature

As I briefly stated earlier, I consider this context to be both literary and historical in character; it is not reducible to Norris's philosophical categorical imperatives or to the misinterpretations that Sokal claims Baudrillard makes. Such 'scientific' criticism of Baudrillard's enterprise is often itself premised on a misconception, which proceeds by repressing the literary dimension and tradition in which he works, and by which his use of scientific terminology must be assessed. In many respects, an account of Baudrillard that attends to his literary context, evident not simply in his style but made explicit in his references, provides the key to understanding how the failure to reflect on the categorisation of his work (which as a hybridous collection of texts resists classification) leads to disapprobation from certain quarters.

Turning again to Sokal and Bricmont's critique, they are at pains to refute arguments against their position on Baudrillard before they have been made. Thus, they confront the question of postmodern theory's literary credentials, by responding to its supposed validity according to its 'poetic licence':

> If a poet used words like 'black hole' or 'degree of freedom' out of context and without really understanding their scientific meaning, it doesn't bother us. Likewise, if a science-fiction writer uses secret passageways in space-time in order to send her characters back to the era of the Crusades, it is purely a question of taste whether one likes or dislikes the technique. (Sokal and Bricmont 1998: 8)

Sokal and Bricmont claim, however, that the examples in their book (Kristeva, Deleuze, Lacan, Baudrillard, and others) use such terms 'in utter seriousness', in order to produce theory. 'Moreover', the two physicists claim, 'their style is usually heavy and pompous, so it is highly unlikely that their goal is principally literary or poetic' (1998: 8–9). Aside from the obvious limitation that their definition imposes on the possible range of literary and poetic style (literature is capable of being pompous), they also refute the role of metaphors and analogy *tout à fait* in these circumstances, and the argument that theorists are merely using turns of phrase and not being literal: 'After all, a metaphor is usually employed to clarify an unfamiliar concept by relating it to a more familiar one, not the reverse'. Their hypothetical case of a physicist using Derridean literary theory to explain 'a very technical concept in quantum field theory' is seen as without purpose. Sokal and Bricmont therefore state that they cannot see the advantage of invoking, even metaphorically, scientific concepts that are understood only vaguely by the postmodern writer when addressing a readership composed almost entirely of non-scientists. The motives, they suppose, are to render banality profound or hide weaknesses in vague theories. They also refuse the contextual argument, pre-empting the allegation that they might be missing something in the rest of these authors' work: 'when concepts from mathematics or physics are invoked in another domain of study, some argument ought to be given to justify their relevance' (1998: 8).

While they concede that many of Baudrillard's terms, such as 'hyperspace with multiple refractivity', are just Baudrillardian inventions, they identify phrases that they choose to interpret as error-ridden, such as 'reversibility of physical laws'. This, they state, has nothing to do with the reversibility of causal order as Baudrillard suggests. Indeed, 'Baudrillard's scientific confusions (or fantasies) have led him to make unwarranted philosophical claims: he puts forward no argument whatsoever to support his idea that science arrives at hypotheses "contrary to its own logic"'. They continue in this vein, pointing out the 'gradual crescendo of nonsense', the high density of scientific and pseudo-scientific terminology, and 'sentences ... devoid of meaning' (1998: 140–142).

Sokal is anxious to point out that he and Bricmont are not so concerned with error but the manifest irrelevance of scientific concepts in the subject under investigation. However, it is apparent that he has omitted a crucial dimension of Baudrillard's work, which has been present since the 1970s (Baudrillard 1993:61). In this respect, Sokal and Bricmont ignore what could be called the third position, which is one that draws on natural and human science, and one in which I suggest Baudrillard's work is situated. This space is scarcely recognised not just by his most ardent critics, but his strident supporters. It is literary through and through, not simply on account of its use of 'metaphor' and 'analogy', but by dint of its specific place in the history of literature. Moreover, Baudrillard not only explicitly refers to a particular tradition of literature in his key texts, but also constucts them according to the specific principles that this literature expounds.

The avant-garde context and challenge of pataphysics

This tradition is made abundantly clear in the title of the first chapter ('Pataphysics of the Year 2000') of Baudrillard's 1994 book *The Illusion of the End*, which attracts particularly virulent criticism from Sokal and Bricmont. The concept of pataphysics (or 'pataphysicks') is, for students of the history of avant-garde performance and literature, a familiar one. Its creator, Alfred Jarry, wrote in the late nineteenth century that

> Pataphysicks is the science of the realm beyond metaphysics ... It will study the laws which govern exceptions and will explain the universe supplementary to this one; or, less ambitiously, it will describe a universe which one can see – must see perhaps – instead of a traditional one, for the laws discovered in the traditional universe are themselves correlated exceptions, even though frequent, or in any case accidental facts which, reduced to scarcely exceptional exceptions, don't even have the advantage of singularity. (Shattuck 1958: 187)

As Shattuck and Watson Taylor noted, pataphysics systematically played with the arrangement of concepts and their significance until the improbable or impossible hypothesis came 'real'. With its emphasis on meaning and creativity pataphysics was, 'despite undertones of spoofing and quackery, a commentary on the other levels of social and historical time, personal biography, and artistic value' (Shattuck and Watson Taylor 1965: 18). The area of scientific imagination (Jarry claimed that there was no other kind) had applications in biographical and literary contexts where the tenets of pataphysics were forged. Pataphysics therefore suggested 'both scientific rigor and farcical wand-waving' (Shattuck 1958: 192) and allowed Jarry to combine the characteristics of comedy and wizardry. As to pataphysics' relationship with other forms of culture, he claimed that it resembled nothing else; rather, it was given dramaturgical form by dint of its fictional exponents, Père Ubu and Doctor Faustroll. The latter took the dream of science (mathematics) and the dream of speech (poetry) and fused them in his own version of 'common sense' (Shattuck and Watson Taylor 1965: 13). It was Jarry's intention to relate the preposterous stories and the experiments of Faustroll in such a detailed, sober and 'scientific' manner that the audience lost sight of the conventional boundary between reality and hallucination. Jarry foregrounded the importance of ambiguity to his style in order to express his passion for the universal principle of convertibility. For Shattuck, Jarry knew that a text 'means all things equivocally; anything may be(come) its opposite: not literature, but living is the supreme pun; writing is a slip of the tongue. Such total literary promiscuity is bound to yield the monstrous' (Shattuck 1958: 187).

It could be argued that Sokal and Bricmont are attempting to separate this unholy mutation from its host (science). However, this procedure is undertaken at great risk, for the tradition is a long one, and has been central to the scientific community as well as the literary one since the mathematician and logician Dodgson transformed himself into Lewis Carroll.

The strategy is further illustrated by Jarry's essay (in response to H.G.Wells's novel), 'How to Construct a Time Machine', in which he demonstrates a practical way to build such a device. He does this with such a conviction in the validity of its scientific and engineering accuracy that the boundary between objectivity and fantasy is disrupted. For Shattuck and Watson Taylor, this text raises the possibility of a 'science-non-fiction'. They suggest, presciently in terms of postmodern theory, that such writing might have its 'satirical-sardonic day and carry such "science" as psychology and statistics and linguistics to their logical and imaginary extremes' (Shattuck and Watson Taylor 1965: 11).

Yet Jarry's purpose is not to claim that science proceeds often by preposterous means (although historically it seems to do just that), but carve out from its discourse and its seriousness a literary space that is closer to allegory than metaphor or analogy. I suggest that it is in this tradition that the 'science' of Jean Baudrillard should be situated. Indeed, even the pataphysical movement should be contextualised: symbolist literature, with its suggestive character in the work of Rimbaud and Mallarmé (the former's apocalypticism would relate to Baudrillard's style); esoteric science, visionary revivals, and the view of science and technology from the perspective of Apollinaire, Artaud, Breton and Duchamp is more germane to Baudrillard's world than that of Euclid, Einstein or Mandelbrot. However, given the wide net that pataphysics casts, it should be no surprise that the latter group often appears in his work, much to Sokal's disgust.

The use of literature in science

Sokal and Bricmont, on account of their relative ignorance of the context in which Baudrillard is working, tend to assume that he, like many other writers they deride in their book, is reducible to discourses of natural or human science such as physics or sociology, and therefore predictably display astonishment that such a heresy of literature's invasion of science could be taking place. Even though they reluctantly admit the possibility of considering science in terms of cultural relativism, where scientific discourse might be conceived as 'nothing more' than a text, it is swiftly dismissed in favour of a model that relegates language and literature to a subordinate and supplementary role. While they acknowledge literature's value (even if they employ clichés such as 'poetic licence' to describe it), admitting that it is 'perfectly legitimate to turn to intuition or literature in order to obtain some kind of non-scientific understanding of those aspects of human experience that cannot, at least at present, be tackled more rigourously' (Sokal and Bricmont 1998: 178), their charitable view is qualified by the assumption that literature is useful only insofar as it precedes the rigorous work of science. Thus, they attempt to preserve the border between literature and science.

However, if they could determine the rhetorical strategies of the text, and the tradition in which Baudrillard's 'scientism' is couched, they would see how certain key terms (e.g. 'gravity') employed in this context cannot simply be adjudged as in error or false to an observable phenomenon or physical law, or be perceived as failing the stringent criteria of scientific validation. Sokal and Bricmont's study therefore relies on a duality, which having constructed science and literature in opposition to one another is too inflexible to permit an adequate explanation of the manner in which Baudrillard's integration of the two cultures (although not necessarily their resolution) occurs both within and on account of historically specific cultural settings. Their dim view of literature ensures that they can blithely censure Baudrillard's pataphysical approach for evincing a low opinion of science. His riposte, surely, would be that they have a low opinion of pataphysics.

Baudrillard's intention runs counter to axioms of pure or applied science. Furthermore, he is not concerned with performing a critique or deconstruction of the discourse and institutions that fabricate or validate the objectivist order of scientific knowledge. Rather, at the heart of Baudrillard's recent work lies the claim that the coercion of the rationalist order of reality is one to which the subject must not give his or her consent. The reality principle, Baudrillard constantly states, denies, regulates and orders the world according to its common denominator. In the pataphysical dimension, Baudrillard wishes to avoid reducing the radical illusoriness of the world, in order to challenge the telos of technology, or the idea that technology has a final purpose.

It is not difficult to view the high-minded objectivity of *Intellectual Impostures* as almost a parody itself, particularly at its most 'analytical', of science's blindness to its assumptions about the language that it employs. The hoaxed text, which inaugurated the subsequent critique of the credentials of postmodern theory, ensured that the subsequent book could be considered as much a burlesque of scientific seriousness as the first had been of postmodern theory. Its lofty, objectivist language arouses suspicion. While Sokal seems noticeably reluctant to include a chapter in their book on Derrida on account of the latter's relatively sparse employment of scientific language, their reasoning might instead be symptomatic of the repressed anxiety that Derrida and his ilk could deconstruct not simply their book, but the texts of scientific communities themselves.

In other words, the language that Sokal and Bricmont employ could be deconstructed to demonstrate the irrationality of their project, which lies at the margins of *Intellectual Impostures*, in its figures of speech, footnotes and anecdotal asides, and above all in its attempts to bring rationality to work such as that of Baudrillard, which is itself built by irrational means. The endeavour to impose scientific rigour on an alien environment (in which the polysemic language of postmodern theory is often illogical by definition) is a doomed one. As John Sturrock argues, while defending 'on principle' Baudrillard from Sokal's claim that his work is 'verbal veneer', 'here, in the marginal lands between the literary and sociological that Baudrillard inhabits, the "verbal veneer" is the very thing, so that to read it as a disguise rather than a display is to misread it in a particularly philistine and irrelevant way' (Sturrock 1998). The associated themes of veneer, mask and illusion constitute the core subject matter of Baudrillard's work. In this light, to criticise Baudrillard's project, which self-evidently embraces imaginary and literary ideas, without registering the historical framework of the text, and the strategy that links cultural history with science's imaginary, is the most irrational enterprise of all.

Additionally, the tactics of pataphysical discussion negate the role that Sokal attributes to the mode of intention and statement within Baudrillard's text. In other words, when, for example, Baudrillard states that his hypothesis on history 'comes directly from physics', it does not necessarily follow that his analogy is meant to be taken as a means of describing history in terms of physics according to an accurate depiction of physical laws. As should be obvious from Shattuck's comments, a crucial element of the literary principles of pataphysics is the assertion of a correlation or association between fields such as history and physics with such conviction that the link should be considered by the reader not just to be preposterous, but to destabilise the authority of the discourse to which it refers. The intention of such language is to pose a challenge to a reality principle, rather than to reinforce the latter by reducing the role of metaphor to its standard function of supplying a set of phrases that merely stands in place of the referent while continuing to reinforce its sovereignty.

Science's reconciliatory moralism and literature's irresponsibility: two models of truth

Returning to the inspiration for the Sokal hoax, we can approach E.P. Snow's original attempt to separate the two cultures in order to subordinate one to the other. He says:

> The clashing point of two subjects, two disciplines, two cultures
> – of two galaxies, so far as that goes – ought to produce creative
> chances. In the history of mental activity that has been where
> some of the break-throughs came. The chances are there now.
> But they are there, as it were in a vacuum, because those in the
> two cultures can't talk to each other. It is bizarre how very little
> of twentieth-century science has been assimilated into twenti-
> eth-century art. (Snow, 1964: 16)

Snow attempts to preserve a permeable borderline between the two cultures, which he sees as potentially permitting a form of communication that is of benefit to both sides. His use of a scientific metaphor for the incapacity of each cultural 'galaxy' to hear the other in the 'vacuum' is striking, for there seems to be no immediate way of separating this linguistic strategy from that of the poets he castigated for misusing terms such as polarised light 'under the illusion that it was a specially admirable kind of light'. To describe speech acts or theories of communication in terms of cosmological laws is to invest in a function of language which is not just metaphorical in character, but rhetorical in operation. It trades under as much an illusion of the function of discourse between the two cultures (by assuming a binary opposition in the first place) as the poets do in their vision of the cosmos.

By way of conclusion, therefore, I suggest that the continuing conflict between science and culture, where borderlines are erected in order to criticise forms of language for being irrational, ethically irresponsible or conceptually conflated, fails to accommodate strategies in which leaps of reason, rhetorical effects and purposive subversions of scientific logic are deployed to certain ends. Indeed, Snow's and Sokal's assumption that a rational, consensual and transparent model of knowledge should be rendered distinct from the cultural relativism that threatens to undermine it, represses the political dimension of forms of literature which emphasise irrationality as a version of truth.

A salutary example of the outcome of this failure to account for the irrational textual form lies in Snow's lecture of the late 1950s, where he claims that literature must share its responsibility for furthering social and political tyranny: 'It was no use denying the facts, which are broadly true. The honest answer was that there is, in fact, a connection, which literary persons were culpably slow to see, between some kinds of early twentieth-century art and the most imbecile expressions of anti-social feeling' (1964: 8).

Thus, for Snow, the influence of Yeats, Pound and Wyndham Lewis brought 'Auschwitz that much nearer' (Snow 1964:7). The moralism of such an observation is obvious, as is the unsubstantiated causal link between their poetry and the death-camp. The political irresponsibility that Snow attributes to certain literary forms is present in Sokal and Bricmont's reproach of 'postmodern' writing for its rejection of 'rational thought'. They consign its 'irrationalism' to a category that reduces it to a quality no less simplistic than Snow's 'imbecile expression'. In doing so, they undermine the history of non-rational thought that I have sketched above, and the force of bogus, rhetorical and 'irresponsible' textual productions, which for Baudrillard constitute not a presentation of the world's pretensions to scientific objectivity, but a challenge to it.

Finally, therefore, we should make Baudrillard less literal and more literary, but not in the restricted way that Sokal or Snow rhetorically suggest. In this setting, the scientist's criticisms of impropriety lose their relevance, because such claims only carry weight if Baudrillard's discourse subscribes to principles of scientific validity. Baudrillard, as should be obvious from his employment of Jarry, science-fiction, and social science demonstrates that it is precisely in the problematic crossovers between science and culture, between fact and fiction, and between falsifiability and fallacy that engagement with his work must take place. This domain is by definition one in which imposture and impersonation of science by culture and of the world by the text supply a form of justification for themselves. Criticisms of Baudrillard by Sokal and others should therefore recognise that Baudrillard's thought stems from a radical literary, poetic and imaginary tradition rather than a positivist and empiricist one. His former tenure as a sociologist may have inadvertently compelled his critics to fight him on the wrong territory, but his literary credentials (as a translator of literature, as diarist and essayist) are demonstrable to the most ardent of scientists. This integration of modes of discourse may render issues of scientific validity irrelevant.

The science of pataphysics, by promoting itself to an 'objective' order (the destiny of technology and science), provokes science's parodic ridicule of itself. Sokal and Bricmont sense the threat of this collapse of science into culture, and respond with a call to meaning and sense. Baudrillard, in an oblique reference to such coercion, chooses impersonation and fakery as a more adequate model of truth:

> A criminal thought which, speaking evil, illusion, seduction, duplicity and the irreconcilable character of the forces which divide up the 'real' world between themselves, is opposed as such to that perfect crime that is the enterprise of the unconditional reconciliation of the world. A thinking that is no stranger to imposture – like truth, which, as we know, is eternally veiled, and is thus itself an eternal imposture. (Baudrillard 1998: 116)

For Baudrillard, it is better to attend to the role of the illusion, the mask, the fiction and the imposter, than seek to expose the latter's fraudulent activity. Baudrillard does not make pataphysics a dogma or doctrine, but treats it alongside physics 'in terms of the game as a whole' (Zurbrugg 1997: 42). Instead, he embraces a form of imposture that does not just challenge the conventional distinctions between modes of discourse, and does not merely constitute an extreme form of relativism, but construes itself as a challenge to scientific models of truth through which science attempts to reconcile itself with reality, and with which it derogates the fictions and illusions that literary culture provides, including those of pataphysics and science-nonfiction. In this context, beyond the strictures of 'The Two Cultures' debate, lies the persistent thought that meaning may operate neither through the languages of scientific truth or cultural relativism, but through artifice. The Sokal Affair, and this summary of a possible defence for Baudrillard's approach, indicates not just the complexities of the links between language and cultures, but the strategies by which these links themselves are placed in the service of conflictual encounters across cultural borders.

References

Baudrillard, Jean. 1976. *L'échange symbolique et la mort*. Paris: Gallimard.

———. 1983. *In the Shadow of the Silent Majorities*, translated by P. Foss, P. Patton and P. Beitchman. New York: Semiotext(e).

———. 1993. *Symbolic Exchange and Death*, translated by Iain Hamilton Grant. London: Sage.

———. 1994. *The Illusion of the End*, translated by Chris Turner. Cambridge: Polity Press.

———. 1998. *Paroxysm: Interview with Philippe Petit*. London: Verso.

Bhaskar, Roy. 1989. *Reclaiming Reality: A critical introduction to contemporary philosophy*. London: Verso.

Callinicos, Alex. 1989. *Against Postmodernism: A Marxist critique*. Cambridge: Polity Press.

Collier, Andrew. 1994. *Critical Realism: An introdution to the work of Roy Bhaskar*. London: Verso.

Feyerabend, Paul K. 1987. *Farewell to Reason*. London: Verso.

Kuhn, Thomas S. 1970. *The Structure of Scientific Revolutions*. Chicago: The University of Chicago Press.

Lyotard, Jean-François. 1984. *The Postmodern Condition: A report on knowledge*, translated by G. Bennington and B. Massumi. Manchester: Manchester University Press.

Norris, Christopher. 1990. *What's Wrong with Postmodernism: Critical theory and the ends of philosophy*. Hemel Hempstead: John Hopkins University Press.

———. 1996. *Reclaiming Truth: Contribution to a critique of cultural relativism*. London: Lawrence and Wishart.

Popper, Karl R. 1959. *The Logic of Scientific Discovery*. 2nd edition. New York: Harper and Row.

Quine, W. V. O. 1960. *Word and Object*. Cambridge, Massachusetts: MIT Press.

Quine, W. V. O. and Ullian, J. S. 1970. *The Web of Belief*. New York: Random House.

Rorty, Richard. 1991. *Objectivity, Relativism, and Truth*. Cambridge: Cambridge University Press.

Shattuck, Roger. 1958. *The Banquet Years*. London: Faber and Faber.

Shattuck, Roger and Watson Taylor, Simon. 1965. *Selected Works of Alfred Jarry*. New York: Grove Press, Inc.

Snow, C. P. 1964. *The Two Cultures: And a second look*. Cambridge: Cambridge University Press.

Sokal, Alan. 1996. 'Transgressing the Boundaries: Toward a Transformative Hermeneutics of Quantum Gravity'. *Social Text* 46/47
(Spring/Summer), 217–252.

Sokal, Alan and Bricmont, Jean. 1998. *Intellectual Impostures: Postmodern philosophers' abuse of science.* London: Profile Books.

Sturrock, John. 1998. *London Review of Books*, vol. 20, no. 14. 16 July.

Zurbrugg, Nicholas. 1997. 'The Ecstasy of Photography', in *Jean
Baudrillard: Art and artifact,* ed. Nicholas Zurbrugg. London: Thousand Oaks.

CHAPTER 6

LANGUAGE, CULTURE, AND GENDER IDENTITIES: EXAMINING ARGUMENTS ABOUT MARRIAGE

Lia Litosseliti

Introduction

My focus in this chapter is on the intersection of language and culture in relation to gender identities: the ways in which sociocultural knowledge, assumptions and expectations about gender are represented and constructed – as well as interpreted and contested – in argumentation discourse. I shall start with an overview of past approaches and current trends in language and gender research, followed by an examination of particular examples of argumentation discourse from focus group discussions on the topic of marriage, looking at both the content and process of talk.

Language and gender: an overview

Since the 1960s, the scope of feminist thought and feminist linguistics has become wider and more diverse. Language and gender research, in particular, has been varied, at times controversial and increasingly interdisciplinary. For my purposes here, I will briefly summarise some of the key concerns in the area.

Past theoretical approaches

Two main theoretical positions have guided the key debate within feminist linguistics on the issue of whether men and women use language differently. These have been based on and contributed to either a theory of dominance or a theory of difference. The dominance approach, which informed earlier (late 1970s) feminist linguistic research, largely sees women as powerless and oppressed, and the differences between women's and men's language as not only reflecting, but also creating, male dominance. This approach was a reaction to the 'deficit' model of analysis (early 1970s), represented especially in Robin Lakoff's pioneering, and widely criticised 1975 book *Language and Woman's Place*.[1] Lakoff presented women's language as lacking and weak, due to their use of, for example, vocabulary (e.g., different colours, use of adjectives such as 'lovely' and 'adorable'), weaker expletives, intonational patterns and tag-questions (both of which, Lakoff claimed, indicate uncertainty), greater numbers of intensifiers and qualifiers (e.g., 'so', 'really', etc., and 'well', 'a bit'), and more polite language than men.

Instead of portraying a negative view of women, the dominance approach places the emphasis on how unequal power relations between men and women are expressed through and affect language usage. This theoretical approach underlies studies by Zimmerman and West (1975) and by Fishman (1983) on interruptions, turn-taking and topic initiation (men seem to be mainly responsible for those), as well as minimal responses ('mm', 'yeah', etc., while someone is talking) and questions, both used more by women in order to provide more conversational support, according to Fishman. These studies place more emphasis on data to support their claims, but overemphasise the subordination of women without providing clear evidence for this. There is also a bias in these studies towards language used by white, middle-class, heterosexual couples.

On the other hand, the difference approach (which started becoming dominant in the early 1980s, and which extends to a cultural difference approach) does not view women's language as inferior or inherently dysfunctional, but values it positively as authentic female speech, with aspects that need to be explored and emphasised. Many studies here focus on interaction in all-female groups; for example, Coates (1986/1993) re-addresses the issues of interruptions, politeness, etc., within female groups, and Holmes (1995) focuses on gossip as a positive aspect of a female 'subculture'. The emphasis

is on a re-evaluation of women's language and an understanding of differences as part of different male/female subcultures (following Maltz and Borker 1982).

The concept of different subcultures is based on the idea
that boys and girls learn to use language differently as they
grow up, because they interact in mainly single-sex peer
groups. Coates (1986/1993) explains that, in addition to children participating in gender-specific subcultures with distinct
male/female styles of interaction, adults provide different linguistic models for children; they talk to them differently
according to sex and respond differently to a similar linguistic
strategy used by boys and girls.

Although the difference approach helped to offset the negative image of women as weak and as victims (maintained by
the deficit and dominance models), it almost ignored the
important power dimension. It also sometimes reduced gender
to an innocent cultural distinction, while not explaining the
existence of separate subcultures in the first place.

The two approaches are not mutually exclusive and there is
evidence of both in feminist linguistics today; however, mainly
because of the overemphasis they have both placed on gender
difference as a binary opposition, their almost exclusive prob-
lematisation of women and disregard for the importance of context (social roles, discourse roles, setting, purpose of talk), they
are not currently influential in language and gender research.

Current trends

The late 1980s and 1990s have seen a move away from deficit,
dominance and difference towards discourse – language as social
practice – and linguistic and poststructuralist approaches to gender and subjectivity. Current research draws attention to gender
tendencies (sex preferential differences) in relation to a variety of
social practices, and is based on an understanding that gender
interpretations construct masculinities and femininities as well as
being shaped by them. The key current tendencies in the study of
language and gender can be summarised as follows:

Theoretical flexibility and more interdisciplinary developments

Theoretical flexibility recognises that different interpretations
of gender can be attached to different, and even to the same,
linguistic resources. The scope of research on language and
gender is becoming wider and more diverse, as it draws upon
and cuts across a number of disciplines: linguistics, sociology,

psychology, education, anthropology, cultural and media studies, literary theory, etc.[2]

The importance of context and an emphasis on specificity and complexity

There is now an acknowledgement of the importance of context – both immediate and sociocultural – and of situated meanings – both complex and context-specific – which goes hand-in-hand with a view of language as a social practice. Context refers to all aspects of social situation, linguistic co-text, and (gender and other) relations between speakers and hearers, writers and readers; also context may often be more important than gender. Looking at studies in context entails an emphasis on specificity (looking at particular men and women in particular settings) and complexity (gender interacting with other aspects of identity categories – such as ethnicity, age, class, disability or sexual orientation – and power relations). Finally, researching language and gender in context has partly led to greater emphasis on written language, which previously had not been as much of a focus as speech.

The centrality of discourse and the emergence of a discourse framework

Discourse analysis has opened up the possibility of exploring an almost infinite range of text types for their contribution to the construction of gender. The key point is that discourses about gender construct gender in different ways. Broadly speaking, the emphasis has shifted to questions about the nature of interpretation and power relations, which in turn lead to the formulation of new, more complex and more nuanced models of ideology and discourse.

The discursive construction of gender identities

Language does not simply reflect social reality; it is also constitutive of that reality. There is an acknowledgement that gender is problematic as a binary, fixed category: male and female linguistic behaviour cannot be viewed as fundamentally different. Instead, recent theories regard gender as fluid and highly contextualised (see, for example, Hall and Bucholtz 1995), and emphasise the concept of performativity: not simply being male or female, but 'doing' or 'performing' one's gender at any one time (Butler 1990).

These conceptualisations of gender have been influenced by postmodernist thinking, understanding people's identities as social constructs, power as productive (people activate power whenever they produce meaning) and discourses as social practices that form what they speak of (for example, what gives meaning to sexism is its practices). The result is a shift of focus from the idea of gender roles to the social and linguistic (i.e., discursive) construction of a range of masculine and feminine identities.

Culture and gender in arguments about marriage

My focus in this section is on the ways in which sociocultural knowledge, assumptions and expectations about gender are represented and constructed – as well as interpreted and contested – in argumentation discourse. By argumentation, I mean the process of argument, through which speakers establish a position and which often takes the form of an interchange or chain of reasoning in discussion (see Litosseliti 1999; also Andrews, Costello and Clarke 1993). To explore these gender assumptions and expectations, or cultural constructs of masculine and feminine identities, I shall draw upon examples from focus group discussions on the topic of marriage. The immediate focus of the analysis is not so much on attitudes towards the institution of marriage, as on the discourses that represent and construct sociocultural knowledge and assumptions in this context. The discussions are not representative or generalisable, but illuminative; the discourses underlying the talk are part of a wider discursive and social formation. First, a brief description of the methodology is necessary.

Methodology and analytical framework

Focus groups are small, structured groups, normally facilitated by a moderator, set up to explore specific topics through group interaction. The two focus groups in this study each had six members, with an equal number of male and female participants. The respective groups consisted of:

(a) *Academics*: social scientists in their late twenties/ thirties, all unmarried; and
(b) *Professionals*: working in industry, consultants, counsellors, or administrators, in their late thirties/ forties, all either married or divorced.

All group members came from the north-west of England, were British citizens (or had been living in Britain for many years), white and heterosexual (by their own description). Their views on marriage were unknown to me before the discussion and they had no prior knowledge of the nature of my research. Participants had met some of the other group members before, but were not aware of their views on marriage.

My approach as moderator was flexible, facilitating discussion so that issues were raised by the participants themselves. I also had an observer present in each group. For a detailed discussion of planning and conducting focus groups, see Litosseliti (1999).

My concern here is to look at examples that offer insight into the discourse practices and repertoires drawn upon by the two mixed-sex groups of speakers, notably sociocultural assumptions about gender. My framework is a synthetic discursive approach to text or discourse analysis, as, for example, in Fairclough (1989), informed by a wider cultural, political and ideological reading of the context in which the texts occur. It attempts to explore both the local organisation of the texts (linguistically) and their culturally charged content: coherent repertoires or themes (sociologically and culturally).[3] Organisation and content are mutually constructed and reinforced: repertoires (and values, ideologies, identities) emerge through specific language use, while the linguistic organisation of the texts constructs, negotiates and changes these ways of seeing the world.

It is important to maintain both orientations in the analysis, since argument is not a straightforward process from premises to evidence, but a battle between discourses in a dynamic relationship with their context. As with any language use, argument '...by selecting its vocabulary from available cultural themes and concepts, and by its choice of their arrangement, makes positive claims to a certain vision of the world' (Antaki 1994: 7).

My discussion of the specific examples in the following sections focuses on arguments put forward by group participants about gender. These draw mainly upon a Change Repertoire (Litosseliti 1999), describing changes in gender roles as part of a broader economic and sociocultural change. I look at the gender assumptions within those arguments – and how these assumptions are realised and reinforced through linguistic resources. Although the categories are presented separately, there is an overlap and a mutually reinforcing relationship between the arguments put forward, the gender assumptions within them, and the linguistic resources used.

Assumptions about dominance and tolerance
in gender relations: the academics

In the group of academics, sociocultural assumptions about gender focused on issues of dominance and tolerance in marriage and men's and women's relations, and on the changes that have or have not happened in these areas. These are illustrated in Table 6.1 overleaf.[4]

The extracts demonstrate two different ways of using assumptions about gender in order to support two partly different arguments (by Tina and Steve).

First, in talking about gender change, Tina raises the issue of power, by referring to the existence of active repression and *domination of women* (Extracts A1 and A3), a stance that is ideologically loaded, and likely to be both familiar and controversial. On the other hand, Steve places emphasis primarily on change in *women's expectations* (Extract A2), rather than their subjection to pressure or discrimination. This shift in emphasis assumes that individuals and the institution can be kept separate, or can be argued in a discussion separately. This assumption becomes more problematic, as Steve's position is largely ideologically dependent on (collectively acknowledged) sociocultural practices surrounding the institution of marriage, some of which are about domination and power along gender lines (Extract A2: 'constraining them', 'put up with it').

Second (and following this pattern of shifting responsibility from 'the oppressor' to 'the oppressed'), the two speakers signal different perceptions of gender change. Tina's language indicates that although such changes have taken place, there is still more to be done (see Extract A1 for use of modals and qualifiers: 'such' pressure). Steve, on the other hand, comes across as assuming change, describing it as something that has indeed taken place. In Extract A2, this conviction is expressed through the use of present tense verbs, adverbs like 'clearly', and phrasing such as 'it must be'.

My emphasis here is on the argumentative effect of these partially different ways of conceptualising and articulating gender. Focusing on women as victims, oppressed in marriage, and seeing gender change as still necessary and ongoing, places gender firmly in the centre of the discussion; gender is then used as a powerful 'weapon' in the service of the anti-marriage argument. However, talking about change in women's expectations, and assuming that such change has naturally and already happened, minimises gender as a crucial factor influencing the institution as well as the actual dis-

Table 6.1: *Gender Assumptions about Dominance and Tolerance in Marriage*

Extracts A1, A2 and A3	Argument(s)	Gender Assumptions	Linguistic Resources
A1. Tina: / [...] there isn't such a MASSIVE societal pressure whatever for women [...] women now have all the choice to. they could survive without having to find someone to marry for financial reasons /	Women are now financially independent and have more choice. Social pressure on women (to marry) is significantly reduced.	a) There has been considerable social pressure on women b) This has changed (positively), but not completely	Quantifiers/ Emphatic use: 'massive', 'all the choice' Time markers: 'now' Tentative: 'such pressure', 'could survive' (modal)
A2. Steve: /[...] fifty years ago women's expectations were very low or they were very constrained / whereas now they don't see their lives in the same way so . they WON'T put up . and rightly so . they won't put up with a situation where the other partner is constraining them / that's clearly a key factor in undermining the institution . I mean it MUST be / it's not really people know that divorce is easier or whatever . it's much deeper than that . it's just that people know that they shouldn't put up with it if it isn't working / [...] so all you've got now is an easier escape route / but the reasons behind it are that people's expectations have changed . THEMSELVES rather than the institution /	Women now have higher expectations themselves, and so, their tolerance of constraint and of unsatisfactory marriages is lower, which in effect leads to higher divorce rates and is undermining the institution.	a) Women's expectations have really changed (are higher) b) It is women who have had to 'put up with' unhappy marriages (Powerlessness) c) It is possible to talk about women and men as separate from the institution	Time markers: 'fifty years ago', 'now'. Contrast: 'whereas', 'in the same way' Conviction about change: present tense verbs (no modals), adverbs ('clearly'), 'it MUST be', 'have changed' Vagueness: 'a situation', 'constraining' Awareness of topic sensitivity; anticipating objection: 'and rightly so', 'women' – 'people'

Table 6.1: *continued*

Extracts A1, A2 and A3	Argument(s)	Gender Assumptions	Linguistic Resources
A3. Tina: *[In response to Steve's point that women/people now know that they don't have to put up with marriage if it is not working]* / but I would wonder how much how seriously people DO take it nowadays . and if they ARE any less serious than people years ago / cause I know a lot of women . you know the generation who would be married in the sixties or seventies who for years in their relationships had separate rooms / there was no way that they would get divorced but as soon as their kids moved out they'd have separate rooms / [...] / I'll tell you one big thing that I think has changed [...] / this issue of duty / particularly as duty on the part of the WIFE /	Counter argument, challenging Steve's claim above: It is doubtful if people (women?) end marriages more easily today. [BUT: argument is framed as whether people do or do not take marriage seriously] Women's sense of duty towards their husbands has changed	Gender and morality are linked b) What is morally acceptable/ desirable differs for women and men, and shapes gender relations c) Keeping up appearances of a marriage (according to the dominant moral code) has primarily been women's task and part of their duty as wives	Tentative/Use of qualifiers: 'I would wonder', 'and if', 'I don't know if…' Shifts from 'people' to 'women' to 'people' Moral discourse: Value laden terms: 'separate rooms', 'duty'

cussion. It also ignores the issue of power relations between men and women.

One reason for this is the potentially face-threatening nature of gender as an area of argumentation. There is evidence of that concern throughout the discussions examined, and in Extract A2 by Steve, in his vagueness and qualifying, which anticipates objection: 'it's much deeper than that' and 'they WON'T put up, and rightly so ...' It is interesting that he begins by referring to 'women' and their expectations, but quickly shifts to 'people' (used three times in this example) and 'people's expectations'. This serves to 'unload' the argument, by distancing it from potentially polarising 'male' and 'female' issues, where gender is seen as a binary distinction.

Contrary to Steve, Tina can be seen to use the sensitivity of gender as a topic to her advantage. In describing gender inequality in vivid ways and by suggesting that gender change cannot be taken for granted, she effectively places gender roles and expectations, as they are embedded within a social and moral framework, in the centre of her argument. These gender roles and social, as well as moral, expectations and understandings are all the more powerful because they are shared knowledge among the group participants (Extract A3: the many women who for years had separate rooms, the issue of duty on the part of the wife).

The participants' shared understanding of the close connections between gender identity and the social and moral status quo becomes evident in the ways the arguments develop. The argument goes that when women had no careers outside the home and no financial autonomy, they tended to stay married, to 'put up with it.' They would adhere to – and often tolerate – their duty as wives, and even in the cases when they would not do so (references to 'separate rooms'), the image of a stable, respectable life and, by association, a morally strong and cohesive society, would be maintained. From an analyst's point of view, the prevalent question here is not the extent to which such sociocultural constructs of gender have become redundant. Rather, the question focuses on how the fact, that these constructs are shared by the focus group speakers, influences their arguments and moral positions. Whether speakers talk about a firmly established and seemingly clear-cut social and moral status quo, or one where men's and women's choices and expectations (and consequently institutions such as marriage) have become 'more complicated', [5] the extracts above illustrate that interpretations of the status quo are almost always tacit.

Assumptions about gender at work and at home:
the professionals

Similarly to the group of academics, sociocultural assumptions, expectations and shared understandings about gender (as these emerged in arguments) were examined through analysis of the group of professionals. A wider variety of gender-related issues were raised by this group in addition to the ones in the first and, in most cases, they were based on and reinforced by personal experiences. Participants' own experiences are not simply informed by existing, often stereotypical, cultural constructs of gender: they also confirm or challenge them. As a result, this focus group discussion was more detailed, often taking the form of long narratives, more graphic and increasingly personalised, compared to the first discussion by the academics. In addition, there is much more agreement among the participants in this focus group.[6]

In the extract that follows overleaf (Table 6.2), Anna has been narrating how, when she was younger, she 'lost a job as a result of being married'. She describes attending a job interview and being asked when her husband's job would finish. After replying 'eighteen months', the interviewer's response was, as she put it, 'thank you very much and goodbye / that was the end!' Extract B1 below begins from that point.

The extract emphasises the importance of gender assumptions for the construction of arguments. Once more, the pro-marriage argument position is effectively undermined (by Anna, Mary and the others) by drawing attention to the ideological constructs of inequality, powerfulness vs. powerlessness and domination. Put simply, if marriage entails different things for men and for women, and if this results in discrimination and gender inequality, then marriage as an institution must be flawed. Irony about common popular notions of gender roles and expectations ('you can't trust women', 'and even if you stay you're gonna have babies') helps to reinforce this argument.

Detailed examination of the talk reveals assumptions about limited change or efforts to alleviate the problems described in the extracts. For example, speakers use mainly present tense verbs to refer to gender values, or roles and expectations for men and for women: 'as a man you're always regarded as...', 'you're a much safer bet', 'it's not symmetrical is it?'. This creates an understanding (further reinforced by generalisations) that this is a current situation that assumes that gender identities are fixed: women as professionally unreliable, primarily as mothers, as 'being a chattel'; men as professionally mobile

Table 6.1: *Gender Assumptions about Double Standards in the Workplace*

Extract B1	Argument(s)	Gender Assumptions	Linguistic Resources
Anna: [...] it took me a LONG time to understand what had happened / and I realised that I could have been any candidate for that job but I was NOT going to get it / I was not going to get it because my husband was likely to complete what he was doing and would be wanting to move and . if he was moving I would be leaving and / you know . *[Ironically]* you CAN'T trust women ! / George: *[Ironically]* and even if you stay you're gonna have BABIES !/ Anna: yes HOPELESS ! HOPELESS ! (...) / *[Laughs]*	As a woman, you run the risk of losing a job 'as a result of being married; (Anna)	Gender is a criterion/ reason for discrimination in the workplace. This is usually unsaid/sensed/ implicit.	Narrative (Personal Experience) Irony used to highlight/ ridicule stereotypical views of gender
		Women may not be trustworthy and reliable at work, or serious in their own right. This is due to their dependence on husbands and due to childbirth. (Marriage disempowers women)	Stereotyping: Gender identities as fixed ('you can't trust women', 'even if', 'you're gonna have babies')
Simon: it's interesting that . because . if that reverses you'd probably expect – Anna: oh what a surprise! *[Laughs]*	On the contrary, there are advantages, at work, for married men (Simon)		Irony (as above): 'hopeless', 'oh what a surprise'
Simon: as a MAN you're always regarded as being . you know the safe option if you were married / if you're a young man unmarried then you will not (...) but if you're married . you have dependants . you have a stable relationship . you're a much safer bet / [...]		Married men, however, are a 'safe option'. Marriage empowers men.	Assumption marker: 'always'
		Being unmarried is likely to mean that one	Moral undertones: 'safe option', 'safer bet'

Table 6.2: *continued*

Extract B1	Argument(s)	Gender Assumptions	Linguistic Resources
George: Matt Busby the famous Man-United manager always encouraged his players to get married / and he was always trying to find suitable wives for them / for that reason cause he didn't want his players out all night – *[Laughs]*		does not have 'dependants' or 'a stable relationship'	Moral undertones: 'out all night'
Me: so in one case being married was an advantage and in another it was a disadvantage /		Unmarried men are uncontrollable and sexually promiscuous	Emotive/powerful language evoking issues/images of power and dominance:
Mary: that's a very common disadvantage for women /			'being a chattel', 'being dragged round' (Passivisation)
Phil: it's not symmetrical is it? /			
Irene: being a chattel /		Discrimination of (married) women is well-established	
Anna: yes /			
Simon: you are more likely to be dragged round the country by your husband than vice versa /			

and promising, as 'safe' and 'stable' once married, but as promiscuous while unmarried. This stereotypical depiction of women as passive and men as active, as a result of different power dynamics, is also obvious in the use of passivisation ('be dragged round the country by your husband'), which shifts the emphasis from who does what to the results of the action, thus obscuring agency and leaving it unquestioned. Moreover, the use of adverbs such as 'always' accentuates the extent to which double standards are socially expected.

This is more of an implicit understanding of the connection between gender identities and the established social and moral values than an explicit discussion of them. It is also an understanding that is necessary for the argument to make sense. When Simon says that a married man is always regarded as 'the safe option' and 'a much safer bet', he may be referring to others' views rather than his own; nevertheless the image he conjures up is one of a morally strong, stable and 'safe' society. The subtle assumption here is, I think, that one way of preserving this kind of society is through 'traditional' gender relations. Although, initially, it is not very clear what Simon means by 'safe', images of morally undesirable and unsafe behaviour start emerging when George develops Simon's point, by referring to the example of Matt Busby. This extract presents men as uncontrollable and sexually promiscuous, unless contained and controlled through marriage. In terms of argument, this stereotypical portrayal helps establish marriage as necessary, not only as far as men are concerned, but for the 'good of society' in general. It acts to strengthen the pro-marriage position, and with it the importance of firmly established sociocultural and moral frameworks.

If marriage entails a different sense of identity and of power for men and for women in the workplace, this becomes even more prominent when the discussion moves to the domestic sphere, as the extracts that follow illustrate (Table 6.3). The specific topic of conversation in Extract B2 (Table 6.3, pages 134–135) is separate surnames for spouses. This is a lengthy discussion, and I will be looking at some key points.

Whereas the first extract explored double standards at work for men and women, and gender assumptions that view women as unreliable, weak and dependent on their husbands, Extract B2 shows the loss of a strong, individual identity for women, as exemplified particularly in the change of name after marriage. Participants seem to agree that the ritualised change of name – strictly speaking, a linguistic change – can represent the loss of identity, individualism or respect for women. George explains that it represents 'owning someone', despite the distancing effect of using 'someone' and 'they', instead of the more potentially emotive 'women'. As Simon adds, the change of women's name after marriage is 'symbolic' of two individuals becoming one, which Irene, Phil and George see as 'a putdown', and not 'being who you want to be'.

It is this symbolic meaning of actions, behaviours, beliefs and values that speakers draw upon in their arguments, and that they often find difficult to describe and account for (see following section). As Van Leeuwen (1996) puts it, following Habermas (1976), speakers' evaluations of what happens around them are typically unclear and abstract, and are the tip of a submerged iceberg of cultural and moral values. Interaction is possible and argument can smoothly progress the way that it does in the extracts examined, because this 'iceberg' exists as shared, if diverse, experience for the participants.

This also became evident in other parts of the focus group discussions, for example in discussing identity loss for women, as a result of their having to cope with many different responsibilities. By analysing that kind of discourse, certain understandings, shared by the speakers, became apparent: that the difficulties and dilemmas of juggling a family and a career, as well as a sense of loss of identity, are more likely to be faced by women; and that the responsibility of nurturing the children lies with the mother. These are assumptions that can be seen to undermine the extent of change of gender roles, values and expectations, as articulated in other parts of the discussions.

Implicitness and inexplicability

The examples presented in Tables 6.1 – 6.3 illustrate some of the ways in which sociocultural knowledge about gender, tacit, assumed and shared, shapes arguments put forward by the speakers. As indicated above, such implicitness can take the form of inexplicability. Speakers are often unable to account for, clarify or legitimise beliefs that particularly draw on firmly established and widely-espoused understandings of how society works and what is expected of its members. Castaneda and Nakhnikian (1965: 206) talk about how in societies people often decide on certain matters of conduct on principles that are unexamined, that is, people acknowledge them as a matter of 'social inheritance'.

Table 6.3: *Gender Assumptions about Identity/Loss of Identity (The case of surnames)*

Extract B2	Argument(s)	Gender Assumptions	Linguistic Resources
George: we've kept our separate surnames / [...]/ it was partly this seventies idea . of you know . not owning someone . not wanting to . they become a chattel and they're just part of you / it is an acknowledgement of that really / [...] EXCEPT that an interesting thing . now this is where you'll shout at me . I was very clear that our children should be called my surname and that was explicit (...) / I don't know . when I'm stuck about those conversations is . you're trying to talk about things in a kind of conscious way but so much of it is intangible and it's feelings and you know / why? why do I want my son to have my surname? / well who knows . but I DO really . I really want my son to be called my surname /	Keeping separate names is one way of being aware of aspects of marriage that may be problematic	Change of name for women after marriage implies more than that: ownership and loss of identity	Distancing: 'this 70s idea', 'someone', 'they', 'they'
			Qualifiers/ anticipating objection (e.g. 'this is where you'll shout at me')
		It is usually explicit/ unquestioned that children take the father's name	Inexplicability

A number of practical reasons for keeping or changing one's surname are mentioned (surnames being difficult to pronounce; surnames being recognisable in work settings; bureaucracy, and so on.)

Me: you mention practical reasons here – Phil: very practical reasons / Simon: no I think it's more than that actually / I think this taking the same name is sometimes a symbolic thing / certainly in my first marriage I wanted my	Women taking their husband's name after marriage can	Marriage entails loss of identity/ individualism	Challenge: 'no', 'actually'

Table 6.3: *continued*

Extract B2	Argument(s)	Gender Assumptions	Linguistic Resources
name to (…) / but my relationship now is very different from my first relationship . it's very much two individuals /	be symbolic	for spouses	Language that evokes issues of power / dominance: 'giving in'. 'giving up'
Irene: I think a side of you feels as if you're giving in/ I feel as if I was giving up something/	This symbolism is negative, as it reveals power asymmetries	Women have had no choice about losing their name	Ideological positioning/ Judgement: 'pretty bad', 'putdown'
Phil: it's pretty bad when you feel that this is your husband's name [Irene: yes] / that strikes me as very much a putdown /			
Irene: I still don't think that it's MY name / my name is X / it's how I was born and it will always be / I like X but it's not my name / [...]			
Simon: I can sympathise with that / I think if the situation reversed I would be very unhappy losing my name /	This becomes even more apparent once gender reversal is imagined (Simon, George)	Men can be in a similar position nowadays	Emphatic use: adverbs ('always') pronouns ('I', 'MY name', 'my own', 'me')
Irene: I was . perhaps I was 36 I think when I got married / and so I had my own name for a long time / it was me /			'I' – 'HER'
Me: [*To George*] you don't seem to agree /			
George: it's just . whenever . the car needs to be serviced and they ring up and they say is it Mr X . and they use her name . and I suddenly become HER / well I say I'm NOT Mr X / but yes you get a glimpse into what it feels like to actually not having . being who you want to be / be symbolic			

Since marriage is a well-established part of life in most societies, it is more likely to be argued with reference to principles that are unexamined and acknowledged as a matter of 'social inheritance'. There are a number of instances of this in the focus group discussions. The following extract is taken from the group of academics:

Fay: it doesn't matter how much I think about [marriage] intellectually and how much I say I don't have time for it and it's never going to happen and everything / I know that if it WERE to happen. it would probably make me really really pleased ! [...] / when you have not been married . regardless of how many marriages you see and how intellectually you look at it . you still have this little part of you somewhere which says well it might be really nice /

Derek: whether it's marriage or some other form obviously /

Steve: I was gonna say / you're talking about an individual rather than marriage. the institution / you said if you met a person you were in love with / so what difference would marriage make? / *[Pause]*

Fay: as in what? / you mean the legal thing? /

Steve: well no. I mean FOR YOU. why are you saying marriage when you can just live with that person? / *[Pause]*

Fay: I have no idea /

Derek: social construction /

Fay: that's social construction I'm sorry *[All talk together]* / no I grew up that way / and I know that it would not make my parents very happy but I think they'll survive it. but they would be HAPPIEST if I was willing to take my love and commitment for someone that one step further /

Me: so you're saying there IS a difference. in that case. for you /

Fay: yes what I'm saying –

Derek: symbolism /

Fay: I'm not saying. I'm just saying PERSONALLY though I can talk about it intellectually. and I'm just thinking that personally despite the fact that I know that it's difficult it's hard and I'm not really sure I really want it . there is that little CORE inside somewhere deep down . that . is rather excited by the idea ! . because it's something I grew up with . I suppose / and it's a funny sort of tension you have because you grow up and your thoughts about it change / and yet there's still that little remnant . from when you were growing up / I mean FOR ME there is /

In this case, acknowledging that preferring marriage to other alternatives as a matter of social inheritance effectively leaves the principles that guide Fay's view unexplained ('I have no idea'). Fay's uncertainty is obvious in her choice of lexis and phrasing ('this little part of you somewhere', 'that little CORE inside somewhere deep down', 'a funny sort of tension', 'that little remnant') and her use of modal verbs, hedges and qualifiers ('might be', 'I'm just saying', 'rather excited', 'I suppose', 'I mean'). Appeals to social inheritance are similar to appeals to convention and history, in that they do not make demands on the arguers for extensive reasoning. As Hampshire puts it, 'justifications that appeal to principles of justice and to utility permit more explicit and more prolonged argument than most justifications that appeal to convention and to history and to a story of personal commitment' (1983: 9).

Inexplicability, as observed in the focus group discussions, was in every case used in arguments in support of marriage. In the group of professionals, for example, Simon supports his argument in favour of marriage by alluding to the mysteriousness of the ceremony: '/ I don't know . it's just the ceremony . it's mysterious really / it's really hard to put your finger on it / '. Here is an extended example of a similar argument by George:

> / but isn't that the thing though / isn't it still true that there's SOMETHING about not being married . it would be difficult to say exactly what it is . financial or other . but SOMETHING about it? / [...] I'm not sure what it is but it's DIFFERENT/ [...] something about the BUSINESS of getting married which is almost a kind of . the entry into the adult world . you think it is / [...] / I think there's still something about the mystique of it which is very difficult to replicate in any other . in any other kind of arrangement really / you know . my PARTNER . it doesn't quite hit it does it . or my girlfriend or whatever /

George's inexplicability effectively makes it difficult for counter-arguments to develop. As an argument in favour of marriage, it is tentative and rather elusive. It is linguistically realised through hedges and qualifiers ('isn't that the thing', 'I'm not sure', 'it's almost the feeling', 'somehow', 'I mean', 'kind of'), and vague lexical choice ('something', 'this is it', 'the business of getting married', 'the mystique of it'). The effect of this is toning down the argument on the topic – with marriage presented in a special, almost mythical light – and minimising the prospect of counter arguments being put forward. There is also an assumption that this 'special' quality of marriage is shared by the others, as George continues:

George: isn't there something about being VERY special to one
          person / that person is willing to give themselves up to
          you which is –
Anna: exclusivity /
George: yeah yeah / there is almost that kind of basic need /

George's framing of marriage as 'that kind of basic need' is characterised both by inexplicability and by 'taken-for-grant-edness'. The speaker realises that this inexplicability also has the potential of being face-threatening, since the other speakers may see the fact that he is not offering tangible support for his claim as inappropriate. He therefore anticipates objections and mitigates his talk by adding 'and I kick myself when I say it / how can I be saying this?' and 'it's really difficult to me to make conscious something that you kind of just do without often knowing why you do it'. In other words, inexplicability can cause a mixture of reactions during argumentation, from an understanding of views that are established and vaguely assumed, to an objection to lack of explicit support of an argument position.

Concluding remarks

Discourse analysis is instrumental in illuminating the ways in which pwer relations, gender identities and ideologies (i.e., networks of beliefs and values held by and attributed to men and women) are constructed and negotiated through discourse. Connecting the analysis of language with the concerns of social analysis (context, belief and ideology, identity, power and social relationships) requires a synthetic approach that analyses language as discourse and is concerned with discourse practices and sociocultural practices embedded in texts.

The examples from the focus group discussions demonstrate how implicit assumptions and shared understandings about gender depend on and at the same time reinforce ideologies about gender identities and power relations between men and women, and about the place of gender in the broader social and moral status quo. Such implicitness is often expressed as inexplicability of a speaker's arguments. The argument process needs to be approached through examining what is said, as much as what is not said.

Notes

1. Criticisms of Lakoff's work address primarily its lack of data and its blindness to both linguistic differentiation (a feature may have various functions) and social differentiation (differences in class, age, etc.). For a detailed discussion of Lakoff's work, see, for example, Talbot (1998) and Romaine (1999).
2. For key discussions of theoretical and interdisciplinary developments, see Romaine (1999), Cameron (1998), Coates (1998) and the edited collections by Hall and Bucholtz (1995) and Bergvall, Bing and Freed (1996).
3. I use the term repertoire to refer to an interpretative frame that speakers impose on discourses. Like discourses, repertoires are 'worlds' consisting of words, acts, behaviours, assumptions, beliefs and values. However, interpretative repertoires are particularly relevant to argumentation (where interpretation and evaluation are crucial), and they belong to society rather than to individual language users.
4. In the tables (...) is used to indicate inaudible, indecipherable speech, while [...] indicates ommited text.
5. I refer here to participants' talk about the lack of fixed categories (such as gender expectations) in contemporary society, which entails what they describe as 'questioning', 'insecurity' and 'the crisis of masculinity'. I have discussed this (Litosseliti 1999) as part of the Moral Decline Repertoire, exemplified in speakers' words, such as 'there are no rules' and 'traditional patterns of being brought up do not fit any more'. People typically draw upon repertoires of social and moral decline, in their attempt to come to terms with, accept as well as resist, change (see also Thompson 1998).
6. Academics are likely to be more accustomed to critically examining different aspects of a topic, to questioning and challenging points of view even as an exercise, if not in earnest. It may also be the case that participants in the second group chose different ways to express disagreement, such as silence. Overall, the professionals may have been less prepared to risk and deal with the face-threat that accompanies sensitive, controversial topics of conversation.

References

Andrews, R., Costello, P. and Clarke, S. 1993. *Improving the Quality of Argument, 5–16 – Final Report*. Hull: The University of Hull.

Antaki, C. 1994. *Explaining and Arguing The Social Organisation of Accounts*. London: Sage.

Bergvall, V., Bing, J. and Freed, A., eds. 1996. *Rethinking Language and Gender Research: Theory and Practice*. London: Longman.

Butler, J. 1990. *Gender Trouble*. New York: Routledge.

Cameron, D. 1998. 'Gender, Language and Discourse: A Review Essay'. *Signs*, I: 945–973.

————. ed. 1990. *The Feminist Critique of Language*, 2nd edition. London: Routledge.

Castaneda, H. and Nakhnikian, G., eds. 1965. *Morality and the Language of Conduct*. Detroit: Wayne State University Press.

Coates, J. 1986/1993. *Women, Men and Language*, (2nd edition). London: Longman.

———. 1998. *Language and Gender: A Reader*. Oxford: Blackwell.

Fairclough, N. 1989. *Language and Power*. London: Longman.

Fishman, P. 1983. 'Interaction: the Work Women Do'. in *Language, Gender and Society*, eds B. Thorne, C. Kramarae and N. Henley. Rowley, Massachusetts: Newbury House, 89–101.

Habermas, J. 1976. *Legitimation Crisis*. London: Heinemann.

Hall, K. and Bucholz, M., eds. 1995. *Gender Articulated: Language and the Socially Constructed Self*. London: Routledge.

Hampshire, S. 1983. *Morality and Conflict*. Oxford: Blackwell.

Holmes, J. 1995. *Women, Men and Politeness*. London: Longman.

Lakoff, R. 1975. *Language and Woman's Place*. New York: Harper and Row.

Litosseliti, L. 1999. *Moral Repertoires and Gendered Voices in Argumentation*. PhD Thesis, Department of Linguistics and Modern English Language, Lancaster University.

Maltz, D. and Borker, R. 1982. 'A Cultural Approach to Male-Female Miscommunication', in *Language and Social Identity*, ed. J. Gumperz. Cambridge: Cambridge University Press, 196–216.

Romaine, S. 1999. *Communicating Gender*. London: L. Erlbaum.

Talbot, M. 1998. *Language and Gender: An Introduction*. Cambridge: Polity.

Thompson, K. 1998. *Moral Panics*. London: Routledge.

Van Leeuwen, T. 1996. *The Grammar of Legitimation*. Unpublished Manuscript, School of Media, London College of Printing.

Zimmerman, D. H. and West, C. 1975. 'Sex Roles, Interruptions and Silences in Conversation'. in *Language and Sex: Difference and Dominance*, eds B. Thorne and N. Henley. Rowley, Massachusetts: Newbury House, 105–129.

PART IV

DIFFERENT LANGUAGE, DIFFERENT THOUGHTS

CHAPTER 7

MANAGEMENT, CULTURE AND DISCOURSE IN INTERNATIONAL BUSINESS

Francesca Bargiela-Chiappini

Introduction

This chapter re-examines the concepts of management, culture and discourse in international business organisations, in the light of research that I have been carrying out since the beginning of the 1990s (Bargiela-Chiappini and Harris 1997). Like Mumby and Clair (1997:181), I take the view that 'when we speak of organizational discourse, we do not simply mean discourse that occurs in organizations. Rather, we suggest that organizations exist only in so far as their members create them through discourse'. Unlike Mumby and Clair, however, I find their distinction between the 'cultural approach' and the 'critical approach' to organisational communication hard to defend. The descriptive emphasis of the former approach does not contrast with the concern for power and control that is the main focus of the latter. These are simply two necessary and partly overlapping stages of a holistic approach to researching organisations as enactments of discursive practices.

Moreover, cultural anthropology and cultural psychology have been contributing insightful discussions on culture that add considerable depth and breadth to Mumby and Clair's position. Heyman (1989: 47) argues that 'culture is an inter-actionally achieved part of a person's identity, not a scientifically knowable, unambiguously objective feature of identity which can be taken for granted as an important variable in every interactional scene'.

Heyman stresses the interdependency between setting and culture, whereby cultural difference is nothing more than a 'reflexive feature of social interaction' (ibid.: 63). Cohen (1994) points out that the interpretative turn in the social science, with its emphasis on culture as the outcome of social interaction, has changed the relationship between individual and society from a deterministic to a problematic one. Culture has lost its role of 'integrator of people' to assume 'an aggregative role' that is founded on the recognition of the *differences* between individuals. These, in turn, have become the locus of culture and cultural differences, so that one talks about *distance between minds, rather than between cultures*. In this sense, 'culture [is] a more or less self-conscious differentiation from a contiguous group' (ibid.: 129). The real contribution to a more fruitful understanding of organisational communication, made by recent developments in anthropological theory is that interpretation of what we observe must be discourse-based: 'we cannot understand cultural boundaries without coming to terms with the discourse they enclose. We cannot do that without sensitivity to the claims and perceptions of those individuals who constitute the discourse' (ibid.:129).

This ties culture to discourse and to the need for self-reflexive methodologies. Cueing into the micro-dimensions of culture enacted by social interactants implies a *self-reflexive* and *relational* concept of the self. This is at odds with the egocentric-rational Western paradigm of understanding and action. The new, individual-based characterisation of understanding is one of a 'mutual process' through which interactants gain access to each other's mental world (Gergen 1990).

This self-reflexive, culture-based approach is poised to develop a critical edge (Mumby and Clair 1997) that is particularly suited to the study of international joint ventures as 'multicultures', a novel perspective in a sparsely researched area.[1] Finally, the case study examined in this chapter shows that the boundaries between descriptive and critical research are indeed blurred ones. During interviews, managers and the researcher, inevitably engage critically and self-critically with issues of status and control, and ultimately power, when they labour on their individual and corporate identities.

The introduction so far has touched on *culture* and *discourse* and will conclude with a reflection on the third key concept in this chapter, that of *management*. We first need to acknowledge that also the concept of management as discourse and praxis is rooted in Western philosophy and hinges on the commonly accepted definitions of the individual as an 'independent self' (Taylor 1989, Triandis 1989, Murthy 1998). Findings from organisational behaviour research are telling on this subject (e.g. Cooper and Rousseau 1995, Chevalier and Segalla 1996, Buchanan and Huczynski 1997), but one does not need to move beyond everyday talk to experience the tentacular influence of management discourse. The most notorious example that comes to mind is 'globalisation', a figure of speech that is now commonplace both in academia and in the market place but still lacking a commonly accepted definition (Bargiela-Chiappini, in preparation). What is becoming more and more apparent is that the alleged universality of management discourse implied in the notion of economic globalisation in fact clashes with local experiences of 'culture', whether national, or regional, or organisational.

This tension between the 'local' and the 'global' could not be more visible in international joint ventures, where many 'cultures' are often subsumed under a new, artificial identity that struggles to gain the loyalty of conflicting parties (Bargiela-Chiappini and Harris 1997). Relativism, then, characterises not only the concept of organisational culture(s) (Wright 1994), but also theoretical developments in management theory, as many textbooks show.

Culture and international joint ventures (IJVs)

Within management research, the most distinctive contribution to the debate on 'culture' comes from organisational studies, where the concept has been extended from *national*, to *regional, group* and *organisational* values. Since the 1980s, the interest in the study of 'organisational culture' has grown into a vast body of literature, a review of which is beyond the scope of this chapter. An ongoing debate that is particularly relevant to qualitative research in organisations in general, and in joint ventures in particular, is whether companies *have* or, in fact, *are* cultures (Sypher Davenport et al. 1985: 13–14).

This question is not only of theoretical interest, but it has wide-ranging implications for managerial praxis in a world where the tangible manifestations of globalisation (i.e., mergers, acquisitions and joint ventures) have impressed an accelerated motion to organisational change. If culture is one of the many components of organisations, practitioners need to take into account its interplay with other factors such as strategy, personnel policies, market orientation, etc. If, on the other hand, organisations are considered to be *cultures*, cultural change can be expected to affect all other aspects of an organisation.

In international joint ventures (IJVs), the cultural question is a multidimensional one, an interplay between group, national or regional cultures, which makes these organisations prime examples of 'multiple cultures'. In published research on joint ventures, there is a noticeable dearth of analysis on the contribution of the so-called 'soft issues', such as cultural values, to the success (or failure) of international partnerships (Parkhe 1980). What is the influence of group, national and regional values on organisational practices? Is management value-free and transferable? Is 'workforce compatibility' a factor in partner's choice and joint strategy making? How managers cope with the changes prior to and following the formation of international joint ventures?

The complexity of international joint ventures, and mergers and acquisitions (M&As), is determined not only by economic, strategic and financial factors, but also by the often ignored 'human dimensions'. Both sets of factors contribute to the higher failure rate of these ventures, ranging from and optimistic 50 percent to a pessimistic 80 percent (Cartwright and Cooper 1994). Recent research shows that mergers and acquisitions (and, by extension, joint ventures) are emotionally stressful events for personnel due to job insecurity and work overload. The same research suggests that if the objectives and the type of merger are two of the crucial elements in successful mergers and acquisitions, the third factor is 'cultural fit', which includes managerial style and corporate culture. It also shows that the protectionist ethnocentrism that precedes mergers tends to obscure similarities between the two companies while highlighting divisive features, so that the success of the merger may depend either on so-called 'cultural fit' or on the degree of autonomy of the two companies (Cartwright and Cooper 1994).

The interpretation of findings from the study of an Anglo-Italian joint venture (which shall be called *Novella)* reported in this chapter require a definition of 'cultural fit' that implies an expanded notion of 'culture'.[2] Furthermore, the experience of *Novella* shows that the process of formation of a joint venture begins well before the actual signing of the agreement and continues for years after. Therefore, longitudinal research is required to illuminate the factors that contribute to the dynamics of international partnership formation and maintenance, among which the human factor plays an (often-underestimated) fundamental role.

Background to the case-study

In 1997, five years after the signing of the joint venture (JV) agreement, both parent companies were able to recognise some of the respective strengths and weaknesses. An earlier tendency to think in terms of future 'cultural integration' was gradually being replaced by belief in a 'hybrid organisation'.

In its early years, *Novella* had had to overcome serious difficulties: drastic personnel cuts, the closure of a plant in Italy and damaging internal conflicts that culminated with the ejection of two top executives. This phase of mutual assessment and adjustment by the two 'cultures' was exacerbated and prolonged by the lack of preparation to the actual JV, so that personnel found themselves 'thrown in at the deep end' with no professional or personal support offered to soften the impact.[3]

A first study carried out in 1993 (Bargiela-Chiappini 1993) to assess the mutual perceptions of selected senior and middle managers revealed that the existing gap between the two national formations was quite wide. Marked defensiveness, even mistrust, were easily detectable, with the British side being overall more pessimistic about the future of the venture. Two internal opinion surveys were carried in 1994 and 1996 respectively, the practical outcomes of which – some managers' cynically remarked – were either long overdue changes, or did not have tangible effects on the employees' working lives.[4] The research conducted in 1997 and reported in this chapter illustrates how the persistence of differing understanding of management and the cultural differences still affected *Novella* five years on.

Methods and their limitations

A questionnaire,[5] originally compiled in English and then translated into Italian, was produced for use both in Britain and in Italy but the experience at the Italian site required more sensitivity in its use due to linguistic and cultural misunderstandings. For example, some Italian respondents preempted some questions, or had difficulty with the semantics of others, especially those relating to 'organisational culture'.[6]

Besides the limitations introduced by cultural influences and preferences, questionnaire-based research critically relies on the honesty of the answers for its overall response reliability. Contrary to what happens in written questionnaires, which provide an anonymous way of expressing one's perceptions without fear of reprisal, recorded face-to-face interviews leave the respondent at the mercy of the interviewer. The establishment of mutual trust is therefore a prerequisite towards reduced response distortion.[7]

Multicultures at work: the case of an Anglo-Italian joint venture

Writing in the mid-1990s, Shuter and Wiseman (1994) warn against a damaging weakness of organisational studies that affects not only research in Multinational Organisations (MNOs), but also, arguably, all organisations that attract the definition of 'multicultures':

> Because the bulk of the research on MNOs has been conducted by business scholars and social psychologists, it is not surprising that the literature on both organizational universals and national cultural influences infrequently focuses on communication issues. What is missing from much of this research is an examination of communication factors that are linked historically to the fields of intercultural or organizational communication. Moreover, it is difficult to locate a dedicated line of research on an organizational communication factor across multiple national cultures. As a result, we know little about communication in MNOs, and even less about multinational communication in specific countries and world regions. (Shuter and Wiseman 1994: 7)

The focus on communication has been an obvious choice in research contrasting national cultural influences on organisational interaction and management practices (e.g. Clyne 1994, Kim and Paulk 1994, Sharpe 1997). 'Communication' is a high frequency item in managers' talk at *Novella*. This confirms findings from previous observation-based research that 'communication', whether formal or informal, is the main managerial activity (Mintzberg 1973, Luthans and Larsen 1986). At *Novella*, both intercultural and intracultural communication issues are brought to the fore in discussion with managers. The following is a summary of their concerns on this subject:

1. the effectiveness and frequency of interpersonal relationships both within and across teams and departments and across hierarchical lines;
2. the role and usefulness of physical communication media such as the new company magazine and the internal projection of the company image;
3. the appraisal and briefing systems;
4. patterns of socialisation.

In order to contextualise communication issues, as well as other salient aspects of multicultural interaction at *Novella*, it is helpful to refer to the history of its early days. Following a notoriously typical pattern, *Novella* had originated from two companies that had undertaken no formal training to assist their employees in the transition towards an ideal 'monocultural' business (Albert 1994). The high degree of uncertainty that individuals and groups had to endure exercised considerable strain particularly in interpersonal relations at middle management level and between middle and top management.

Personal narratives revealed that uncertainty had caused a split within top management ranks, too. The Italian *dirigenti* (senior executives) were ready to admit that the climate at the beginning of the joint venture was stormy and that two or three of their Italian counterparts had experienced it as a great culture and power clash – one director could not adapt and was eventually 'removed'. However, in the early days, pessimism on the fate of the joint venture was much more tangible on the British side, possibly because of the severe staff cuts and the 'culture of decline' that had affected the British parent company. By contrast, a long tradition of capital investment at the Italian parent company had contributed to reassure the Italian *dirigenti* that it would only be a question of time before major differences would be resolved and that the joint venture would indeed survive (Bargiela-Chiappini 1993).

Five years on, at the time of the research reported here, uncertainty being a lesser factor, the Italian personnel continued to be more positive about the joint venture than their British colleagues. This, despite marked self-criticism among the Italians, was partly caused by persisting complaints, by their British counterparts, of poor meeting management, lack of teamwork, acts of autocratic power, little respect for rules and regulations, excessive bureaucracy, etc. A British director summed it all up as follows: 'it's organised chaos ... Italians survive in spite of everything and seem to do very well'.

Regarding interactional practices, the British perception of Italian managers centred on the degree of formality of work interactions and relationships, and the predominance of vertical (top down) communication. The structured nature of many meetings, which did not allow humour or joking, the use of professional titles, and the deference shown by managers to *dirigenti*, was incomprehensible to the British. At company level, this was matched by lack of cross-functional communication on the Italian side of the JV. Despite the awareness of some serious flaws in the Italian way of doing business, only one Italian strongly advocated a 'one culture, one soul' *Novella*. The general consent seemed to be that best practice from both sides should be drawn upon, whilst maintaining effective distinctive features. Flexibility was the quality generally praised in the Italian approach to management. An Italian *dirigente* thus described the commercial reality at *Novella*:

> the reality of this company is complex. Here [in Italy], we are capable of delivering what in England couldn't be delivered, but in England, delivered goods are always perfect. Here, something which is impossible today may become possible tomorrow; a product isn't available today but can be bought tomorrow. For the English mentality, this is something totally unacceptable.

Managing entails a large amount of time spent in meetings, which, in an Italian company, may become arenas for (apparently violent) personality clashes (Bargiela-Chiappini and Harris 1997). This, combined with the Italian habit of 'flexible punctuality', turned meetings into patience tests for the British managers at *Novella*. On the other hand, British reluctance to speak up against the boss at meetings was chastised by Italians as the 'yes culture'. It was observed that it was more often the case in Britain than in Italy that 'the boss is always right', and this was attributed to the fact that British employees are less protected against dismissal than their Italian counterparts. In Italy, it was not uncommon for a *dirigente* to have to sustain repeated verbal attacks from his collaborators, particularly when they thought that they had a good case. Consistently with this, there would be no need to invite reactions from participants at Italian meetings: these were often too many for the chair to cope with, whereas it appeared that British collaborators were more restrained, particularly when the boss was Italian. On the other hand, the stereotypical trait of English self-control seemed to hold true:

> it almost seems as if the British can forget about their status when they work together, and are able to be on the same level and deal with problems together; this is completely remote from the Italian culture where people say 'I am responsible for this only, I don't agree with what you say, I am responsible here'. I couldn't manage like them; I believe this is a cultural trait. (an Italian manager)

Negotiating complementarity in intercultural management

The Italian contribution to the joint venture in terms of *advanced technical expertise* was looked upon by the Italians as a complement to the *managerial skills* provided by British personnel: it was claimed that both were needed in the textile sector. Motivation was said to be 'quite good', with few exceptions, where personal history and the legacy of the past were still considerable stumbling blocks to the acceptance of inevitable change. Awareness of the need to change management style to accommodate the Anglo-Saxon model was high, and Italian top management paid lip service to it. Pockets of muffled personal resistance to the consequences of such a change still existed among Italians and were expressed in contradictory statements such as full support of more open interpersonal relations while protecting one's own right to choose what information should be released and when.

Language matters appeared to concern the British much more than the Italians, but it was an Italian director who remarked that the unilateral choice of English as the language of executive board (OpEx) meetings was not matched by visible efforts to learn Italian by British directors. Inevitably, intercultural meetings came under heavy criticism. Having to endure a mix of delayed starts, the interruptions of telephone calls, the side conversations in Italian, and the disappearance of individuals half-way through the proceedings was still a cause of frustration among the British directors who, however, had learned to exclude plain rudeness as an explanation for the Italians' behaviour. One *dirigente* had this to say on the subject:

this bothers us Italians too, but we accept it after all. It's part of our organisation; we are benchmarked on it. All that's around us is benchmarked on it; otherwise, we wouldn't manage to do all that we usually do.

The Italians' notorious reluctance to 'own problems' and take binding decisions militates strongly against management tools such as appraisals and briefings that rely on power sharing and active involvement of the first line managers. The appraisal system was heavily criticised by middle managers on the grounds that top management would tend to use it as a tool for quantitative assessment, which brought back school memories of a dreaded scoring system that most adult Italians would rather see laid to perpetual rest. Briefing, like appraisal, could run the same risk, of becoming a tool drafted onto an organisational culture that was not ready to receive it.

The issue of problem ownership had two other manifestations in the corporate life of the Italian sites, which attracted the criticism of the British team: (1) the use of consultants when major organisational changes were necessary; and (2) the *dirigenti*'s involvement with (allegedly) trivial or routine tasks. These two aspects, the British claimed, could be explained with the Italians' concern for the preservation of one's own position, at the expense of expected involvement in strategic management. Limited corporate awareness and participation was often symptomatically expressed in the individualism of the *dirigenti*'s language. Only one explicitly pointed out that it was time that they (the *dirigenti* and the middle management) began to use 'we' to refer to *Novella*, rather than the impersonal '*l'azienda*' (the company), as if they did not actually belong to it. Indeed, the collective 'we' was much stronger in the discourse of the British, as it was the perception that the British team were more openly committed to the Chief Executive's directives and therefore to *Novella*'s corporate policies.

The implications of the individualism in the Italian culture were used as an argument against forced cultural integration. Managers acknowledged that, whilst whole areas of the company were still isolated, and not only by their logistics, pursuing the myth of full integration would be the most serious corporate mistake that *Novella* could make. The Italians expressed the need for sharing in a common mission and common objectives; the British seemed to take these as already in place. The preservation of distinctive cultural preferences could be of mutual advantage: for example, manufacturing could benefit from the more methodical approach of the Anglo-Saxon management style, whereas the commercial function could be run following a revised version of the Italian customer-oriented approach. This marriage of necessity would not be an easy one to realise, and some pessimistic notes were sounded from both cultures:

> it's clear that if we marry a very individualistic culture as is the Italian one, characterised by few rules and much intuition, with the Anglo-Saxon culture that, on the contrary, relies less on intuition and much more on accurate organising, obviously these two cultures won't always match.

Another factor that had militated against integration was, among others, the long-standing friction between two culturally distinct functions, the *commercial* and the *production functions*, which were often perceived to be working against each other:

> in my opinion, in our company there are two important areas: sales and production. Given that we are a manufacturing business, these two areas must be fully integrated, and all the rest is to revolve around them.

In Italy, 'the factory', that is, the production site, was still quite a separate entity from the rest of the organisation. Logistics at the Italian site had contributed very little to the call for integration, with the three main buildings proudly bearing historically meaningful labels such as *la sede, la direzione* and *la fabbrica* (offices, headoffice, factory). Moreover, the almost divine status of the *direttore di fabbrica* (factory manager) presented a typical British manager with a puzzling example of anachronistic autocratic behaviour.

Back in Britain, the nerve of the organisation, the operations (or manufacturing) function, expressed very positive feelings towards the joint venture, after experiencing years of little capital investment and very little expenditure on maintenance. Consequently, severe job losses, which would have been politically unacceptable in Italy, were accepted as the necessary price to pay for the survival of the factories and there was a perception that more 'streamlining' might be necessary if the business was to survive a probable cyclic market crisis. The experience of being able to exercise control over performance and investment was also praised as another positive outcome of the joint venture, alongside with the face-lifting of the British factory buildings.

In Italy, the picture was somewhat different. Being based on a customer-oriented culture, the Italian company prided itself on flexible customer service policies. However, the British contribution to the joint venture was to impose restrictions to what was seen as excessive flexibility. Following British practices, customer service would contain an element of 'education' of the demanding Italian customers to a new type of service that would include planning and scheduling, two aspects of management praxis that, traditionally, had not met with favour among 'imaginative' and 'creative' Italian middle managers.

Managing in the middle

It was the CEO's (Chief Executive Officer's) own admission that middle managers are the people with the heaviest burden of work and responsibility in a joint venture (and in companies in general). A glance at the literature on middle managers confirms the accuracy of this analysis (e.g., Dopson and Stewart 1990, Wheatley 1992, Jackson and Humble 1994). The problem of ill-defined managerial identities and roles in a national company is exacerbated by intercultural contact. The introduction of job descriptions had not helped the identity crisis that plagued Italian middle managers. Substantial discrepancies had begun to emerge between the new managerial profiles and job descriptions imposed by the joint venture and what was expected of them in real life. Attempts to translate practical necessities and concerns into a pragmatic model outlining managerial competencies for each of the new roles had met with only partial success.[8]

The most visible manifestation of the confusion over managerial competencies in the new venture was typified by the 'titles war' in the Italian company. The new titles, often in English, did not describe the duties fulfilled by Italian middle managers prior to the joint venture, nor did they match the expectations of British managers working with their Italian counterparts. So, for example, the 'responsabile della produzione' became a 'production manager'; the 'responsabile della qualita' was renamed 'quality control manager': their titles had changed in line with their British counterparts, but their competencies and power had not, thus creating a gap between (Italian) performance and (British) expectations. The title switch had but deepened the identity crisis of the Italian *quadri* (middle managers) and left them to juggle with the continuing autocratic practices of their Italian superiors and the new demands imposed by their British colleagues. The discourse of Anglo-

Saxon management, although competently mouthed by Italian managers, had turned out to be a failure in its practical applications. It was clear that *Novella's* culture, as well as the Italian and regional cultures, were too distant from the expectations built into the language of British management praxis.

The effect of English terminology on perceptions of self-identity was not limited to job titles. Words such as 'appraisal', 'briefing' and 'focus groups' had also become part of the Italian managers' idiolect. The identification of the terminology with the source of a new (British) way of doing business affected mainly, but not only, Italian middle managers. The senior managers appeared to have *adopted* the discourse but not *adapted* their behaviour.

Uncertainty fuelled by terminological vagueness and fluid role attributes and competencies favoured the strong perception among the Italians that the British were 'in control'. However, alongside envious remarks about British managers enjoying more benefits (e.g., company cars), there was an acknowledgement among Italians of their British colleagues' managerial skills and their organised way of working. Somewhat expectedly, the three features that impressed Italian mangers who had visited the British production sites were all missing in the Italian company: a more efficient organisation, a clear definition of roles and expectations and respect for rules. By contrast, Italian managers underlined their own ability to react to problems or unexpected situations in a more flexible and imaginative manner, a fire-fighting approach to managing.

In all of their struggles, Italian middle managers, and some of their British counterparts, often referred to the gap between them and the top management as a major contributing factor in their identity crisis and inability to operate more effectively. Despite (or because of) token gestures of 'goodwill' and 'openness' towards managers and other staff, top management were seen to occupy an unreachable corporate Olympus. A typical example of their elitist attitude was the 'one o'clock club', i.e., top managers going to lunch all together at one o'clock and sitting at the same table in the staff canteen.

Conclusion

Intercultural management combines the issues and problems of managing a national company with the impact of cultural differences and preferences, the complexity of which is often appreciated only when a new company is already signed into existence, and then it might be too late. The literature on cross-cultural management (e.g., Mead 1990 and 1998; Usunier 1998) often explores the many pitfalls, imparts prescriptions on how to avoid them and, sometimes, presents case-studies of successful companies. By contrast, one could cite research that quotes the strikingly high percentage of companies who fail the merger or acquisition test through lack of consideration for the influence of the 'human factor' (Cartwright and Cooper 1994).

As a linguist who came to organisational communication from mainstream discourse analysis, I have become very conscious that future theoretical development in organisational communication in general, and in intercultural organisational communication in particular, depends on increased multidisciplinary collaboration and interdisciplinary exchange. Both substantial rigorous empirical work and innovative theoretical insights are needed that build on the richness of many established disciplines such as sociology, social psychology, anthropology, linguistics and organisational theory.

The case-study considered in this chapter is a preliminary investigation that has highlighted areas of concern that would require further micro and macro analyses within a longitudinal research project in order to deepen the understanding of joint ventures as prime examples of 'multi-cultures'. Questions of organisational communication, identity and management styles have emerged as most pressing to the people who had lived through the first five years of an Anglo-Italian joint venture. As expected, the case study shows that the strongest sense of corporate identity in a new joint venture is found at top management level, with some important qualifications. There remained, both among directors and *dirigenti,* pockets of resistance to the process of new identify formation instigated by the British team. Allegiance to the old system values appeared to be a posture aimed to safeguard one's own position of power and authority (Italian side). As suggested by several interviewees, when 'personal conversion' to the new set of unwritten values fails, 'natural waste' could be the only alternative in a labour protectionist system such as, for instance, the Italian one.

The joint venture case-study has also highlighted critical deficiencies at middle management level (mainly in the more conservative Italian company), confirming findings from previous research (Dopson and Stewart 1990, Wheatley 1992, Jackson and Humble 1994). The contact with the British managerial culture, more used to empowering its middle managers, had led to a sharp identity crisis among the Italians, exacerbated by the persisting hegemonic power of the top management. The expertise and interest that middle managers were (potentially) capable of offering were only partially exploited for corporate aims; much effort seemed to be wasted in bureaucratic procedures and the management of tense interpersonal relations. Often, middle management roles were fulfilled *despite* all obstacles, which put the organisation and the individuals under an unnecessary degree of strain and pressure

Although there was quite widespread (verbal) support for the British way of managing the business, real intercultural contact and exchange over the first five years had remained confined to the top management and to few middle managers. Moreover, senior management had been notoriously absent in the promotion of intercultural management.

The internal tensions between attitudes and practices especially at middle management level, and the mixed success of the expatriates experiences, were the most visible, but not the only, signs that learning about cultural diversity in an international organisation requires both preventive and supporting action. The former includes an early assessment of the projected impact of cultural differences and management styles on all the individuals who are likely to work with their counterparts across linguistic and cultural barriers. The latter builds on the feedback and results of the induction plan to provide training and continuous learning to enable individuals to contribute fully to the business.

To understand the role of culture(s), from which differing understandings of management are derived, is not only a challenging topic of continuing academic research (Meschi 1997), but a requirement on which the success of a business may ultimately depend. *Listening* to what people have to say and *watching* them work is the necessary first step in that direction.

Notes

1. I was not able to find empirical studies on Anglo-Italian joint ventures, which may only mean that research published in languages other than English is not listed in English bibliographies. By contrast, there is by now an established body of research on American-Japanese and American-European joint ventures.
2. Typically, however, *Novella's* management had set up no plan to cope with the repercussions of the joint venture agreement on its personnel, and had

adopted a reactive stance following the difficulties experienced, particularly at middle management level.

3. At the main British plant, managers were given the opportunity to attend a course of Italian language and culture during working hours that was meant to equip them with sufficient skills to cope with frequent intercultural contact. This did not continue beyond its second year and never developed into a learning programme specifically aimed to facilitate managers' cross-company activities.

4. Such a design reflects the nature of the issues to be analysed, which are neither static nor simple. The pace of change experienced by *Novella* in the first five years of its activity renders one-off samplings of corporate perceptions quickly dated, and therefore of little practical use to the company.

5. In this research, the questionnaire was both a tool and a 'pretext' in that, in the author's own experience (Bargiela-Chiappini and Harris 1997), she was expected to behave 'professionally' – which includes the display of appropriate tools such as a written questionnaire – and yet tactfully, to avoid alienating the sensitised respondents already suffering from 'survey fatigue'.

6. This difficulty is probably due to the fact that the concept of 'corporate culture' has appeared only relatively recently in Italian undergraduate and postgraduate business courses, following the adoption of American management study programmes.

7. At *Novella,* whilst it would be possible to quote one or two examples of individuals who 'waffled', in general, the author felt that the longer she spent with the interviewees, the more open and honest the discussion became. In this respect, the findings reported in this chapter, derived from interviews ranging from one to three hours, are probably more reliable, and certainly more detailed, than the quantitative findings provided by statistical methods.

8. The use of English job descriptions was not making the task easier: in fact, it could have been seen as the attribution of empty categories to individuals whose corporate roles were far from clear. When asked to explain what the new job titles actually meant to them, interviewees often recited what sounded like quotations from a management book, followed by their own perceptions of who they were actually *allowed* to be in the organisation.

References

Albert, R. Daskal. 1994. 'Cultural diversity and intercultural training in multinational organizations', in *Communicating in Multinational Organizations*, eds R. L. Wiseman and R. Shuter. Thousand Oaks, California: Sage. 153–165.

Bargiela-Chiappini, F. 1993. 'Issues in international business communication', paper read at the 5th ENCoDe International Conference, Preston, UK.

———. In preparation. 'Think globally, act locally: competing discourses of economic globalisation'.

Bargiela-Chiappini, F. and Harris, S. 1997. *Managing Language. The Discourse of Corporate Meetings*. Amsterdam: John Benjamin.

Buchanan, D. A. and Huczynski, A. 1997. *Organizational Behaviour: Integrated Readings*. Hemel Hempstead: Prentice-Hall.

Cartwright, S. and Cooper, C. L. 1994. 'The human effects of mergers and acquisitions', in *Trends in Organizational Behavior*, vol. 1., eds C. L. Cooper and D. M. Rousseau. Chichester: John Wiley and Sons.

Chevalier F. and Segalla, M., eds. 1996. *Organizational Behaviour and Change in Europe: Case Studies*. London: Sage.

Clyne, M. 1994. *Inter-Cultural Communication at Work: Cultural Values in Discourse*. Cambridge: Cambridge University Press.

Cohen, A. 1994. *Self-Consciousness: An Alternative Anthropology of Identity*. London: Routledge.

Cooper C. L. and Rousseau, D., eds. 1995. *Trends in Organizational Behavior*, vol. 2. Chichester: John Wiley and Sons,

Dopson, S. and Stewart, R. 1990. 'What is happening to middle management?' *British Journal of Management* 1: 3–16.

Gergen, K. J. 1990. 'Social understanding and the inscription of self', in *Cultural psychology. Essays on Comparative Human Development*, eds J. W. Stiegler, R. A. Shweder and G. Herdt. Cambridge: Cambridge University Press.

Heyman, R. D. 1989. 'Cultural difference as topic, not resource, in comparative studies'. *Discours Social/Social Discourse* II, no. 3: 47–65.

Jackson, D. and Humble, D. 1994. 'Middle managers: new purpose, new directions'. *Journal of Management* 13, no. 3: 15–21.

Kim, Y. Y. and Paulk, S. 1994. 'Intercultural challenges and personal adjustments: a qualitative analysis of the experiences of American and Japanese co-workers', in *Communicating in Multinational Organization*, eds R. L. Wiseman and R. Shuter. Thousand Oaks, California: Sage. 117–140.

Luthans, F. and Larsen J. K. 1986. 'How mangers really communicate'. *Human Relations* 39, no. 2: 161–178.

Mead, R. 1990. *Cross-cultural Management Communication*. Chichester: John Wiley and Sons.

———. 1998. *International Management: Cross-Cultural Dimensions*, (2nd edition). London: Blackwell Business.

Meschi, P. X. 1997. 'Longevity and cultural differences of international joint ventures: toward time-based cultural management'. *Human Relations* 50, no. 2: 211–228.

Mintzberg, H. 1973. *The Nature of Managerial Work*. New York: Harper and Row.

Mumby, D. K. and Clair, R. P. 1997. 'Organizational discourse', in *Discourse as Social Interaction*, vol. 2, ed T. van Dijk. London: Sage. 181–205.

Murthy, P. N. 1998. 'Leadership: A comparative study of Indian ethos and Western concepts'. *Journal of Human Values* 4, no. 2: 155–165.

Parkhe, A. 1980. '"Messy" research, methodological predispositions, and theory development in international joint ventures'. *Academy of Management Review* 18, no. 2: 227–268.

Sharpe, D. R. 1997. 'Managerial control strategies and subcultural processes: on the shop floor in a Japanese manufacturing organization in the United Kingdom', in *Cultural Complexity in Organizations*, ed. S. Sackman. 228–251.

Shuter, R. and Wiseman, R. L. 1994. 'Communication in multinational organizations'. in *Communicating in Multinational Organizations*, eds R. L. Wiseman and R. Shuter. Thousand Oaks, California: Sage. 3–11.

Sypher Davenport, B., Applegate, J. L. and Sypher, H. E. 1985. 'Culture and communication in organizational contexts', in *Communication, Culture and Organizational Processes*, eds L. P. Stewart and S. Ting-Toomey. Beverley Hills: Sage. 13–27.

Taylor, C. 1989. *Sources of the Self: The Making of the Modern Identity*. Cambridge: Cambridge University Press.

Triandis, H. C. 1989. 'The self and social behavior in differing cultural contexts'. *Psychological Review* 96, no. 3: 506–520.

Usunier, J. C. 1998. *International and Cross-Cultural Management*. London: Sage.

Wheatley, M. 1992. *The Future of Middle Management*. Corby: B.I.M.

Wright, S. ed. 1994. *Anthropology of Organizations*. London: Routledge.

CHAPTER 8

INTERCULTURAL COMPETENCE: THEORIES INTO PRACTICE

Libby Rothwell

Introduction

It is perfectly possible to live alongside another culture without ever acquiring the ability to communicate effectively in that culture. Effective communication between cultural groups does not just happen as a result of exposure to other cultures; it has to be learnt. A good example of this is the case of students spending part of their study period abroad. Research on undergraduate students who spend part of their studies abroad has shown (Coleman 1996) that they do not universally appear to benefit from the exposure to a different culture in terms of a heightened cultural awareness of the reasons for differences they have observed. A minority of them return with a more negative opinion of the target country, and of its language, people and culture. A different approach to teaching language and culture is needed, linking formal learning to what is learned through experience abroad. Given that language teachers have to teach both language rules and 'the context of understanding of culturally defined aspects of a communicative event' (Saville-Troike 1989: 258), pedagogy needs not only to value 'facts', but to encourage their relativisation by fostering a diversity of experience, and the ability to reflect on that diversity (Cormeraie 1997). This has been called 'intercultural competence' (Coleman 1996: 15).

Byram and Zarate (1997) define intercultural competence in terms of five kinds of knowledge (five *savoirs*) or skills that offer a framework for language teaching in general, but specifically, for visits abroad and exchanges. They can also be used to evaluate the cultural learning that has been achieved. This framework is summarised below:

Savoir être

An ability to abandon ethnocentric attitudes towards and perceptions of other cultures, and to see and develop an understanding of the differences and relationships between one's own and a foreign culture; this involves affective and cognitive change in learners.

Savoir apprendre

An ability to observe, collect data, and analyse both how people of another language and culture perceive and experience their world, and what beliefs, values and meanings they share about it; this involves practical skills and a readiness to decentre and take a different perspective.

Savoirs

The knowledge of aspects of a culture, i.e., a system of reference points familiar to natives of the culture, which helps the natives to share beliefs, values and meanings, and to communicate without making explicit those shared assumptions.

Savoir faire

The ability to draw upon the other three *savoirs* and integrate them in real time and interaction with people of a specific language and culture.

Savoir s'engager

An ability to evaluate – critically, and on the basis of specific criteria – perspectives, practices and products in one's own and other cultures and countries.

It has been noted that, despite recent interest in the language and culture nexus, no theory of culture learning has yet emerged (Byram et al. 1994). Culture learning has been said to be a special type of Kolb's experiential learning (Bennett 1986). Whalley (1997) uses Mezirow's (1991) theory of transformative learning to draw up a typology of forms of intercultural learning, based on the analysis of journals kept by

Canadian students in Japan and Japanese students in Canada, on a residence-abroad programme. Mezirow identifies three forms of reflection involved in transformative learning: reflection on the content of the problem, reflection on the process of problem-solving and reflection on the premise of the problem itself.

In recent years, a variety of research and teaching approaches have emerged that seek to build on the learner's experience. Some focus on the content of what students say about their experiences of other cultures in diaries and logs (e.g., Whalley 1997). Others take the learner's own culture as a starting point for ethnographic enquiry (Jordan and Barro 1995). Kramsch (1993) demonstrates how both teacher and learner can reach the 'third place' between their own and other cultures, by exploring conflicting interpretations of literary and other texts in their language class.

My aim is to show how cultural learning can be better understood by paying attention to both the *content* of what learners say about their own and other cultures and the *manner* in which they express themselves. The insights of cross-disciplinary theoretical perspectives can be translated into teaching and learning activities for the critical analysis of cultural identity and difference. To this end, I will briefly outline five theories of culture as they relate to language, before considering the implications of an interdisciplinary approach to language and culture.

To illustrate my argument I shall use extracts from informal debriefing sessions with British undergraduates studying French with German or Spanish, and ERASMUS exchange students at Kingston University (UK), during and after residence abroad.

Culture as socialisation

The study of language and culture arises from anthropology. The early linguistic anthropologists Edward Sapir and Benjamin Whorf focused on how different cultures use language to classify and categorise their experience of the world (Sapir 1931/1964). The Sapir-Whorf hypothesis postulates that every language embodies a specific worldview, and that speakers of one language cannot fully understand the perspective of speakers of another language. A weaker version is now more readily accepted: languages do influence our perceptions of the world, or 'reality', supported by findings that common concepts evoke different semantic associations in different cultures (Wierzbicka 1992).

As a child learns to speak the language of its parents, it learns to view the world according to the categories and patterns encoded in that language – for example, what type of animal and vegetable are considered 'food'. The grammar of a language also encodes social distinctions in specific ways (e.g., through the system of address forms such as the *tu/vous* distinction in French). A study of the 'gaps' between languages is very revealing of the worldview of that culture. There is, for example, no word for 'privacy' in some languages (Duranti 1997), and English, unlike Spanish, has no separate words to distinguish animal and human parts such as mouths, backs, necks and legs. This different classification of 'animal' can explain the different cultural meaning of, for example, bullfighting to a Spaniard and to an American. If culture is something one learns along with language, it follows that in learning other languages, one has the ability to put aside one's own way of seeing the world and take on the perspective of the speakers of those languages. Some words are rich in associations for a particular culture; the extent to which students identify and make sense of these 'rich words' (Agar 1980) provides an interesting perspective on their cultural learning. For example, students frequently note that the concept of vegetarianism in the way they understand it seems to be absent in some cultures. If the word itself exists, it is 'borrowed', and therefore does not provide a perfect fit with its English counterpart; there is a lexical gap. Such lexical items are hard to translate precisely because they are 'rich': '... the problematic bit of language is puttied thickly into far-reaching networks of association and many situations of use' (Agar 1991: 176). For this student returning from Spain, one such rich word was *guiri:*

Extract 1:
Anyone who's not Spanish is called that name, it's called guiri. They're so proud of their culture, they're so proud of where they come from and anyone who's not Spanish or even not from where they come from is .. an outsider.

Such insights can act as the focus for the exploration of otherness and belonging as it is encoded in languages, and from there, the cross-cultural analysis of the different meanings of related concepts, such as stranger/acquaintance/friend. It seems that the British students' conception of 'friend' differs from the French. Ardagh (1990: 352) argues that there are three levels in the two cultures. The first level is the casual, anonymous chat with a stranger, in which no personal questions are asked and there is no presumption of acquaintanceship. The second level is where new acquaintances are made, whom the British and Americans quickly transform into 'friends' by swapping personal details, using first names and so on – a level that takes longer to reach in France. The French, Ardagh maintains, distinguish more sharply between acquaintances, and so the third level – *les vrais amis* – is for enduring friendships often formed in youth or over a number of years as professional colleagues. It would be possible to investigate the extent to which this claim could be substantiated. One way to explore different cultural conceptions of common concepts is to trace the semantic maps around the concept as they appear in a variety of texts, remembering, however, that text selection cannot be 'neutral'.

The discipline of anthropology offers a wealth of divergent theoretical perspectives, which can contribute to the development of a language-and-culture pedagogy. Linguistic anthropologists see the study of language as a cultural resource, speaking as a cultural practice (Duranti 1997). Speakers are social actors, members of communities with similar beliefs and moral values. They focus on language as a set of symbolic resources that make up the fabric of society and the way individuals represent actual or possible 'realities'. Cultural anthropologists, on the other hand, focus on universal categories of human behaviour, such as time orientation, power distance, uncertainty avoidance, individualism and masculinity (Hofstede 1980). Uncritical application of Hofstede's theories could encourage the 'product' view of cultural identity as something static and unchanging, reducing cultural identity to nationality ('the French are like this, the Germans do that'). However, it is my contention that a combination of the 'top-down' approach of cultural anthropologists such as Hall (1964) and Hofstede (1980), complemented by the 'bottom-up' approach of linguistic anthropology, affords effective methods to explore and critically reflect on cultural identity and difference. The following example may help to clarify how this can be done.

I had noted that students returning from residence abroad repeatedly referred to points of difference between the host cultures and their own concerning laws and other forms of regulation of behaviour, as exemplified in the next extract.

Cultural anthropologists maintain that the interpretation of written, or statutory law, and unwritten rules can provide a key to the culture, or standardised values, of a community. Douglas (1966: 40) claims that culture, in this sense, provides in advance some basic categories, a positive pattern in which ideas and values are tidily ordered. Above all, it has authority, since everyone is obliged to assent because of the assent of others. The categories are rigid because of their public nature. Actual laws tend to reflect 'living law' or unwritten societal norms (Northrop, cited in Hofstede 1980: 136). Several students described occasions in Germany when they were made aware of the workings of 'the law'. In contrast, the descriptions concerning infringements or compliance during residence in France centred on contacts with representatives of 'the law'. In Spain, students remarked on the areas where there appeared to be less legislation (or observance of it) than in Britain. Hofstede (1980: 135) notes that Germany has an extensive set of laws for emergencies that might occur (*Notstandgesetze*), whereas Britain does not even have a written constitution. Legislation is a consequence of a highly developed need for uncertainty avoidance, but even in cultures where uncertainty is tolerated more readily, the pattern of legislation may provide an insight into the cultural value system. The following extract shows how interpretation of foreign laws could be seen to as revealing the value systems of the student's own culture. In it, the speaker describes her reaction to the German system of sorting domestic waste into different coloured bins:

Extract 2:
We were shocked about that. ... Well, I must confess we didn't [sort waste] and there was a grey one and she said right at the end of the conversation 'there's this grey er bo – big carton that you can put ... everything in' and my flatmate and I just kind of looked at each other and ... just this first common ground that we first got to know each other on as well for was : ' put it in the grey one'

Viewed from the perspective of cultural anthropology, the issue behind the law in this extract, environmental protection, might be interpreted as revealing culture-specific values. Countries that prioritise economic growth, achievement and excellence display essentially 'masculine' values, whilst those that favour the protection of the environment equate with traditional 'feminine' values, according to Hofstede's fourth societal norm, which he calls 'Masculinity' (Hofstede 1980: 178).

The Masculinity-Femininity polarity is defined as a tendency to assertiveness versus nurture. Britain and Germany are both revealed as having more 'masculine' values. Every developed society is faced with the conflicting needs of economic growth and the protection of the environment. In Germany's case, a solution to this problem has been found by the Green movement; their extensive recycling programme is primarily an economic solution.

The British student's 'shock' seems to be caused, not by the idea behind the law, but by the 'complicated' system of rules to follow in order to comply with the law. It could be argued, following Hofstede, that she and her French flatmate found 'common ground' because as representatives of highly individualist cultures, they were instinctively reacting against what they felt to be excessive restriction on their independence imposed by 'community law'. However, other factors could be at play here, such as the gender of the participants, personality and the context of the interaction. Through discussion of situations such as these, the concept of social identity and its relationship with national identity can be explored.

Individualist values, it is claimed (Hofstede 1980: 164), manifest themselves, among others, in driving behaviour. In more individualist countries, drivers show a more 'calculative' involvement in traffic, which leads to safer driving. One student, in describing how frightened she was when being driven home by her Spanish friend who had had too much to drink, put his behaviour down to a lack of statutory law. In Britain, 'calculative' involvement in driving has been enshrined in extensive legislation, backed up by publicity campaigns. To express the belief that a law would have prevented this incident may be seen as naïve, or, taking the perspective of linguistic anthropology, it may be interpreted as the 'public voice' used by the student to construct her social identity. Whatever our interpretation of the speakers' comments, they are a telling example of culture as process; we are both products and producers of cultural norms.

Culture as a communication system

The belief that each language produces its own distinct conceptual world was taken up at the turn of the century by the Swiss linguist Ferdinand de Saussure, called the father of structural linguistics, for whom language was a system of signs, since the connection between a word and its meaning is arbitrary. So language is cultural, not natural, and so too are the meanings it generates. Language is a system of relationships that sets up categories and makes distinctions through webs of difference and similarity or binary oppositions (Lèvi-Strauss 1968). This structuralist view has given us a key concept in the understanding of the production of meaning: interpretation involves comparison and entails differentiation. Whereas structuralism tries to explain cultural differences in terms of general laws of behaviour, others see them as examples of human beings' never-ending process of interpretation:

> The concept of culture I espouse [...] is essentially a semiotic one. Believing, with Max Weber, that man is an animal suspended in webs of significance he himself has spun, I take culture to be those webs, and the analysis of it to be therefore not an experimental science in search of law but an interpretive one in search of meaning. (Geertz 1973: 5, cited in Duranti 1997: 36)

In any culture, a 'sign' (be it a lexical item, a custom, a practice, etc.) may have many meanings, but it has been argued that one dominant meaning will emerge, to become a cultural 'myth' (Barthes 1957/1993). The identification of these dominant associations can provide a useful starting point for reflexive discussion on the dynamic nature of cultural value systems and on the process of intercultural learning itself. The following two extracts are taken from a discussion in a mixed nationality group on the practice of going barefoot. In Extract 3, the speakers are Spanish (S) and French (F):

Extract 3:
S: I would like to mention something (laughter) how English people love .. to walk without shoes ..
F: it's true you know.
S: Yeah it's really true without shoes to go in the kitchen without shoes and without ..socks something like that I don't understand even .. in the street you can see the girls with their shoes in their hand or walking without shoes ..here is incredible the amount of people that are .. without shoes even in the home.
F: Maybe they were just brought up like that, I don't know.

The Spanish and French speakers here found the habit of going barefoot 'dirty and dangerous'. Douglas (1966: 36) argues that dirt is 'matter out of place' and that our ideas of what is dirty and dangerous express symbolic systems; the difference between pollution behaviour in one part of the world and another is only a matter of detail. Distinctions between 'dirty' and 'clean' objects and behaviour within a culture are invaluable for the insight they afford into that culture's values: what is considered 'sacred'.

The Spanish and French speakers' interpretation of the meaning of going barefoot can be compared to this British student's account of an incident that happened in her hall of residence while she was studying in France:

> *Extract 4:*
> I walked down I had my pyjamas on and just like a dressing gown and didn't have any shoes on, went to collect my mail so I could read it in bed and the cleaner followed me all the way downstairs and went 'A –, are you … are you feeling … feeling ill' sort of thing and I was like 'No no' (laughs) 'I'm fine'

The student accounts for the cleaner's consternation by supposing that it was caused by her lateness in getting dressed. For the student, bare feet signalled merely the intention to go back to bed to relax. British Rail and Virgin Atlantic have both exploited this association of bare feet with relaxation in advertising campaigns in recent years. Not wearing footwear may also symbolise freedom from constraint in a culture that values personal independence (cf. the expression 'footloose and fancy-free', in French, simply: *un coeur à prendre*). Students and other young people may see it as a mark of nonconformity (cf. the controversy caused by the popstar Sandie Shaw appearing without shoes on British television in the 1960s). In Spain and France, however, wearing shoes or slippers may symbolise cleanliness, health, safety and a good upbringing. Such a contrastive approach can help students identify one of the major sources of intercultural misunderstanding, namely the interpretation of target culture behaviour according to the norms of one's own culture, and encourage reflection on the norm-making process.

Culture as shared knowledge

Another theory, arising from psychology, sees culture as knowledge:

> whatever it is one has to know or believe in order to operate in a manner acceptable to [a society's] members and to do so in any role that they accept for any one of themselves. (Goodenough 1957, in Hymes 1964)

We can ask students to apply Goodenough's definition to any situation where they have had to operate in another culture. Do they believe that there exists a body of knowledge that one can learn in order to become accepted into that culture? By comparing his with other definitions (including students' own), we can illuminate the difference between positivist and interpretivist conceptions of reality and the implications this has for them when they read published research and when they design their own language-and-culture projects.

This can be followed by an examination of the categorisation process. The world is too vast for us to be able to experience everything differently, so we group our experiences into categories, to which we assign labels. When we meet new phenomena, we look for similarities with items in an existing category so that we can slot new experiences in to our existing knowledge. Categorisation is fundamental to the process of making sense of the complexities of the world, to the organisation of 'what one has to know'. It simplifies things and makes them more predictable. Categories activate expectations or schemata (a mental picture of some area of experience), which in turn may help explain the process of stereotyping. When new things do not conform to our schematic knowledge, we have several choices: we can reject the new information, reassign it to a different category, adapt the information to fit the category, or alter an existing category to fit the new information. We use the resources of language in everyday conversation to maintain or reinforce cultural norms:

Extract 5:
(a) We thought, Germany – height of communication and technology, but it wasn't, except Bamberg was the exception to the rule.
(b) I think I could have been misled into thinking they just like studying all the time – which seemed to be the case in Toulon, but that wasn't the case, erm, it really does depend on which part of France you're talking about.
(c) She used to strip her bed each day and she'd sit there and eat walnuts and tomatoes all evening. It really annoyed me, and she went to bed at 8:30 every night, but she wasn't typical, that wasn't typical German.
(d) You can't just stereotype a French person as being, you know, the lot there, just because our experience has, er … I agree, it's just the people of Nancy.

How do the speakers' linguistic choices display a change in thinking? It is clear that all the statements involve the manipulation of stereotypical categories. In (a) and (b) the stereotype is modified without being abandoned, whilst in (c) there is ostensibly a refusal to stereotype, whilst still depending on stereotypical classification; by describing a stereotypical example, there is an assumption that there is a unified entity that is 'German'. When we construct and organise categories, we centralise some elements as being 'prototypes' (Rosch 1978), or best examples of that category. We also marginalise or mark others as being exceptional, different or poor examples of a given prototype. We assign typical behaviours or 'scripts' to members of our categories, often in contrast with atypical examples. In (d), there is an interesting self-contradiction: a metalinguistic reference to the stereotyping process itself followed by a modification of a stereotype. Here again, contextual factors must be taken into consideration in the analysis of language and culture: since it is a university student talking in a group with the tutor, the speaker may be influenced by an awareness of the undesirability of stereotyping within an academic context.

Culture as language-in-action

The concern for what people do with language is central to ethnomethodology (Garfinkel 1967), which looks at the methods used by a social group to make their words and actions accountable, or meaningful. Accountability is analysed via the concepts of stake, interest and footing (Goffman 1981). These are linguistic devices speakers use to create a sense of authenticity, or to indicate how their words are to be taken. There are several examples of narratives in the data, that is, instances where speakers tell the story of an experience that was in some way important for them: a critical incident. An initially puzzling feature of these accounts was the number of 'stereotypical' comments they contained that seemed to be at odds with the stated reason for telling the story: as an illustration of how experience had caused them to 'see things differently'. However, cognitive script theory postulates that people have mental 'scripts', or expectations of how things should happen based on everyday experiences. When they encounter variations, their schematic knowledge structures are automatically updated. A discourse analytic approach may provide an answer to the puzzle. Sacks (1992, cited in Edwards 1997: 164) emphasises how robust and normative such cultural knowledge is, and how impervious it is to the dictates of personal experience. Its frequent invocation in conversation is pragmatic, he maintains; it has to do with accounting for actions. Edwards (1997: 165) suggests that

> the intelligible orderliness of social life stems not from a set of updatable knowledge structures in a sense-making cognitive being, but from how social actions flexibly unfold, as situated performances.

In the following extract, the speaker describes a brush with the German police, and what she learned from it. The analysis that follows examines the account from the perspective of a 'situated performance' (certain excerpts are emphasised and numbered for reference):

Extract 6:
It's actually quite embarrassing. We went out for an *evening just getting to know the town* [1] and we were on our way home /??/ some friends that I'd met out there and we were *just sort of messing around being silly* [2], next thing I know, in Germany particularly in Bamberg where I was they have it was beautiful, absolutely beautiful town and they were very proud because it was /??/ as well they were very proud of their sort of town and everything, and there was this lovely sort of big sort of flowerpot, not little flowerpot, this big concrete thing and lovely flowers and next thing .. anyhow *I ended up* [3] sort of flat in this flowerpot thing *I got sort of pushed in* [4] and um .. I said 'Look somebody help me out here' and then right .. must have been about thirty seconds later, this police car turns up and out come the old German policemen and um I just stood up and I was like 'oh no this is awful' *because of the way I suppose Germans are* [5] in a way um they were very .. (mock official tone) 'What's going on, what's happened here?' It was like 'Just a moment .. this was just an accident I just fell in .. I'm very sorry' er but you know they wouldn't have it and *I suppose because they realised as well that we were foreign* [6] it might have had something to do with it but they were taking our names down wanted our addresses and um it was all very formal and they were like radioing through and everything to see if there was any trouble anywhere else or something and it was just so... it was no no.... and we thought if that was in England um *I suppose the Police would have been able to have told you off or something 'stop being stupid' or whatever* [7] but they wouldn't have gone so far because like two weeks later we had a letter from the police and

we had to go to the Police Station and we had to like write a statement basically they wanted a statement of what went on why I ended up in the flowerbed (laughter) and I was just so .. *I couldn't believe* [8] it how sort of bureaucratic I suppose in a way 'cos they wanted, you know, everything had to be written down and it all had to be .. just right sort of what to explain why this happened.... and *we thought I mean at one stage I really did think* [9] I was going to get charged for .. squashing some flowers (laughs) This is awful I mean I didn't break the plant you know it was nothing like that, just squashed a few flowers, that was it, but I think that was just like I thought, *I think you know that really sort of brought down to everybody* [10] really like hhh they really are .. quite you know .. they do care about their community and that (.) really care.

The assertions in excerpts [1] and [2], 'just getting to know the town' and 'just messing around being silly' act both as a frame for our interpretation of what is to come and a denial of responsibility for any charge of 'criminal damage'. The absence of an agent in excerpts [3] and [4] ('I ended up', 'I got pushed in') have the effect of reinforcing their right to be seen as blameless. One expects people in certain categories to have special rights and knowledge, such as the right of policemen to impose the law. By introducing the category 'policemen' with the qualifiers 'old German', this right is undermined, which also diminishes comeback (Potter 1996: 135). Tautological statements such as 'because of the way I suppose Germans are' in excerpt [5] have the effect of appearing to be invoking self-evident, undeniable, obvious knowledge (Edwards 1997: 256). The suppositions in excerpts [6] and [7] come at a point in the narrative where the speaker's motives might be questioned, that is, when the German police would not accept her apology that leads to the summons to the police station. Whereas the first supposition appears to be accusing the policemen of prejudice ('they realised we were foreign'), the second appears to be excusing them on the grounds that they had no choice, unlike British policemen who 'would have been able to have told you off or something'. Such devices have been termed stake inoculation (Potter, in Silverman 1997) in that they limit the ease with which speakers' talk and text can be undermined by creating the appearance of neutrality. The offence itself is represented in a chain of terms that cumulatively diminish its seriousness: messing around-accident-being stupid-squashing some flowers-not breaking-just squashed. Other references to mental processes weave first person singular with first person plural perspective: 'I couldn't believe' (excerpt [8]), 'we thought I mean I really did think' (excerpt [9]), 'I think.. that really brought down to everybody' (excerpt [10]). This gives the meaning that the speaker attributes to the incident the status of shared knowledge, which increases the appearance of authenticity.

Thus we can see that the learning here does not consist of an abandonment of 'old' knowledge structures; in fact, these meaning schemes are essential to the process of creating an orderly reality, of trying to make sense of a lived experience. The meaning scheme is transformed in that it allows a more flexible interpretation of the new experience: bureaucracy, but in a good cause, i.e., caring about the community.

Conversation Analysis (CA), which developed out of eth-nomethodology, focuses on the sequential structure of conversation: turn-taking, openings, closings and adjacency pairs and repetition. McCarthy and Carter (1994) show how CA can be combined with Speech Act Theory (Austin 1962/1975) for the contrastive analysis of differences in realisations in discourse, which may reveal cultural differences. They maintain (1994: 192) that interviewing learners in the target language, recording their own perceptions of their performance and exploring their possible cultural motivations, is just as important as analysing the product of their performance of a specific task. I would suggest that this approach can usefully be extended to recording language learners' reflections on personal experiences of cross-cultural misunderstanding. These could include occasions when what they said or did was misinterpreted, or when they misinterpreted someone else's words or behaviour. Many such misunderstandings are easily recalled because they challenge the participants' concept of politeness and personal values.

The 'ritual' nature of interpersonal politeness has been developed into a theory of linguistic politeness based on the notion of 'face' (Brown and Levinson 1987) that can be used to analyse incidents of cross-cultural miscommunication. Face is claimed as the determining, universal factor in social relations, although the current definition may apply to Western societies more than it does to other cultures. Conflicting 'positive' and 'negative' face wants have to be negotiated in social interaction, and there will be cultural variations in the assessment of what is seen as face-threatening. Topics, which are taboo or touchy will differ according to cultures, and according to the social distance between speakers; some things can be discussed only between close friends or relations. Whilst it is perfectly acceptable in Britain to ask a stranger for the time, it is less usual to ask a stranger for a cigarette, unlike in Spain, for example. Brown and Levinson maintain that it is the calculation of all these variables that determines the amount of 'face work' or linguistic politeness strategies that speakers use in interaction; the more 'face-threatening' the act is estimated to be, the more redressive action will be needed to preserve face. Speakers can be direct (on-record), with or without face-saving redressive action, or indirect (off-record), in which case the hearer has to interpret speaker meaning. Since going off-record gives the hearer more options, it is usually considered more polite. Requests and orders are intrinsically face-threatening speech acts (Austin 1962/1975, Searle 1969) since they seek to impose the will of the speaker on the hearer. Giving an on-record direct order is risky: the speaker has to accept responsibility for issuing the directive and the hearer has to comply or challenge it. In general, bald, on-record directives in the form of imperatives are rarely used in conversational English, even in transactional situations such as shopping and asking the time, whereas this is not the case in languages such as French, German and Spanish. Brown and Levinson's theory, although open to the accusation of Western bias, provides a useful framework for advanced learners to examine misunderstandings across cultures.

Thomas (1983) has outlined two distinct types of cross-cultural miscommunication. The first type, pragmalinguistic failure, occurs when the pragmatic force mapped by the speaker onto a given utterance is systematically different from the force most frequently assigned to it by native speakers of the target language, or when the speech act strategies from one language are inappropriately transferred to the other. Mistakes in judging the parameters of 'face' constitute sociopragmatic failure. She maintains that this type of miscommunication is the most problematic since it stems not from differences in language forms alone, but from culture-specific belief and value systems. Although advanced language learners will have explicit knowledge of the grammatical forms involved in making requests, invitations, and other everyday functions in the second language, they may still be surprised to experience the extent to which they are affected by cross-cultural failures. Reflecting on the taken-for-granted assumptions that have directed our previous reasoning, we begin to question our own stereotypes. This type of learning is valuable because it involves a transformation of meaning schemes (Mezirow 1991). It has been argued, however, that the most significant form of intercultural learning consists of perspective transformation (Whalley 1997: 111). Perspective transformation occurs when learners become aware of the presuppositions upon which a distorted or incomplete meaning scheme is based and then transform that perspective. This type of learning relates to Byram's (1997) fifth objective: *savoir s'engager.*

Culture as system of social practices

Savoir s'engager involves critical evaluation of perspectives, practices and products of one's own and other cultures. In this section, I shall show how the bottom-up approach of discourse analysis can be used to contribute to our understanding of this aspect of intercultural learning.

Savoir s'engager may or may not lead to a transformation of one's perspectives as exemplified in the two following extracts from the data. A linguistic analysis of such data allows us to see this meaning-making process in action. In the first extract, the speaker develops a powerful critique of the Spanish domestic cleaning routine. A number of devices are used to 'abnormalise' this routine, to recategorise 'spring cleaning, being houseproud' as 'going beyond that ... a bit excessive ... obsessive' behaviour. Key devices are the overlexicalisation and repetition of items in the semantic fields of 'clean' and 'time':

Extract 7:
They really are hot on cleaning and not like just you know doing the hoovering once a week or whatever but we each had a week to clean the entire house as if you were doing the spring cleaning, not just mopping the marble floors, and doing a bit of polishing. I had to bleach the kitchen cupboards once a week, clean the entire bathroom, all the tiles you know, every week,.. excessive. They're not just houseproud it goes beyond that. ...you know we used to clean literally an afternoon a week for like four or five hours.

But then I saw that these two girls really did everything together; they went shopping together, they did the laundry together they did everything together, that's when I sort of realised it's because they want the whole.. family .. you know .. unit to be together

Grammatical devices in narrative can be used to highlight what was done (Act), who did it (Agent), when and where it was done (Scene), how it was achieved (Agency), or why it was done (Purpose) (Riessman 1993). The web of overlexicalisations and repetitions above serves to emphasise Act, Scene and Agency because these are the important dimensions of understanding in her meaning scheme. In the evaluation section (Labov 1972) of this narrative, the repetition highlights Agent and Purpose as the speaker realises the 'other's' meaning of 'cleaning'. Although the speaker understands the meaning scheme of the other culture, she resists the practices she identifies. Douglas (1966: 129) maintains that as a social animal, man is a ritual animal and we recognise ritual as an attempt to maintain a particular culture, a particular set of assumptions by which experience is controlled. The student goes on to resist these assumptions in her rejection of the role expectations of Spanish girls:

Extract 8:
I respect their culture and everything but when it comes to completely changing my personality to fit in with them I'm sorry I couldn't not be .. I was used to doing things for myself.

Before we can hope to understand foreign cultures, we have to be aware of our cultural myths and 'common sense' notions, which may affect the way we interpret others' practices. Systems of belief are more easily exposed in contrast with each other, as in extract 8. In a multicultural environment, advertisements facilitate this process. By contrasting different cultural groups' reactions to and interpretations of such 'cultural products', we can 'better link language and culture in an exploration of the boundaries created by language itself in the cultural construction of reality' (Kramsch 1993: 225). Critical discourse analysis provides us with the tools to examine this link between language, taken-for-granted assumptions and systems of beliefs within a society.

Conclusion

We have looked at culture as a form of socialisation, a communication system, shared knowledge, language-in-action and as a system of social practices. The case study of students going abroad clearly shows us that acquiring facts about a language and culture, although important, may not be enough to achieve intercultural competence. We have shown that it is essential for students to develop an open attitude, the ability to reflect upon experiences of intercultural interaction, and a capacity for critical evaluation of difference. We have demonstrated that any approach to intercultural education should be multidisciplinary, drawing on theoretical perspectives from sociolinguistics, cultural studies and anthropology.

These conclusions are valid not only in the case of students. They give good pointers for a wide range of other social groups, who are being brought together in a variety of contexts. In the contemporary world it is increasingly important for people to be able to interact effectively within and across cultures and languages. Any efforts to improve intercultural communication between these groups should develop a strategy which includes tools for learning intercultural competence.

References

Agar, M. 1980. *The Professional Stranger*. New York: Academic Press.
———. 1991. 'The Biculture in Bilingual'. *Language and Society* 20: 167–181.
Ardagh, J. 1990. *France Today*. Harmondsworth: Penguin.
Austin, J. L. 1962/1975. *How To Do Things With Words*. Oxford: Oxford University Press.
Barthes, R. 1957/1993. *Mythologies*. trans. Annette Lavers. London: Vintage.
Brown, P. and Levinson, S. 1987. *Politeness: some universals in language usage*. Cambridge: Cambridge University Press.
Bennett, J. M. 1986. 'Modes of Cross-Cultural Training: conceptualizing cross-cultural training as education'. *International Journal of Cross-Cultural Relations* 10: 117–134.
Byram, M., Morgan, C. and Colleagues. 1994. *Teaching-and-Learning-Language-and-Culture*. Clevedon: Multilingual Matters.
———. ed. 1997. *Face to Face: Learning 'language-and-culture' through visits and exchanges*. London: CILT.
Byram, M. and Zarate, G. 1997. 'Defining and Assessing Intercultural Competence.' *Language Teaching* 29: 14–18.
Coleman, J. 1996. *Studying Languages: A Survey of British and European Students*. London: CILT.
Cormeraie, S. 1997. 'Cross-Cultural Conflict Resolution: What is involved?' in *Developing Cross-Cultural Capability*, eds D. Killick and M.Parry. Leeds: Leeds Metropolitan University.
Douglas, M. 1966. *Purity and Danger: An analysis of the concepts of pollution and taboo*. London: Routledge.
Duranti, A. 1997. *Linguistic Anthropology*. Cambridge: Cambridge University Press.

Edwards, D. 1997. *Discourse and Cognition*. London: Sage.

Fairclough, N. 1992. *Discourse and Social Change*. Cambridge: Polity Press.

Garfinkel, H. 1967. *Studies in Ethnomethodology*. Englewood Cliffs: Prentice Hall.

Goffman, E. 1981. *Forms of Talk*. Oxford: Blackwell.

Hall, E. 1964. *The Hidden Dimension*. New York: Doubleday.

Höfstede, G. 1980. *Culture's Consequences*. London: Sage.

Hymes, D. ed. 1964. *Language in Culture and Society: A Reader in Linguistics and Society*. New York: Harper and Row.

Jordan, S. and Barro, A. 1995. 'The Effect of Ethnographic Training on the Year Abroad'. in *The Year Abroad: Preparation, Monitoring, Evaluation*, eds G. Parker, and A. Rouxeville. London: CILT. 76–90.

Kramsch, C. 1993. *Context and Culture in Language Teaching*. Oxford: Oxford University Press.

Labov, W. 1972. *Language in the Inner City*. Philadelphia: University of Pennsylvania Press.

Lèvi-Strauss, C. 1968. *Structural Anthropology*. London: Penguin.

McCarthy, M. and Carter, R. 1994. *Language as Discourse: Perspectives for Language Teaching*. London: Longman.

Mezirow, J. 1991. *Transformative Dimensions of Adult Learning*. San Francisco: Jossey-Bass.

Potter, J. 1996. *Representing Reality*. London: Sage.

Riessman, C. K. 1993. *Narrative Analysis*. London: Sage.

Rosch, E. 1978. 'Principles of categorization'. in *Cognition and Categorization*, eds E. Rosch and B.B. Lloyd. Hillsdale, New Jersey: Lawrence Erlbaum. 27–48.

Sapir, E. 1931/1964 . 'Conceptual Categories in Primitive Languages'. Reprinted in *Language in Culture and Society: A Reader in Linguistics and Anthropology*, ed. D. H. Hymes. New York: Harper and Row. 128.

Saville-Troike, M. 1989. *The Ethnography of Communication*. Oxford: Blackwell.

Searle, J. 1969. *Speech Acts: An Essay in the Philosophy of Language*. Cambridge: Cambridge University Press.

Silverman, D. 1997. *Qualitative Research: Theory, Method and Practice*. London: Sage.

Thomas, J.1983. 'Cross-Cultural Pragmatic Failure'. *Journal of Applied Linguistics*, vol. 4, no. 2: 89–112.

Valdes, J. M. 1986. *Culture Bound*. Cambridge: Cambridge University Press.

Whalley, T. 1997. 'Culture Learning' Face to Face: Learning language-and-culture through visits and exchanges, ed. M. Byram. London: CILT. 102–119.

Wierzbicka, A. 1992. *Semantics, Culture and Cognition*. New York: Oxford University Press.

PART V

BEYOND THE LIMITS
OF LANGUAGE

CHAPTER 9

EMOTION AND LABOUR IN CULTURAL COMPARISON

Stephen Lloyd Smith

Between looks and deeply held *belief* lies an intermediate zone – the zone of emotion management. (Hochschild 1983:104, emphasis added)

[Emotional] labour requires one to induce or to suppress feeling in order to sustain the outward countenance that produces the proper state of mind in others […] This kind of labour calls for coordination of mind and feeling, and it sometimes draws on a source of self that we honor as deep and integral to our individuality. (Hochschild 1983:7)

The very idea that social forces, rather than one's uniquely personal needs and desires, might have shaped the form of one's love seems like an *infringement* of personal liberty, an intrusion into that mysterious, private world, the irrational splendor of one's finer feelings. (Sarsby 1983:1, in Jackson 1993:201, emphasis added)

Introduction[1]

Western identity is contained in the shape of the person, 'I'. Hospitable emotions are pictured in the *heart*, associated with the *soul*, conferring the *e* in humane. 'Base', 'bellicose' hostility, bad-temper, 'bile' and hatred of a person's 'guts' show intestinal associations. Emotion is distinguished from thought (the head) and dexterity (the hands). Metaphysical map-locations indicate that emotion is more central and fundamental than thought or dexterity. Picturing manual labour as the work of *hands* at the periphery, requiring comparatively little thought or feeling (just coordination, aural-, optical- and touch-sensation) underlines the centrality of emotion.

Rule by the heart is distinguished from rule by the head. Value is central, heartfelt, passionate, but often implicit in discussion. Theory commands high status and attention. Data is pictured as the mundane material of fieldworkers, empiricists and bench-scientists, as if obtained manually by 'going into the field', getting 'hands' or sometimes 'boots' 'dirty' while 'gathering' data. These distinctions bear imperfect comparison with the high status of mental work and of manual work (typically lower). The division is manifest from Valentine cards to boardrooms, placed inconveniently on *top* of soulless, *head*-quarters buildings, from where emotion is supposed to be banished (Fineman 1993, 1996; Newton et al. 1995; Fineman and Gabriel 1996).

Westerners see this as unremarkable; but many non-Western cosmologies – as I shall call them – exhibit differences, sometimes in the absence of a word for 'I' and in a mass of terminological differences around thought, physicality and feeling.

This chapter calls for a re-examination of service in the West. Here emotions become commodities: the hospitable or hostile work done on and through the emotions by flight attendants, debt collectors, sales workers, holiday guides, undertakers and so on, which alter the mood of the customer – sacred 'hearts' brought into cosmological proximity to money.

Many emotions do not translate between languages, cultures and cosmologies and neither does service. Our purpose here is to question Western cosmology's precious treatment of emotion. We depart from Hochschild, who sees emotional labour as an intrusion on the heart by soul-stealing customers and corporations (Hochschild 1983; see also Smith S 1999a, 1999b). Instead it is suggested that skillful emotional labour might be welcomed.

Alien perspectives

Humanity as an imperial notion

Research and common sense observation are often used to provide plausible theoretical and empirical support to cherished ideals. This occurs in domestic arguments, playground disputes and public politics. Such processes enliven the study of methodology. Even mundane decisions require us to step between values, theory and evidence, or to fuse them into potent arguments.

Biological thinking that emotions offer adaptive advantages (Darwin 1859, 1872) might lend comfort to those who cherish the idea that human beings have passions in common, pictured as deeper and more fundamental than methodologies for everyday life. Humanity, divided by language, economy, polity, history and culture, but united by universal emotions, experienced, expressed and understood everywhere, through smiles and grimaces (Lazarus 1991:73).

There is a coincidental convergence between biological claims for universal emotions and metaphysical conceptions of emotions as central to one's being, constituting the universal core of humanity, in the region of the heart.

The notion that humanity is tied up with both inner emotion and biology, lends an imperial quality to Western culture because the powerful sense of identity which it gives rise to is experienced as natural, indisputable, unproblematic and universal. Capital 'I' defines psychological and metaphysical variants of the imperial model: *I* feel; *I* think; *I* run. 'I' experiences spontaneous emotions 'on the inside', again suggesting natural origins to emotion. It would follow that other 'I's in other places share similar internal emotions.

Although selfhood and emotions are supposedly universal, each 'I' is also thought of as special in a double sense: as *unique* and *precious* (a problem in mass service systems). Possession of an 'I' is presumed universal, but engenders *individuality*. Hochschild questions the apparent discreteness of subjectivity (also Bordieu 1984), pointing to socially constructed 'feeling-rules' (Hochschild 1979, 1983) which shape emotion, prompting it in various settings like weddings and funerals. Feeling rules and cosmology are surreptitious elements in infancy. There is fleeting awareness of 'I' as a construction: '*I* is *me*! *I* is *Deborah*! *Deborah* is *me*!' a child exclaimed, beaming with self-discovery, aged three. 'When I grow up where will be Daniel?' asked her brother.

The notion of 'core and periphery', introduced earlier, was reinforced by Freud's and Simmel's accounts of 'inner' and 'outer' components. The outer, *intellectual* self is supposed to monitor the more basic *innerself*, protecting it from 'external threat' and internal 'annihilation' (Simmel 1909/1950; Freud A 1936/1993; Freud S 1984; cf. Tonnies 1887/1950; Wirth

1938). The rapid acceptance of Freudian notions shows that they lend themselves to a Western sense of being, composed of universal metaphysical structures and individual differences.

The self-regarding self may seem unusual to non-Westerners seeking to understand the cult of the individual, narcissism and economic theory – which idealises perfect competition between economic entities behaving as if they were *individuals*. The 'I' which is writ large for Westerners and pervades Western theory is less salient in other cultures, some of which have no such unambiguous and direct equivalent word. Even if emotions *were* universal among those without an 'I', they would not necessarily be experienced in the same place (such as the 'heart'). Many describe thought as coming not from the head, but from external sources. Instead of 'I remember', they may speak of a distant place or event acting upon them and, instead of 'I'm angry', express the idea that there is annoyance present.

Similarity and difference

The linguist Wierzbicka (1999:19–31) criticises psychologists like Ekman (1989, 1992, 1994) for discussing emotions only in an English vocabulary. She argues that there are no universal emotions as concepts, but rather 'prototypical cognitive scenarios for feelings'. There is nothing quite like German *angst* or Polish suspicion of compliments. Iordanskaja and Paperno (1996) pinpoint 'all the information [...] on the body and emotional expression [...] necessary for the correct use of the corresponding Russian words and expressions [showing that] we live in different worlds' (Wierzbicka 1999:216–217). Wierzbicka defines emotion concepts using a relatively small set of semantic primatives, coming closest to stating that certain emotions are recognised only if they also exist in language. Language translates 'prototypical cognitive scenarios' for feelings into lexicalised emotion. She writes

> because every natural language contains it's own 'native picture of the world' [...] by relying [...] on ordinary English words we unwittingly fall prey to the 'naïve picture' that is reflected in them [...] The approach to 'emotions' adopted [...] seeks to break the dependence on any one natural language as the source of 'common sense insights' by anchoring the analysis in universal human concepts and their 'universal grammar' [...] arrived at by empirical cross-linguistic investigations carried out by several linguists [...] and based on work with typologically diverse and [...] unrelated languages [...] Most words in any language are specific to this particular language [...] and

are not universal [but] the concepts of 'good' and 'bad' [...]
'know' and 'want' [...] are universal, and can, therefore, be
used as elements of a culture-independent semantic meta-lan-
guage. (Wierzbicka 1999:34–35)

The anthropologist Lutz finds 'pleasant' and 'unpleasant',
'comfort' and 'discomfort' to be universal (Lutz 1986:278). The
distinction between prototypical scenarios and distinct emotion words compliments Levy's anthropological claim that cultures which describe emotions through vague terminology
cannot evaluate them sufficiently for them to be felt clearly.
Wierzbicka and Levy share the postmodern notion that
thought is inseparable from the impermanent languages that
convey it. Emotions need words.

Levy offers a reversible three-way model. Cultures that
describe an emotion through vague terminology are unable to
evaluate it sufficiently for it to be felt clearly. (Examples might
include 'agapic' and 'chivalrous' love, which have fallen into
disuse in the West.) Such emotions are termed 'hypocognised',
while those that are clearly described in language are 'hypercognised'. Sorrow, which is hypocognised for Tahitians, is
hypercognised in English and dissected into fine gradations of
positive and negative value (Levy 1973, 1978, 1984). Self-pity
is reprehensible, depression and melancholy forgivable; sorrow and grief are virtuous, even ennobling.

Levy and Heider, another anthropologist, do not deny that
emotion has some biological basis, but argue that language
and culture give emotions their register. Wierzbicka and others
(McRobbie 1982; Crawford et al. 1992; Duncombe and Marsden 1993) have also searched for gender differences in language and emotion, supposing that they contribute to
inequality. Heider is more optimistic: 'cultural consensus is the
result of overt use of, even discussion of, emotion words'
(1991:91), implying that innumerable conversations shift
emotion-language imperceptibly, as meanings are challenged
and new sensibilities added (cf. Lutz 1990). Heider's principle
focus is however on differences rather than change:

Angek ati (hot heart) is in the 'Happy' cluster in Minangkabau,
but its cognate pana hati is in the 'Anger' cluster in both Indonesian maps. Bangga and berbesar (both proud) are tightly tied
into the 'Happy' cluster in Minangkabau maps. But in Javanese
Indonesian they form an isolate. Suko in the Minangkabau
maps is more closely linked to 'Desire', but in Javanese Indonesian it is in the 'Happy' cluster, which is an isolate with no links

to 'Desire'. The 'Fear' cluster in Minangkabau is in the 'Worry' area, but in Javanese Indonesian it is in the adjacent 'Confusion' area. *Binguang* in Minangkabau is in the 'Indecision' area, but in the Indonesian maps it is in the adjacent 'Confusion' area. The 'Poignant' cluster in Minangkabau Indonesian is in the 'Anger' area, but in Minangkabau and Javanese Indonesian it is more closely tied to 'Sad'. (Heider 1991:93–94).

Minangkabau words for jealousy 'have much sharper, more malicious outcomes in Indonesian, with relatively little of the contemplative hurt and sadness, which are the most typical outcomes of [the] English emotions.' (1991:221). Language defines emotional consensus: grasping the meaning of a word that defines an emotion makes it accessible. Indeed bilingual Indonesians switch language to express different emotions.

However a virtuous, hypercognised Japanese emotion, *amae* (Morsbach and Tyler 1986), approximating to 'sweet childishness and lifelong dependency', cannot be learned by Westerners, probably because of the importance they attach to independence. 'In Castillian, courage (*coraje*) has a connotation of aggressiveness, which it appears to lack in English' (Crespo 1986:216), implying different sensations. Welsh *hiraeth* pictures place, culture and the past, but English *homesickness* less so.

Connections between language and emotion raise questions about what happens to emotions when languages spread or die out. Which comes first: hypercognition, evaluation or linguistic-emotional competence? What historical forces promote an emotion from hypo to hypercognition? What is acting on what? How are emotion-ideologies promoted or cast off?

In some cultures, concealment and extreme internal regulation is required: Among Chewong,

> ...the *punen* [...] rules [forbid] what they call 'speaking badly'. [They] make it unacceptable [...] to express desires which are as yet unfulfilled [or to] express pleasure at the thought of the meal to come, [to make] any emotional outburst when you injure yourself [or] to discuss emotions at all [...] To do so is thought dangerous [...] you will be attacked by an animal [...] If not [...] by an actual tiger or snake, you may still sicken and die, because the soul of the tiger can attack you too. (Wetherell 1991:72 after Howell 1981)

Anthropologists and linguists report variation in the imagery used to express emotion and within a culture there may be marked variation in emotional evaluation and expression between individuals, classes, age-groups and the sexes (Crawford et al. 1992), even cross-cultural emotional variation in drunkenness (MacAndrew and Edgerton 1970).

The 'cosmological positioning' of the subject in relation to emotion, is most untranslatable. On Ifaluk, a Micronesian atoll, governed by reciprocity, emotions are treated as statements about the relationship between the person and the event rather than as descriptions of internal states (Lutz 1986). While

> Harré [...] points out that [...] *Innuit* [...] language [...] doesn't emphasise personal identity [...] and talks about qualities or states of mind which incidentally happen to find expression in individuals. Thus to feel indignation is not 'I feel angry' but 'there is annoyance [...], [t]he Dinka of Southern Sudan [...] do not posses a concept of mind as an internal self which stores up memories. [...W]hen 'remembering' something the Dinka regard the place where the event happened as the agent which then acts upon the person 'remembering [...]. From a Western perspective autonomy, self control, uniqueness, separateness and mastery over the world seem like facts of nature [...] It is hard to treat this view as an assumption, an idea, a theory, a representation which so firmly structures the way we understand ourselves that it seems as though we must have always thought this way. (Wetherell 1991:70–71, 72)

In public societies, outbreaks of 'bad' and 'unpleasant' emotion prompt demands for 'more rites and rituals', while Western miscreants are ordered to 'get a grip of themselves'. Milton captured this idea of self-mastery in *Paradise Lost, Book 1*, writing that 'The mind is its own place, and in itself/ Can make a Heav'n of Hell; a Hell from Heav'n' (cited in Burrel 1997). Clearly, by the late-mediaeval period, Europeans placed emotion internally and had become personally responsible for happiness – an assumption foreign to many cultures. One elderly Asian grandmother regards herself as 'located in her throat, because that is where words come from'.

Westerners do experience externally located emotion in 'the atmosphere' at football matches, concerts and other person-dissolving gatherings. However, what if everyday life was person-dissolving?

Cosmologies and emotion also shift over time. Tracing 'the meaning of the word *soul* before Plato', Claus (1981) finds that it has migrated around the viscera and once had no specific bodily location but occupied the blood. Soul has meant 'life force', 'after-life soul', 'a balance between reason and desire', 'a comprehensive personal self', something 'separate to body' and eventually 'subject to therapy' in a 'fully realised psychological version' (1981:180–183). Milton's dictum and the discipline of psychology rest on this shift.

Accidie, nicknamed the 'noonday demon' in the Middle Ages, was a form of clinical depression

> [...] closely bound up with changing conceptions of religious duty. [...] Hermits who found it difficult to keep up their devotions through boredom were victims of it. But the boredom was not touched with guilt or shame. Rather, it was qualified by despair and sadness, the gloom that comes over one who has lost the warmth of God's regard. (Harré 1986:11, also 220–233)

Accidie cannot be experienced by non-believers, whose depression must take other forms, nor among believers, as Christian theology no longer pictures God as uncaring.

Function, history, structure, agency

Those who agree that emotion is socially constructed often run into problems of the 'chicken-and-egg' type: the question of 'structure and agency' and the circular reasoning found in functional explanation. In describing the 'social-construction-ist' account of emotion, Harré reminds us that:

> Aristotle proposed a cognitive account of emotion in which factual beliefs and moral judgements have a central role in the causation and individuation of emotions. On Aristotle's account, while emotions give rise to affective impulses, they are generated by a state of mind, involving cognition-based construals and evaluations of some state of affairs in the world. 'Fear' said Aristotle ([McKean (ed)]1941 edition), 'is a mental picture of some destructive evil in the future'. (Harré 1986:2)

Aristotle, Levy, Heider and Wierzbicka agree that emotions involve cognitive evaluation, here, negative evaluation of fear. In Aristotle the subject seems to be the agent making the evaluation, whereas for Levy and more arguably Wierzbicka and Heider, cultural structure comes first, because cognition is taken to depend on given language qualities which define emotional experience. The tension between the priority given to cultural 'structure' and 'agency' – the capacity to take part and make a difference – occurs throughout social science.

Sympathetic to Wittgenstein's mind/brain distinction (Wittgenstein 1953), Geertz is clear that 'the mind' in all its variation is indeed subject to 'evolution' by social activity (Geertz 1973/1993:55–83, 142–169). Different minds in similar brains. He pursues a variant of 'functionalism', arguing that all cultures have developed theoretical, religious and emotional systems that *function* to supply a methodology for navigating everyday choices. While a causal explanation for events can usually be found, emotions clarify courses of action – as do Wierzbicka's and Lutz's universals 'good', 'bad', 'know', 'want', 'pleasant' and 'unpleasant'.

A static model of a universal function does account easily for particular and evolving differences. Geertz's explanation for how 'minds' evolve, is convoluted. The keyword seems to be 'incongruity':

> [...] disruption [...] may be traced to incongruity between the cultural framework of meaning and the patterning of social interaction, [for example] an incongruity due to the persistence in an urban environment of a religious symbol system adjusted to peasant social structure. Static functionalism, of either the sociological or psychological sort, is unable to isolate this kind of incongruity because [...] it fails to realise that cultural structure and social structure are not mere reflexes of one another. [...] The driving force in social change can be clearly formulated only by a more dynamic form of functionalist theory, one which takes into account the fact that man's need to live in a world to which he can attribute some significance, whose essential import he feels he can grasp, often diverges from his concurrent need to maintain a functioning social organism. (Geertz 1973/1993:169)

Rosaldo (1997), feels that Geertz's

> cultural systems appear impervious to change [partly because] few of his works explore differences or variations in the beliefs, values, or idioms embraced by different groups within societies.[...] Probably the most important source of the interest in difference has been feminist anthropology, which has problematised the apparent unity of cultural systems by demonstrating that cultures look very different from the perspective of women than they do from that of men. (Rosaldo 1997:49)

Sewell concurs:

> Rather than conceptualising culture as a [given] text, Roseberry suggests, we should think of it as a 'material social process,' as 'production' rather than as a 'product', constantly asking how,

by whom, and for what ends it is being produced. (Sewell 1997:36, after Roseberry 1982:1020–23)

While it is defensible to use functional explanations for the handful of universal emotions, functionalism fails to deal with purposeful social change and the process of social construction of emotion. The post-war replacement of 'in-betweenies' by teenagers was an emotive revolution; indeed moodiness, rebellion and resistance was its marketing motif. If the Western mind, however, had evolved in a different way, we would be deceived by functional analysis into privileging, (say) greater emotional neutrality, stoicism, compliance, serenity, politeness, respectfulness, stiff upper-lip, anonymous courage, deference, modesty, propriety and calm with some different 'systems purpose', treated, like biological function, as given.

Emotion wars should be understood, not functionally, but in their own terms as winnable and loseable. Innovations like rock and roll sensibility, jazz 'cool', rave culture, pay and pray cable television, shock-jocks, gay-pride, shopping, evangelical sales technique, ideological arousal, new forms of comedy, horror films, total war and enduring peace, were forged by the activity of individuals, political parties, interest-groups, corporations, musicians, charismatics, comedians, drug-dealers, genders, classes, age cohorts, armies and diplomats, pursuing various interests; often beset with failure.

The Western association between emotion and the inner heart-soul

As the 'centre' of Western identity, the heart-soul calls for historical research. The soul is implicated in the notion that we each have an authentic, precious, individual, emotional, private and deep inner self located in the region of the heart and that this is at stake in emotional labour.

In a complex way, late-mediaeval 'disciplinary control' (Foucault 1977:170–177) may have given rise to modern conceptions of individuality, self-possession, preciousness, uniqueness, privacy and personal freedom. Among cultural historians, the late-medieval period is known for developing new techniques of governance and for the 'discovery of the individual'. This author wishes to stress connections between governance and individuality in the mediaeval legacy and that they underlie the incongruent evaluations we make of emotional labour today.

The church sought to measure time and establish rules governing periods of work, rest, prayer and eating, market activity and holy days for which accurate clocks and calendars and the Book of Hours were developed (Giddens 1987:140–165). Modern freedom and personal mastery is an inadvertent outcome of this mediaeval attempt to 'govern the soul' by shaping a soul which was susceptible to governance through self-consciousness, discipline and internal regulation. The soul and holy days were double-edged. They exposed individuals to efficient, centralised, yet personalised governance of each soul through church services. These developments were protective and of some advantage to individuals. The soul was seen as precious enough to deserve both pastoral protection and self-care; hence the 'guarding' of the 'inner self' by the 'outer self'.

Fine one-room, hall-houses were modernised with internal walls, cross-passages and two or three floors separating private and public activities into bedrooms, servant quarters, outhouses, kitchens and living rooms (Smith, Peter 1975). Thus rules governing all kinds of public and private activity through clocks and calendars and the division of the self into layers were complimented by architectural conventions that provided greater privacy. The industrial revolution separated work from home, underscoring the privacy of home, subjecting work to centralised factory surveillance.

This division of the self into private, sacred, inaccessible, inner, soulful parts and public, accessible, outer and secular elements probably established the 'core-and-periphery' or 'deep and surface' levels that Westerners find in themselves today.

Cultural cosmologies, then, are not fixed. Levy's circle of interchangeable variables, beginning or ending in hyper or hypocognition, are not the permanent features they appear when viewed through functional analysis at a distance from the Society Islands or when looking back at mediaeval Europe. A negative evaluation of anger or violence, a positive evaluation of gentleness (and vice versa) or the shaping of the self, are the temporary, deliberate or inadvertent features of transient 'civilising processes' (Elias 1978). Cosmologies have histories.

Western emotional labour from an alien perspective

Incongruity

Having described other cultures and past times, we can appreciate the particular qualities of Western cosmology and how it intervenes in the evaluation of emotional, mental and manual labour. Take the standpoint of an alien and infer our cultural rules around labour. The alien sees that, though vivid and compelling, Western cosmology creates anomalies for owners, managers and emotional laborers in establishing workable divisions between what is for sale and what is not; eliciting emotional labour without exhaustion; giving appropriate depth to the acting; avoiding intrusion on customers' sense of privacy and avoiding embarrassment. The rules are inferred from Western identity comprising 'I' (inner and outer), thinking heads, emotive hearts and transforming hands.

Rule 1: Mental labour is excellent because 'I' is in control and because the head is pictured above hands. Mental skills are best.

Rule 2: Unskilled manual labour, is undesirable because the worker becomes a 'hand', or machine 'appendage' (Braverman 1974; Cooley 1987). Heidegger (1926/ 1962) defines authenticity partly in the avoidance of being turned into the tool of others.

Rule 3: Skilled manual labour is good – hands under the control of 'I'. The 'responsible autonomy' of the craft worker preserves against alienation and 'direct control' by capital (Friedman 1977).

Rule 4: Because emotional labour 'draws on a source of self which is deep and integral to our individuality' (Hochschild 1983: 7), film stars, singers and nurses enjoy high public esteem.

However, an alien might find it odd that the emotional labour of the cheery sales worker, holiday rep, receptionist, repossession agent, credit controller, doorstep canvasser or prostitute is not always given the highest ranking among all forms of labour. There must be another rule. By picturing emotional labour as the inner work of the heart an anomaly is created. On the one hand emotional labour is riveting and positive when performed by skillful stage actors – the willful, courageous exposure of self – and negative if unskilled, mechanical, mannered and scripted, showing obvious manipulation of 'I' by the employer. This is because 'skill is good' and 'tool-likeness is bad'. Standardised, deskilled surface hospitality, 'upselling', 'suggestive selling' and 'speed-up' (which concerns Hochschild) is distasteful. *'With* fries? ...Is that a *large*? Have a nice day.'

But for Hochschild commodifying inner feelings – the product of the heart – is worse than commodifying the manual labour of factory hands. This concern is captured in the title of

The Managed Heart; the commercialisation of human feeling (1983): when the heart is being called on to labour, the genius of capitalism for selling everything has trespassed too far into the 'core' of humanity. She is more disturbed when flight attendants' inner, 'heart-felt' feelings of hospitality are for sale through 'deep-acting' than where manual labour is applied to wallpaper production. Deep-acting flight attendants draw on their 'repertoire of emotion memories' at work and report difficulty 'turning off' at the end of a shift, smiling inappropriately in the street during private, non-contracted hours. For Hochschild service corporations demand too much and deep-acting labourers deliver too much.

Factory workers, whose hearts are not put into the product, are not engaged by work because it demands less of them: they engage their bodies and, to a lesser extent, their minds, but not their hearts. By disassociation, the unskilled factory worker's precious heart is untouched by work, which is then not soul-destroying. The consequence of Hochschild's argument is that surface-acting emotional labourers, with smiles 'just painted on' and disassociated from inner, heart-felt feelings, are better protected than deep-acting co-workers. Hence:

Rule 5:   Refuse to work heart and soul.

Reminiscent of the 'unmerciful matter-of-factness' and 'blasé attitude' in Simmel's urbanites (Simmel 1909/1950), indifference and guile become *good* things, while authenticity places guileless individuals at risk of manipulation, exposure and ridicule by those eager to trespass on simple souls.

> As mobility became a fact of urban life, so did guile and people's understanding that it was a tool. [...] Sincerity for its part came to be seen as an inhibition of the capacity to act before a multiplicity of audiences or as an absence of the psychic detachment necessary to acting. The sincere 'honest soul' came to denote a 'simple person, unsophisticated and a bit on the dumb side' [...] It was considered dumb because the art of surface-acting was increasingly understood as a useful tool. When mobility became a fact of urban life, so did the art of guile, and [...] interest in sincerity as a virtue disappeared. (Hochschild 1983:191)

Deep-acted emotional labour is pictured as more invasive than surface-acting, manual and presumably mental labour and there is a health and safety risk to the 'heart' in contriving authenticity among strangers. However Hochschild writes:

As enlightened management realises, a separation of display
and feeling is hard to keep up over long periods [...] Maintaining a difference between feeling and feigning over long periods
leads to strain. We try to reduce that strain by pulling the two
closer together either by changing the way we feel or changing
what we feign. When display is required by the job, it is usually
feeling that has to change; and when conditions estrange us
from our face, they sometimes estrange us from feeling as well.
(Hochschild 1983:90)

Hence:

Rule 6:   Deep acting is good, enabling an improved degree-
          of-fit between countenance and feeling.

The alien sees that Hochschild's evaluation of emotional
labour is incongruous. Under rules 4 and 5, deep-acting is
both riveting and unfortunate and surface-acting advisable,
but also tool-like, inauthentic and undesirable. Under rules 5
and 6, the guileful managers of emotional labourers place
them in the invidious position of having to resort to deep-acting, to access emotion and avoid strain. Rules about correct
display and the possession of a feeling-heart-soul give managers leverage because in combination they regulate emotional labourers' inner/outer congruence and composure.
There is semblance between the governance of emotional
labour and the governance of precious mediaeval souls. In a
complex way, the rules pull emotional labourers between
composure through concealment ('urbanite' superficiality)
and composure through exposure (deep-acting).

Note the location of skill, not just in heads, hearts and hands,
but in public and private settings and spaces: skilful craft workers are admired during factory 'open' days and at 'craft-centres'.
Here commodification of labour is overlooked, especially in
cases of self-employment. Sex workers are objected to even if
private and self-employed, although a group of British nurses
who volunteer sexual services to the disabled are regarded more
positively. The Samaritans are revered but not paid.

Lawyers invite suspicion by performing commodified emotional labour on juries in open court, while managing their
belief in the guilt or innocence of defendants. Street beggars –
whose pleas for money constitute the most immediate commercialisation of feeling[2] – attract momentary sympathy.
Among public conviction workers, politicians are reviled and
revered about equally, by members of their own party.

In Europe, the emotional skills of nurses are rewarded more highly in the pay of private hospitals than in public health services, but nurses with no greater skills and less time to practice them, but working in public services, are esteemed. Alternative therapy and complimentary medicine, containing much emotional labour, while invariably commodified and practiced openly at 'alternative fairs' and in private, is blessed with considerable confidence and suspension of disbelief. Histrionic confessional television shows and pray-and-pay cable evangelists – in publicly accessible but privately owned settings – fascinate and repel.

Objections to making money in public are overlooked if the activity is mental: there are no objections to the commodification of the architect's imagination: fine buildings in public places. Cosmological incongruities make it difficult to devise policies that promote the interests of emotional labourers. These contribute to the high pay of 'gifted' private sector architects and to the high praise and low pay of gifted public carers.

Why is the principle that skill-is-good often violated in evaluating skilled emotional labour? These cases suggest that emotional labour entails proper and improper access to

- the labourer's inner, sacred, private self and the other party's inner self,
- ownership of the space for the encounter,
- access to this space and
- the proper and improper 'cosmological positioning' established between feelings and workers, managers, customers, clients, guests, patients, passers-by and public or private capital. Hence the hospitality of the public sector nurse or the courageous battlefield projection of hostility by the volunteer soldier are praised, while the hospitality of the private sector nurse, flight attendant or prostitute, or the courage of the mercenary are questionable and particularly questionable if genuine.

Emotion: special stuff from a special place?

There is little research on emotional labour outside care (James 1986, 1989; Hochschild 1989, 1995, 1997; Walter 1990; Smith, Pam 1992; but see Morris et al. 1996). Service management texts make no reference to it. Among innumerable work studies, many cover emotions at work, not in terms of labour but in order to identify high and low 'motivation', 'morale' or 'stress', often with a view to extracting more manual or mental labour.

This silence suggests the 'enchantment of sociology' (Flannegan 1996) and adherence to the map which places the passions near the heart, denoting emotion as sacred, magical, meta-physical, spiritual, non-rational, splendid, not knowable, inner and other worldly; beyond reasoned analysis or measurement; the natural art of women. The mass of research on mental and manual 'heads' and 'hands' reveals a preference to look away from, in silent recognition of, precious hearts. This could explain why so few have looked at emotional labour and why Hochschild is troubled by its commodification. This omission does not assist emotional labourers or their managers.

Hume treated reason and passion as inseparable. The American philosopher Solomon (1993) finds passion reason-able. Feelings turn out to have been correct and reasoning mistaken; going in the right direction requires and supplies confidence; nonsense is accompanied by self-doubt, derision and worrying-through. Reason and passion are proximate. The agreement between romantics and rationalists that emo-tions are spontaneous, irresistible, uncontrollable, irrational and natural is spurious, because thoughts are as hard not to think as emotions are hard not to feel; thoughts and emotion are instantaneous. They are equally suggestible. Emotions are prompted at funerals, during aircraft flights, just as lectures, reading and conversation prompt thoughts. Thought and feel-ing are all in the mind but pictured separately.

Evaluating passionate labour as favourably as mental and manual labour means abandoning the head, heart and hands distinction and asking new questions.

Conclusions

Language differences indicate emotional differences. Groups of emotions distinguished by many words in some languages, which shift over time, conveying variations in experience, have little or no equivalence in other languages. It is wrong to assume that we can read and share 'emotions' across lan-guage divides any better than we can translate their proxi-mate 'thoughts'.

Even convergent claims for the universality or otherwise of emotion must be treated with caution. Linguists welcome anthropological research because the discovery of difference is evidence that emotion is socially, not biologically constructed. But while linguists and anthropologists have joined the 'relativist' attack on the idea of scientific evidence in social science – a criticism directed at positivism – they treat data about cultural and language differences as significant – which is a positivist conception. Constructionists hint at functional explanation (Harré 1986:13) as does Rose (1990) who pictures individual absorption in freedom as a control tool. This is having it all ways: embracing emotional differences as scientific fact *and* anti-rational, romantic relativism; teleological structural-functional explanation *and* sensitivity to shifting, thinking, feeling agents of meaningful change. We need a better, historical method, for explaining difference.

Biologists, theologians and economists – unlikely allies – are captivated by axiomatic explanations for universal similarities and psychologists show more interest in universal similarities than particular differences. That similar and different arrangements can be explained by the function they serve is a common thread, yet this method is questionable when applied to non-biological systems.

Notwithstanding these sources of confusion, we doubt universalistic Western cosmologies describing how thought and emotion arise and see the 'I' and the heart-soul as a mixed blessing for emotional labourers. Hochschild's concern for hearts is partly misplaced. Emotional labourers are better-off than manual workers because they are often sustained through immediate, direct, positive, hospitable face-to-face feedback from the consumer. Working 'heart and soul' is a damn good thing.

The reader may be unhappy at these arguments, or share linguists' and anthropologists' celebration of differences and wonder at the extensive implications. In supplying and receiving service within and across cultures, we should question whether we understand what is going on and above all, expand our understanding of why our grasp of what seems obvious has not been questioned more thoroughly. The abandonment of cosmology might enable a more sophisticated, comprehending and aversion-free handling of emotional labour.

Notes

1. The author dedicates this chapter to the memory of Gerralt Jones, an inspirational teacher, who might have disagreed, but who encouraged him to explore.
2. I thank Scott Dixon for pointing this out.

References

Bordieu, P. 1984. *Distinction: a social critique of the judgement of taste.* London: Routledge.

Braverman, H. 1974. *Labour and Monopoly Capital; the degradation of work in the twentieth century.* New York: Monthly Review Press.

Burrell, G. 1997. *Pandemonium,* London: Sage.

Claus, D. B. 1981. *Towards the Soul; An Inquiry into the Meaning of Soul Before Plato,* New Haven: Yale University Press.

Cooley, M. 1987. *Architect or Bee?* London: Hogarth Press.

Crawford, J., Kippox, S., Onyx, J., Gault, U. and Benton, P. 1992. *Emotion and Gender; Constructing Meaning from Memory.* London: Sage.

Crespo, E. 1986. 'A Regional Variation: Emotions in Spain'. in *The Social Construction of Emotions,* ed. R. Harré. Oxford: Blackwell.

Darwin, C. 1859. *The Origin of Species,* London: Murray.

———. 1872/ 1965. *The Expression of Emotion in Man and Animals.* Chicago: University of Chicago.

Duncombe, J. and Marsden, D. 1993. 'Love and Intimacy: The Gender Division of Emotion and 'Emotion Work'; A Neglected Aspect of Sociological Discussion of Heterosexual Relationships'. *Sociology* 27, 2: 221–241.

Ekman, P. 1989. 'The argument and the evidence about universals in facial expression of emotion', in *Handbook of social Psychophysiology,* eds H. Wagner and A. Manstead. New York: Wiley. 143–163.

———. 1992. 'An argument for basic emotions'. *Cognition and Emotion* 6, 3/4. 169–200.

———. 1994. 'All emotions are basic', in *The Nature of Emotion: Fundamental questions,* eds P. Ekman and R.J. Davidson. Oxford: University Press. 15–19.

Elias, N. 1978. *The Civilising Process.* Cambridge: Polity Press.

Fineman, S. ed. 1993. *Emotions in Organisation.* London: Sage.

———. 1996. 'Emotion and Organising', in *Handbook of Organization Studies,* eds in S. Clegg, C. Hardy, and W. Nord. London: Sage.

Fineman, S. and Gabriel, Y. 1996. *Experiencing Organisations.* London: Sage.

Flannagen, K. 1996. *The Enchantment of Sociology; a study of theology and culture.* Basingstoke: Macmillan.

Foucault, M. 1977. *Discipline and Punish.* London: Allen Lane.

Friedman, A. L. 1977. *Industry and Labour,* London: Macmillan.

Freud, A. 1936/1993. *The Ego and the Mechanism of Defence.* London: Karnac Books/Inst, Psychoanalysis.

Freud, S. 1984. *On Metaphysics: the Theory of Psychoanalysis.* London: Harmondsworth.

Geertz, C. Q. 1973/1993. *The Interpretation of Culture.* London: Fontana.

Giddens, 1987. A. *Social Theory and Modern Society.* Cambridge: Polity/ Blackwell.

Harré, R. 1986. *The Social Construction of Emotions*. Oxford: Blackwell.

Heidegger, M. 1926/1962. *Being and Time*. London: SCM Press.

Heider, K. G. 1991. *Landscapes of Emotion; Mapping Three Cultures of Emotion in Indonesia*. Cambridge: Cambridge University Press.

Hochschild, A. R. 1979. 'Emotion Work, Feeling Rules and Social Structure'. *American Journal of Sociology* 85: 551–575.

———. 1983. *The Managed Heart; The Commercialisation of Human Feeling*. California: University of California Press.

———. 1989. *Second Shift; Working Parents and the Revolution at Home*. New York: Penguin.

———. 1995. 'The Culture of Politics: Traditional, Post-Modern, Cold-Modern, and Warm-modern Ideals of Care'. *Social Politics* Fall: 331–346.

———. 1997. *The Time Bind; when Work becomes Home and Home becomes Work*. New York: Metropolitan Books.

Howell, S. 1981. 'Rules not Word', in *Indigenous Psychologies*, eds P. Heelas and A. Lock. London: Academic Press. 133–143.

Iordanskaja, L. and Paperno, S. 1996. *The Russian-English Collocational Dictionary of the Human Body*. Columbus Ohio: Slavica.

Jackson, S. 1993. 'Even Sociologists Fall in Love: An Exploration in the Sociology of Emotions'. *Sociology* 27, 2: 201–220.

James, N. 1986. *Care and Work in Nursing the Dying*. Doctoral Thesis. Aberdeen: University of Aberdeen.

———. 1989. 'Emotional labour, skills and work in the social regulation of feeling'. *Sociological Review*, 37, 1: 15–42.

Lazarus, R. 1991. *Emotion and Adaptation*. Oxford: Oxford University Press.

Levy, R. I. 1973. *Tahatians: Mind and Experience in the Society Islands*. Chicago: Chicago University Press.

———. 1978. 'Tahatian Gentleness and Redundant Controls', in *Learning Non-aggression*, ed. A. Montague. Oxford: Oxford University Press.

———. 1984. 'Emotion, Knowing and Culture', in *Culture Theory: Essays on Mind, Self and Emotion*, eds R. A. Shweder and R. A. LeVine. Cambridge: Cambridge University Press. 214–237.

Lutz, C. A. 1986. 'The Domain of Emotion Words on Ifaluk', in *The Social Construction of Emotions*, ed. R. Harré. Oxford: Blackwell. 267–268.

———. 1990. *Language and the Politics of Emotion*. Cambridge: Cambridge University Press.

MacAndrew, C. and Edgerton, R. B. 1970. *Drunken Comportment: a social explanation*. London: Nelson.

Marglin, F. A. 1990. 'Refining the Body; Transformative Emotion in Ritual Dance', in *Divine Passions: the Social Construction of Emotion in India*, ed. O. M. Lynch. Berkeley: University of California Press.

McKean, R., ed. 1941. *The Basic Works of Aristotle*. New York: Random House.

McRobbie, A. 1982. 'Jackie: an ideology of adolescent femininity', in *Popular Culture Past and Present*, ed. B. Waites. London: Croom Helm.

Morris J. A.and Feldman, D.C. 1996. 'The Dimensions, Antecedents and Consequences of Emotional Labour'. *The Academy of Management Review* 21, 4: 986–1010.

Morsbach, H. and Tyler, W. J. 1986. 'A Japanese Emotion: Amae', in *The Social Construction of Emotions*, ed. R. Harré. Oxford: Blackwell.

Newton, T., Fineman, S. and Handy, J. 1995. *Managing Stress: Emotion and Power at Work*. London: Sage.

Rosaldo, R. I., Jr. 1997. 'A Note on Geertz as a Cultural Essayist'. *Representations*, 59: 30–34.

Rose, N. 1990. *Governing the Soul; The shaping of the private self*. London: Routledge.

Roseberry, W. 1982. 'Balinese Cockfights and the Seduction of Anthropology'. *Social Research* 49, 4: 1013–1028.

Sarsby, J. 1983. *Romantic Love and Society*. Harmondsworth: Penguin.

Sewell, W. H., Jr. 1997. 'Geertz, Cultural Systems, and History: From Synchrony to Transformation'. *Social Research*, 49, 4: 35–55.

Simmel, G. 1909/1950 . 'The Metropolis and Mental Life', in *The Sociology of Georg Simmel*, ed. K. Wolf. New York: Free Press. 409–424.

Smith, Pam. 1992. *The Emotional Labour of Nursing*. Basingstoke: Macmillan.

Smith, Peter. 1975. *Houses of the Welsh Countryside*. London: HMSO.

Smith, S. L. 1999a. 'Arlie Hochschild: Soft-Spoken Conservationist of the Emotions'. *Soundings* 11, Spring: 120–7.

———. 1999b. 'Theology of Emotion'. *Soundings* 11, Spring: 152–8.

Solomon, R. C. 1993. *The Passions*. Indianapolis/Cambridge: Hackett.

Tonnies, F. 1887/1950. *Community and Association*. London: Routledge.

Walter, T. 1990. *What Makes a Good Funeral?* London: Hodder.

Wetherell, M. 1991. *Identities and Interaction*, DIO2, Block 5. Milton Keynes: Open University.

Wierzbicka, A. 1999. *Emotions across Languages and Cultures; Diversity and Universals*. Cambridge: Cambridge University Press.

Wirth, L. 1938. 'Urbanism as a Way of Life'. *American Journal of Sociology*, 44, 1, 1–24.

Wittgenstein, L. 1953. *Philosophical Investigations*. New York: Prentice Hall.

CHAPTER 10

LANGUAGE ABOUT GOD: MEETING THE OTHER

Ben Wiebe

Introduction

Language about the divine has its own importance, that is, the communication about the significance of the divine for its own sake.[1] However, it also has importance for communication between people and communities. In reality, they are not separated. If understanding others is to understand what is formative and vital to them, then understanding them in terms of their religion is essential. With all their differences, people at the same time share common concerns in their different religions, especially as we speak of the great world religions. There are inevitable differences: different ways of understanding the divine, different views of life, different customs and different cultures. Nevertheless, we live more and more in one world.

One possible outcome is that this will mean further domination of some by others and increasing conflict. If we seek another way, what is the alternative but conversation in which we take account of one another? The question is whether within the religions themselves there are circumstances and concerns similar enough to make conversation possible. Authentic conversation calls for recognising what we share in common, and at the same time, being clear about the differences. To presume 'we are all the same' without taking account of difference can only keep us from meeting the other. This continues in hidden form the pattern of exclusion or domination over the other.

The first concern therefore is the use of language about God. This is a question not only of the use and the limits of language, but about how language relates to the divine. This study will proceed by reference to Christian faith and Hinduism. Each in its own way gives a central place to the divine, yet within a very different framework. They therefore clearly show the way language is used to express the divine within two quite different worldviews. We will then examine the use of language as a sign of the way people think of God and human relationships. In light of this, we will consider the relation of mystery and metaphor in speaking of God, taking account of similarity and difference.

The use of language about God

This is first a question of how language relates to reality. According to one view, language, rooted and shaped in social context, is no more than a creature of culture. On the one hand, the question of God is clearly not limited to one or another culture. On the other hand, taking into account differences in language and culture, we face the wider challenge of the many ways of speaking about the divine, about God. God is not to be counted as one among the many 'objects' in the world. This itself poses the question of how language relates to God. Further, is it possible at all to convey enduring meaning through language?[2] This is not merely about whether language develops or words are conventional, but whether language is capable of carrying enduring meaning over time from the past into the present.

The place of language is therefore a matter of primary importance. In particular, if language expresses and simply reflects experience, how is one to know whether one's religious experience is experience of the divine? That is, how can we ever know that religion is anything more than our aspirations or desires? By intention, the doctrine of creation is about what God did at the beginning and about his sustaining of all things in the present. If this cannot be meaningfully affirmed in some straightforward way, then what point does the doctrine of creation have apart from expressing the inner state of a person? How can language itself, on this understanding, serve as actual communication between people? Can the doc-trine be of more than passing interest to anyone else? In accord with the postmodern emphasis, understandings of the divine are embedded in a larger framework that incorporates particular ways of reasoning and making sense of the divine.

Language and worldview

We understand within 'a context'. To speak the same language as the other is an important step into the world of the other. That is, to learn a language in the fullest sense is to learn a worldview. We can talk at length about something or other and make no headway in understanding each other. Until our 'worlds' con-nect, we literally do not know where the other person is coming from. Beyond the conversation partners there must also be something of a shared horizon to enable meaningful communi-cation. Coming from a shared background, as part of a more comprehensive framework for thought and action, people may expect to hear one another with understanding,[3] whereas when two people from quite different backgrounds meet, communica-tion may be difficult. Each of them speaks from his own frame-work, and interprets the other from his own framework.

The presuppositions within the different frameworks, devel-oped over long periods, are deeply rooted and influential, whether on the conscious or unconscious level. Authentic encounter and understanding between people can only begin as they deal with their deeper difference of framework. It is therefore important to attend first to the larger issues – our place in the world, our relation to God and to others – in order to arrive at some idea of what the possible options are. Until we do this, communication will remain largely a matter of projection without common context: we cannot expect to understand or enable another to understand concretely our meaning about the divine and much else until we deal with these presuppositional matters.

The fact is that as humans, we make choices and take actions based on a sense of our place in the world and our understanding of God and others. For those who discount God, something else fills in as ultimate. In the West, this for some has been materialism; that is all reality from origins to ends has been reduced to matter. It is therefore very much a ques-tion of how this sense is formed and informed. From a prelim-inary standpoint, a person's worldview can be defined as all he knows and cares about. However upon further thought, reflec-tion, or new insight that person's worldview can change or be enlarged. A person making choices and taking actions does so within a certain understanding of existence and of the world. In the words of Alasdair MacIntyre, human conversation and actions are 'enacted narratives' (MacIntyre 1984: 211).

Therefore, a key feature of any worldview is story, the account in which the worldview finds expression. As the framework for what a person knows and cares about, worldviews reflected in stories (sometimes embodied in literature) are expressed through intentional actions. In turn, worldviews through story address the basic questions of human existence: where are we, who are we, what is wrong, what is the solution (Middleton and Walsh 1995: 19)? There are in all cultures deeply rooted beliefs as part of the worldview that can be called on in answering these questions. For most, these deeply held beliefs are related to some form of the divine.

God in the Christian and the Hindu worldview

To begin with, then, what is the 'story' Christians or Hindus tell that reveals the meaning of the divine? This is to take up the central feature within the worldviews considered here. As a prelude, we should recall that before and beyond the fragmentation of modernity, the Christian religion cultivated an understanding of existence rooted in the order of being as a whole. The immanent God upholds this order in being: 'for in him we live and move and have our being'. God as the transcendent One can be truly immanent to particular events and persons within the created order. The One does not swallow up the many, but rather makes room for the other to be. The vision is one of the full dignity and partnership of women and men, a hope-directed reality coming to be in Christ (cf. Galatians 3: 26–29).

In contrast to the position of sheer immanence, God's freedom in relation to creation is precisely what makes possible his presence to it, and is itself the source of freedom of all particular things. This is an 'integrated' understanding of reality not determined by 'hierarchy or dualism'. Further, God is not exhausted by being the origin of the world or of its ever repeating processes and events. As transcendent, God keeps the future open and is the ground of hope that in God's faithfulness creation is on the way toward healing and peace (cf. Romans 8: 18–27).

This is against the grain of much recent thinking in the West. Out of the Enlightenment, there was a move toward pantheism in understanding God and world. It coheres with the view of reality as a closed continuum of cause and effect. This rules out particular divine action, whether in the making of a covenant through Moses or the raising of Jesus from the dead. Within the inner contradictions of modernity, it is far from simple to elucidate a doctrine of God and creation. On the basis of classical theism we can – indeed, must – affirm that all creatures enjoy the sustaining presence of God. According to biblical tradition, God out of his own purpose summons the whole created order into being by the power of his word. Scripture thereby affirms transcendence of the One (God) and the contingency of the many (creation). This is in contrast to both the mother-matter-matrix view of static immanence and the spiritual-beyond-the-cosmos view of a remote transcendence.

The basic question is how we are to think of God. It matters whether we think of God as an aloof monarch or as a generous caring parent who is responsive and open, who as a personal being (rather than a metaphysical principle) experiences the world, who relates to and interacts out of love with humans. The creation accounts dramatise the sovereignty of God. God alone is 'the Lord of all the earth' (Psalms 97: 6). To recognise God as sovereign is to affirm his freedom in relation to the world as in Genesis 1. The 'openness' of God invites attention at the same time to the mode of God's presence to the world. It includes both 'distinction and presence, freedom and embrace' (Scott 1994: 97).

Much Christian reflection has been in terms of God's mastery and control over creation. This has been to the neglect of God as triune, creating a world with openness and with freedom so that loving relationships can flourish. God is one who delights in his world and brings into being creatures with the independence and the freedom for significant action. So humans are able not only to act in accord with, but even against God (i.e., the meaning of sin). This gives 'scope' to sovereignty. This is to speak not simply about the power of God, but about the way God uses power determined by love, making room for and waiting upon humans.

Hinduism, in representing the divine, represents first great diversity along with elements of unity. There are various understandings of the divine. More recent study makes clear that Hinduism was and is a culture with distinct forms of religion within itself. Certain conceptions or ways of thinking of ultimate being may hold across main forms of religion, though various gods may be worshipped as the 'highest' god. Within an understanding of many gods, there is recognition of the one or 'highest' god. This is a power that works behind all and out of which the whole universe and the gods themselves emerged (Hiriyanna 1995: 116, 117).

A basic understanding of the divine refers to *Brahman* as *sat-cit-ananda* ('being-consciousness-bliss'). This is not to compare *Brahman* with other beings, but to recognise *Brahman* as an entity existing in its own right. This entity is indeed other than the known and cannot be defined (Arapura 1986: 13, 29), so that even to discuss the being of this entity calls for care: if being is identified with phenomena of this world, then *Brahman* may be defined as non-being. Rather, *Brahman* is 'alone being' and that without which there is no being ('being alone ... was this in the beginning, one without a second' (Sankararya 1942: 6.2)).[4] Relation to *Brahman* reveals the possibility of enduring being.

How then are we to think of the divine in relation to worldly reality? This world is passing and transitory, and according to one main school of Hindu thought, 'illusion'.[5] It comes into existence; true perception reveals that it exists in relation to true being present in *Brahman*. There is another form of Hindu thought that represents thoroughgoing dualism: worldly reality (*pradhana*) is co-eternal with the other ultimate reality of Spirit. In some ways, the whole universe actually emerges from *Brahman* and therefore participates in the character of reality. There is an endless cycle of 'creation' and of dissolution, a complex of returning to and emerging from *Brahman*. We might speak of *Brahman* as Cosmic being; it is the universe and the universe is its form.

Therefore, it is not proper to think of this being as a deity who purposes and creates the world. It creates and destroys in accord with its own nature. At the same time, there is an emphasis on the changeless reality beyond activity and beyond substance. This reality is more than the world or its creator and is the source of both (Danielou 1964: 44,46). Thus *Brahman* is understood as the eternal principle realised in the world as a whole and as the essence of the human self. There is no point in proving the reality of the world (we live and assume it). The task is to explain the way the world is as part of the search for meaning and liberation. The world itself cannot offer knowledge; it can only offer analogies in distinction between fact and non-fact. True knowledge depends on revelation, which can be aided by analogies from the phenomenal world (Arapura 1986: 27). Therefore, knowledge even about worldly realities is only possible as part of knowledge about *Brahman*.

The intent is not denial of the world. The ultimate 'non-being' of the world is apparent by definition in comparison to

Brahman. The connection between the divine and the human is consciousness. In this sense, there is an equation of the human soul with the divine. In humans, consciousness is oriented to the transcendent and unchanging entity, because this is the essence of the self (*atman*), in 'the struggle to free itself from the bondage of phenomena' (Arapura 1986: 116).

In the world, observation of changing forms cannot provide true knowledge; this is possible only in perception of the changeless and permanent that gives shape to these forms. This knowledge can be achieved by humans, but only in accord with (*Vedanta*) revelation. The achievement depends on union with the absolute wherein the knower and the known become one. Solution is related to plight; humans recognise themselves as essentially alien in this phenomenal world. Their consciousness in kinship with the divine is the bridge to oneness with ultimate reality. Accordingly, language itself is rooted in this consciousness and finally in *Brahman.* Human reasoning is therefore always dependent on the divinely given word (Prakash and Vidyalankar 1977: 1.164).[6] Language and consciousness belong together.

It is apparent, to note here briefly the account of the divine in Christian faith and Hinduism, that there are important connections: the recognition of an ultimate self-existing reality that is the source of all things. There is also some common understanding on the nature of this ultimate reality as the centre of truth and light. That right relationship to this reality brings wholeness or peace. However, as soon as we think about how the relationship is constituted and what the substance or meaning of peace is, there is difference. From the first there is deep divergence: God as personal being and the creator of all things in Christian faith, and the divine as 'metaphysical principle' in Hinduism behind all and somehow immanent in all things. Now, this divine reality takes on 'personal character' in various forms depending on the particular god or gods that people may worship. Therefore, language about the divine reflects both important connections and deep differences. Language about the divine functions in each case within a quite different worldview as a whole.

Language, mystery, and metaphor

How does language relate to the transcendent mystery of God? Some ways of referring to God are clearly more adequate, more in accord with the divine reality, than others. This provides one test for the use of language within a particular religion and also in the dialogue between religions.

Language and the real

We recognise that language is rooted and shaped in social context. 'The only true form of theological discourse will be one that recognises the determined nature of all discourse' (Scott 1994: 80, 87). On the one hand, this is to recognise that language is subject to potential distortion or ideology. On the other hand, this is to recognise that the world has its own form and character; it is structured independently of our conception of it. That structure can impress itself upon us and become part of the content of thought. Since there is no direct correspondence between word and world, however, this relation is necessarily elusive. Words do not function like a mirror in relation to things in the world. How do we come to be in tune with the real? How do we know and affirm the real? Only in answer to this question does it become possible to give account of the way words 'fit' the world. Animals 'see' and 'sense' the objects out there in the world. In that respect they live in the 'real world'. However, they do not wonder about or affirm the real in judgement. Accordingly, they do not live in the world as 'real'; they merely adapt to their surroundings. Insight into what is true is not a simple passive registering, but involves converting wonder into a focused question, finding a promising answer, determining how good the answer is. What is 'objective' is not simply the registering of 'bodies' out there, but that for which there is sufficient evidence (Meyer 1994: 67).

A naïve realism may issue in two sorts of opposite conclusions. One is to suppose a complete or exact fit between language and world, for knowing is simply a matter of registering sense data. A second, based on the realisation that there is no direct relation between word and world, is to interpret words as a merely human imposition. Knowledge is humanly created: the reality remains essentially unknowable and unknown. The first form of naïve realism ends in presumption; the reaction to it ends in resignation. So in speaking of God, there is the presumption that human language may directly comprehend God, or there is the resignation that human words or images speak of God, who in actuality remains wholly unknown.

Language and metaphor

Central to the whole is the issue of language and the use of metaphor. Language is the primary mediator of meaning for humans, and so is constitutive of experience and knowledge. This is to recognise that all understanding is embedded in a particular language that uses concepts and symbols that have been developed in particular communities.[7] Still the question remains: does language relate to something beyond itself or not? The claim that all understandings are culturally and historically embedded does not entail the claim that none of them make contact with reality (Newbigin 1995: 74).

At the same time, since there is no direct connection between words and world, our words cannot simply be equated with God; literalism will not do. There is a general human sense of ultimate reality as the source of 'created' things. In the Christian context, there is the record of scripture as testimony to the history of God with men and women. It is in this way the awareness of God emerges. God is at once close, but not simply included as one of the 'objects' or 'beings' within creation. Creaturely being is derived. While creatures 'have' existence, God 'is' existence. This is part of an understanding of the 'transcendence' of God. Certain implications for language about God follow from this.

If language about the world is indirect, this is certainly so of language about God. Metaphor, by its nature indirect, is in some ways the most appropriate way to speak of God. At the same time, there is a long tradition that certain forms of speaking are superior to others. In particular, there is the view that meaning and truth can only be expressed by concepts or abstract logical statements.[8] In this vein, the metaphor or symbol has no value of its own in speaking of God.[9]

Now, it has been noted that theology is not alone in its dependence on analogy or metaphor to express the substance of its reflections. Metaphor is a way to gain and express new understandings of the world. Science as well speaks of one entity in terms of another to make clear what is unclear or unknown; metaphor in particular is important to express what cannot be directly perceived as in the case of the light 'wave' and magnetic 'field' (Soskice 1985: 103). What is more, in both science and theology, there is reliance on a variety of metaphors or models for the partial contribution each can make in understanding the subject.

Language, consciousness and enlightenment

In Hindu thought, the claim is that knowledge of *Brahman* is objectively given, not developed from human thought in reflection upon the world or existence. The idea of being follows from the knowledge of *Brahman* through the word; *Brahman* is the source of scripture, and scripture is the source of the knowledge of *Brahman* (Arapura 1986: 9, 10). Since, however, we do not know being (*Brahman*) directly, it comes to us in the self-revelation of *Brahman*, that is, through the word that originates with *Brahman*. The problem of 'ignorance' (*avidya*) is underlined as central in *Vedanta*. It is closely aligned with 'illusion' (*maya*). It refers primarily to the absence of metaphysical knowledge of *Brahman*. It is the centre of the human plight. Humans arrive at a seeming impasse. If there is, however, the desire to know, that is, the desire to know *Brahman*, the person is reoriented and can begin to move out of ignorance.

The vehicle for this movement is language. Language is closely identified with human consciousness and finally has its source in *Brahman*. Emphasis is on the mystery of language and on language as the source of knowledge of the divine. Language brings the revelation of ultimate reality and is the framework in which the entire knowledge of reality is made possible (Arapura 1986: 157). There is recognition of different levels in the use of language. There is the level of ordinary use, and there is at another level the use of language to probe the depth of consciousness. This is in accord with language in speaking of the transcendent. Essentially, language is one with the divine. This receives strong and clear emphasis: the supreme *Brahman* 'is attained by the discipline of grammar'. It is therefore not surprising to read that language is the gateway to enlightenment (Arapura 1986: 159).

If language is identified with consciousness and consciousness with the divine, then to possess the language is in some way to be in possession of ultimate reality. One expression of this is in the use of 'AUM' in chant.[10] This term represents both the unity of language by recognising it for what it is and the Supreme Self. This AUM reveals the mystery of language in directing a person and bringing the ultimate unity of *atman* and *Brahman* (Arapura 1986: 169, 174).

At the same time, we do not know being directly. It is not known through analogies of being. Transitory phenomenal reality cannot provide knowledge of ultimate reality. Being in that respect always remains hidden. In the face of divine mystery, human reason is limited. Some forms of this thought come close to saying ultimate reality is unknowable, or that what can be known is so covered by conceptual or cultural distortion that there can be no true or certain knowledge of the ultimate. It may be that this position not only says something about human limitations, but raises a question about the source of our knowledge of the divine. A prevailing form of thought is that this knowledge comes to us in the self-revelation that originates with *Brahman* (Arapura 1986: 41).

Since language is closely identified with ultimate reality, there is no hesitation in main forms of Hindu thought of believing that language can reveal this reality. Transcendent knowledge through Vedanta is entirely within human capability. True knowledge is not only possible, it is the path to release and enlightenment.

It becomes apparent that in Christian faith and in Hinduism, language is decisive for relation to the divine. Each has a place for the language of revelation. In Hinduism, this is closely bound up with human consciousness corresponding to the varied and vast literature making up its scriptures. In Christian faith, revelation is bound up with God's activity and his presence with his people in history (e.g., God's activity in the liberation of Israel out of Egyptian bondage, in the work and teaching of Jesus, in the beginning of the Christian community, etc.). Human language for Hinduism itself participates in the divine. In Christian faith, language says something about humans created in God's image as a whole. Language is one expression of this human reality. The view of language itself differs because in each case, it functions within a different worldview.

This can perhaps become more concrete by briefly examining the place of gender in language for the divine. There has been intense discussion in recent times among Christians on gender as it relates to God. Two observations have figured prominently in the discussion. First, God transcends, or is 'beyond', sexuality. Properly speaking, God is neither masculine nor feminine. Second, scripture uses both masculine and feminine images to refer to God. In Genesis 1: 26–27, human beings, one male, one female, are created 'in God's image' (cf. Genesis 5: 1–3). God is reflected in both. Human beings are accordingly created to reflect God fully in complementary fashion. The human twoness in Genesis 1 intimates love or community is present in God. The point is not to say that God is masculine or feminine; God, rather, is sovereign, creating all things but unidentifiable in this way with the limits and processes of created nature. As sovereign, God is free to act with life-giving involvement ('let there be light ... and there was light') and work in covenantal ways.

There is the bold use of the masculine image to speak of God (Hosea 2: 16–20). In accord with covenantal faithfulness, God will bring peace and safety to Israel. This means God will take Israel as 'wife' and God will be to them a 'husband'. The point is not to say God is male, but that he will relate to Israel 'in justice and in steadfast love', and in that respect be a faithful husband to them (Hosea 2: 19–20). Again, God, in his care for Israel in and beyond the ordeal of exile, is compared to a woman nursing a child. Even if she should forget the child of her womb, God will not forget his people (Isaiah 49: 14, 15).

In the scriptures, the reference to God as 'Father' or 'Lord' has its own specific significance within the larger understanding of God. 'Father' was used in Greek religion of Zeus, as one of the gods, the first among equals but not as creator. The reference to God as 'Father' does not indicate primarily God's transcendence and certainly not God's maleness, but his relationship with Jesus Christ. Who is this God acknowledged by Israel and the Christian Church? It is this God of exodus and covenant who sent Jesus Christ and who raised him from the dead to enact his purpose. God as Father is then understood not as the solitary absolute nor simply as the source of all things, but as the first person of the divine triune reality, as Father with the Son and Holy Spirit in a communion of love. 'Father' is not a general reference to the divine essence but the specific personal name for God in dynamic relationship. This is God not simply as transcendent and removed from the world, but God who interacts with and loves the world.

Scripture, in describing God, abounds in the use of masculine and feminine images. These ways of speaking can and have been used to reinforce a patriarchal system. The use of one or the other in describing God is not neutral; through them we come to understand God in particular and specific ways. Language restricted to a neuter form or abstract statement will not do to express adequately the character of God. That calls for a range of language in human, and therefore masculine and feminine, terms (just as both bear the image of God).

In Hindu thought, the primary gods are considered male. Important for all these gods, Brahman, Shiva, Vishnu, are consorts with whom they are paired. For example Shiva, as the reconciliation of opposites, is both male and female, creator and destroyer, eternal rest and ceaseless activity. He can be described in relation to his consort, but in another way she is understood as being actually part of himself. She is his 'power' (*sakti*) by which he creates, sustains or destroys. These female consorts, sometimes mild as Parvati but also dreadful and destructive as Durga or Kali, are also the focus of worship.

In Hinduism, with its male and female deities, there is a strong hierarchy. In this and other ways the gods are very much like humans in their form, and sometimes their conduct. In this worldview there is a merging between the divine and human. Among the gods, the male is primary, and, without now taking the time to discuss this in detail, this must be reckoned with as a factor in a strongly patriarchal society. The language about the divine in male and female form may indirectly honour both in human form. It all depends on the relationship between them as this is embodied in story within the larger worldview.

Conclusion

It is apparent that there are connections as well as differences between Christian faith and Hinduism. The language about the divine points to some common understanding. It is also true that language can sometimes be similar, but the meaning can be quite different. This indicates that understanding is not first of all a matter of comparing particular points, but calls for a comparison of wholes as two largely different worldviews. So Christian faith and Hinduism have a place for revelation, but there are real questions: What is the origin of revelation? The meaning of revelation involves the issue of the nature of the divine. If this is some kind of ultimate power or metaphysical principle behind and in all things, revelation will take a certain form; if this is purposeful, personal being it will take another. Accordingly, is revelation primarily a matter of what takes place in human consciousness and reflection, or response to divine action and communication with humans and in human history?

In both Christian faith and Hinduism, in their own way, there is respect for the 'otherness' of God. In each case, this raises the question of how language relates to the divine. In Hindu thought, there is a close connection between language and consciousness, but access to the divine is darkened because of existence in a world of 'illusion'. In Christian faith, this darkness is first a matter of human choice or sin that separates from God. More, as transcendent being the divine is beyond human comprehension. We can, however, speak truly of a subject without claim to definitive knowledge. Beyond presumption in speaking of God, there is the more realistic and more modest possibility that respects our knowing with its limits; 'we know in part' and 'darkly'.

The test of coherence and adequacy of language can be used within a particular religion and also in dialogue between the religions. This means taking both similarity and difference seriously. Questions then about the meaning of the divine, of salvation and human destiny, are unavoidable. Dialogue may focus on understanding the worldview one of another, and then on how these and other matters can be most coherently and meaningfully addressed. Has a tradition the resources to solve its own major problems? The criterion might be 'how has each accounted for different aspects of the problems sharpened by hearing the other, and dealt with them'? This is at the centre of our different worldviews.

Notes

1. At a number of points in this essay I have depended on work done for an earlier essay, Wiebe (1997).
2. (cf. Johnson 1992: 6.) There is wide agreement that language, and in particular symbols, are open to 'interpretation'. To what extent are they also open to 'transformation'? Rebecca S. Chopp makes the statement that symbols have no 'essential' meaning that endures through Christian history. Without attention to 'continuity' in the mediation of meaning the emphasis is all on change or transformation of language (Chopp 1995: 47–63).
3. 'Background', 'framework' and 'worldview' are here related terms. Background is more limited; framework would, for example, also include expectation. Framework is almost a synonym for worldview.
4. This is a Hindu 'scripture' commentary.
5. Immanuel Kant comes close to this thought in saying that what we can theoretically know is limited to mere appearances (Kant 1965:29).
6. This is reference to an authoritative document for Hindu thought.
7. (cf. Scott 1994: 80, 87.) The issue is can there be a criterion that is more than or other than our 'circle of interest'? If not, this just becomes one more group seeking to impose their view on the rest (cf. Thiselton 1992: 440–462).
8. The modern source for much of this begins with Rene Descartes with his emphasis that only what can be conceived with clarity and distinctness can be true (Descartes 1998).
9. Certain thinkers emphasise the symbolic character of reference to God as a human construct receiving its content from human imagination. How it refers to the real beyond imagination is therefore discounted (cf. Eck 1993: 46).
10. AUM, also sometimes transliterated as OHM, is a word identified with the divine in Hinduism and, when chanted in meditation, makes the worshipper one with the divine.

References

Arapura, J. G. 1986. *Hermeneutical Essays on Vedantic Topics*. Delhi: Motilal Banarsidass.

Chopp, Rebecca S. 1995. 'Feminist Queries and Metaphysical Musings'. *Modern Theology* 11, 1: 47–63.

Danielou, Alain. 1964. *Hindu Polytheism*. Bollingen Series LXXII. New York: Pantheon Books.

Descartes, Rene. 1998. *Discourse on Method and Meditations on First Philosophy*. Translated by D.A. Cress. Indianapolis: Hackett Publishing.

Eck, Diana. 1993. *Encountering God: A Spiritual Journey From Boseman to Banaras*. Boston: Beacon Press.

Hiriyanna, M. 1995. *Essentials of Indian Philosophy*. Delhi: Motilal Banarsidass.

Johnson, Elizabeth A. 1992. *She Who Is*. New York: Crossroad.

Kant, Immanuel. 1965. *Critique of Pure Reason*. New York: St. Marten's Press.

MacIntyre, Alasdair. 1984. *After Virtue*. Notre Dame: University Press.

Meyer, Ben F. 1994. *Reality and Illusion in New Testament Scholarship*. Collegeville, Minnesota: The Liturgical Press.

Middleton, J. R. and Walsh, Brian J. 1995. *Truth Is Stranger Than It Used To Be*. Downers Grove, Illinois: Intervarsity Press.

Newbigin, Lesslie. 1995. *Proper Confidence*. Grand Rapids: Eerdmans.

Prakash, Satya and Vidyalankar, S. 1977. *Rigveda*. New Delhi: Veda Pratishthana.

Sankararya. 1942. *Chandogyopanisadbhasya*, Jha, Ganganatha, Sir, 1871–1941, Poona: Oriental Book Agency.

Scott, Peter. 1994. *Theology, Ideology and Liberation*. Cambridge: Cambridge University Press.

Soskice, Janet Martin. 1985. *Metaphor and Religious Language*. Oxford: Clarendon.

Thiselton, Anthony C. 1992. *New Horizons in Hermeneutics*. Grand Rapids: Zondervan.

Wiebe, Ben. 1997. 'Gender as a Theological Issue: How Can We Speak of God?' *Asia Journal of Theology* 11, 1: 3–19.

LIST OF CONTRIBUTORS

Francesca Bargiela-Chiappini is Research Fellow in the Department of English and Media Studies, Nottingham Trent University, England. Her work on business discourse and international communication in organisations has appeared in academic journals and in three recent books, *Managing Language. The Discourse of Corporate Meetings* (1997), *The Languages of Business. An International Perspective* (1997) and *Writing Business. Genres, Media and Discourses* (1999). She can be reached by e-mail at <francesca.bargiela@ntu.ac.uk>.

Teresa Dobrzyńska is a professor in the Institute of Literary Research of the Polish Academy of Sciences in Warsaw, Poland, and a leader of the research group on Theoretical Poetics and Literary Language. Her research interests include the pragmatics and semantics of natural language, poetics, metaphor and discourse analysis. Among the books she has published in Polish are two monographs on metaphor: 'Metaphor' (1988) and 'Metaphorically speaking: Studies on metaphor' (1994). She has also published journal articles in English, German, Russian, and Czech.

Chris Horrocks is Senior Lecturer in Art History at Kingston University in Surrey, England. His recent publications include *Introducing Baudrillard* and *Postmodern Currents: Baudrillard and the Millennium*. He is also publishing his research on Marcel Duchamp for the forthcoming book *Secret Spaces and Forbidden Places: Rethinking Culture* (Berghahn). He can be reached by e-mail at <C.Horrocks@kingston.ac.uk>.

Sakis Kyratzis is currently teaching linguistics at Kingston University in Surrey, England. His research interests include the use of metaphors in public and private discourse, the cognitive study of metaphor, the semiotics of intimacy and the construction of in-group identity. He can be reached by e-mail at <Sakis.Kyratzis@kingston.ac.uk>.

Lia Litosseliti is Senior Lecturer of Linguistics in the Dept. of English and Media Studies at Nottingham Trent University, England. Her research interests range from critical linguistics, discourse analysis and language and gender, to more interdisciplinary developments within feminist and cultural theory, media discourse and social psychology. She has published in the areas of moral argumentation, media debates, and gender identities in spoken and written argument. She can be reached by e-mail at <lia.litosseliti@ntu.ac.uk>.

Jim Miller has a personal chair in Linguistics and Spoken Language at the University of Edinburgh, Scotland. His research areas are the semantics of grammar (particularly case, tense and aspect), spoken and written language (from clause structure to literacy) and Russian. His published works include *Semantics and Syntax: Parallels and Connections* (1985) and *Spontaneous Spoken Language: Syntax and Discourse* (1998, with Regina Weinert). He can be reached by e-mail at <jmiller@ling.ed.ac.uk>.

François Nectoux is professor of Contemporary European Studies at Kingston University in Surrey, England. Before becoming an academic, he was a research consultant on international environmental issues, and he also thought in Algeria. He has published papers on environmental policy as well as on economic and cultural issues in Europe. He can be reached by e-mail at <F.Nectoux@kingston.ac.uk>.

Libby Rothwell is Principal Lecturer in the School of Languages at Kingston University in Surrey, England, where she teaches courses in Applied English Language and Linguistics and in French. Her research interests include language and culture learning and teaching, discourse analysis, and cross-cultural communication. She can be reached by e-mail at <l.rothwell@kingston.ac.uk>.

Stephen Lloyd Smith is a member of the School of Business and Management, Brunel University, England, and has published papers in urban history, power structures, inter-firm collaboration, and what he terms the 'technical impact of new society' in banking, retailing, and new technology home-based working. He has presented courses in emotional labour for several years and is collaborating with Pam Smith, Professor of Nursing at South Bank University and a team lead by Geraldine Cunningham at the Royal College of Nursing on clinical leadership and ward management. He can be reached by e-mail at <Stephen.Smith@brunel.ac.uk>.

Magda Stroińska is Associate Professor of German and Linguistics at McMaster University in Hamilton, Ont., Canada. She works closely with the School of Languages at Kingston University in Surrey, England. Her research interests include both theoretical linguistics and sociolinguistics, in particular academic discourse, language and ideology, bilingualism and language-based stereotyping. She can be reached by e-mail at <stroinsk@mcmaster.ca>.

Ben Wiebe received a Ph.D. from McMaster University in Hamilton, Ontario in Judaism and Christianity. He has done some special study of Asian religion and taught in India for three terms in three different years. He combines teaching, ministry and writing. He has published on interpretation and Christian ethics. He can be reached by e-mail at <wiebe@mcmaster.ca>.

INDEX